到美国去

GO TO AMERICA

投资移民与二代培育**实用指南**

方 向 著

ZHEJIANG UNIVERSITY PRESS
浙江大学出版社

目录
contents

第六章 CHAPER6
移民初期的生活安排与创业拓展

后　记
曼哈顿法则,"狼狗式"生存　245

自 序
移民过程是人类历史的合理构成

2007 年的春天，大学发榜了。

亲朋好友相聚，经常重复下述对话。问：闺女上哪所大学呀？答：她个人决定去哈佛，我主张她上麻省理工，不过她妈倾向普林斯顿，三选一，真难。最终的结局是，我们以同学挚友般的美式风格，尊重了女儿的选择。

2006 年圣诞前夕，女儿高中期间最后一个隆冬，我们收获了史上最贵重的一份圣诞礼物，那就是从女儿书房传来的，因被麻省理工学院提前录取而发出的惊叫声。记得那天中午 12 点，离网上发榜还有三分钟，闺女决定把自己反锁在屋内。她的理由是：在接下来的几十秒里，只会发生梦想成真或期望落空两种情况，无论是哪种冲击，都将一瞬间砸向头顶，她决意独自承担一切。

结果好事如愿。

在接下来的常规大学申请中，基于已经获得了麻省理工学院的录取承诺，女儿继续大胆地冲刺哈佛大学和普林斯顿大学。在这个繁忙的大学申请季节里，我们没有花费太多额外精力，播种三回，"连中三元"。

2011 年春天，临近哈佛大学毕业季，女儿的最新决定是，暂时放弃美国法学院入学考试（LSAT）的成绩——177 分（180 满分）这样一个千里挑一的高分，不惜中断连续完成法学院学业的金色梦想，决意投身华尔街的一流投资银行，先实现财富梦想。

1

　　这就是美国。21世纪的精英学子们知道，只有追求职业甚于追求学业，方能立足于激烈竞争的现实社会生态中。下一代从他们自己的视角，重新掂量学位与职位的分量，挑战上一辈的学位越高越优秀的传统观念。我们最终决定，还是尊重她的选择，哈佛闺女已经长大。

　　多年前，就有不少熟悉我们家庭故事的世交，包括出版界的朋友，一直怂恿我们整理一册《哈佛女孩》或者《哈佛家长》之类的指南用书，与其他家庭分享育儿经验。我们仨轻重自知，婉谢再三，免得贻笑大方。

　　2009年起，我开始担任上海交通大学海外教育学院高层管理人员工商管理硕士(EMBA)的讲座教授。课余时，我与学员们闲聊，发现话题基本与课业无关，主要围绕着出国移民和子女教育这类问题在深入探讨。难道是我的授课内容出现了问题，以致出现交流隔阂？又或许是我旅美学者的履历和年近半百的年岁，让同学们另有所问？相处久了，我知道学员们有着更深层的想法。

　　有位同学说，他遇到过几次同样的经历。往往约好了与国际商业领袖洽谈商务，结果发现，在一小时的会谈中，真正涉及合同细节的时间不到20％。对方关注的是历史、文化与哲学。自己只顾得上倾听、理解和消化，却无以对答。新钱拥有人与旧钱拥有人之间，横隔了深壑。

　　有位同学说，自己的公司已经度过了公开上市辅导期。董事会的许多成员，开始更多地考虑善后问题：如何面对可能的公众追问，即第一桶金的合法来源；如何解决个人的资金流向，即资产爆发增长与长期持有的矛盾。创业原罪和守业难题，真是一胎双生。

　　有位同学说，我的事业日趋成熟，主观上极不愿意改变已有的生活，放弃既得利益，有所异动。但是，最见不得子女们的学习环境和日趋严峻的生存压力，他们其实比父母还难，孩子们无忧无虑的岁月，消耗在现代"八股"的考分主义竞争中。为孩子择校海外的需求，一天天紧迫。

　　诸如此类,世上真的是有那么多成功者的烦恼? 或者,这种移民倾向正是人类的一种生存本能和社会属性,我的电脑屏幕上显示着 300 万年来人类基因从非洲东部,漂泊移民至全球各地的模拟轨迹,其中蕴涵了惊人的密码。

　　一次偶然的机会,蓝狮子财经出版中心得知我正在用功,试图依据国内精英的困惑与个人旅美的经历,梳理出一部中国精英人士可持续生存发展的实用建议小册子时,他们热心地将吴晓波先生的杰作《跌荡一百年》送我参考。这部近代百年财经史让我体会到,看来真的出现了读书人所处竹林不同,思路却不约而同的现象。吴晓波先生努力发掘的那个曾经辉煌,而今"下落不明"的政商阶层,正是我赖以预警的史实依据之一:富不过三代。三代之外,多在海外。①

　　由此看来,出国移民和子女教育事由,已经走出家庭,上升到了社会关注的理性高度。一位著名的社会学家这样认识最近热议的海外移民问题:当下发生的向海外移民的浪潮是中国历史上第三大移民潮,此前的两次分别是 1644 年前后和 19 世纪中后期的移民潮。② 2010 年 6 月 10 日,《环球》杂志与新浪网联合进行调查,截至 6 月 11 日 19 时,7 000 余名受调查

---

　　① 吴东平著:《走近现代名人的后代——名人后代丛书》,湖北人民出版社 2006 年版;布鲁斯·爱德华·何著:《茶壶烈酒:一个唐人街家庭的回忆录》,珠海出版社 1998 年版;等等。笔者自 2009 年起,编撰用于上海交通大学海外教育学院 EMBA 课程的讲义时,特辟专章与学员分析研讨,中国大陆每年公布的各种富翁榜上为何数年难见一位名贾巨商的后代。关于晚清以降名人之后的产业遗存研究,业已成为上海交通大学海外教育学院产业发展研究的专项课题,有关内容见笔者相关论文。

　　② 清华大学社会学教授孙立平在 2011 年"两会"前夕,特意接受《经济观察报》记者采访。在一篇《社会失序是当下的严峻挑战》的专栏文章中,他总结了 30 年来我国社会转型的特点,并就国内当下的富人移民热潮,表达了学术观点。详见 http://www.eeo.com.cn/Politics/by_region/2011/02/28/194539.shtml。

者中有移民意向的高达 88.2%。汇丰银行的一份调查显示,月收入在 1.2 万元以上或流动资产在 50 万元以上的中国内地富裕人群中,60% 在未来 10 年有移民计划,移民目的国或地区前四位为:澳大利亚、新加坡、中国香港、加拿大。而且还有调查表明,在最近短短一年的时间里,移民的动机发生了明显的变化,原来移民第一位的动机是子女的教育,而在 2010 年,移民的第一位的动机已经变成了安全。

过去一段时间,我在主业以外,认真筹划完成一部涉及两类人士的移民路径实用指南。两类人士即富裕的中产阶级和接班的第二代,同时也将自身经历的 20 年海外生活融入书中,将详尽的表格程序和生活经历合二为一,作为后来人借鉴参考的第一手资料。值得指出的是,在这本书里,被媒体广泛渲染的亿万富翁的海外生活,不是讨论的主题,这些权贵富豪的生活,对于中产阶层而言,没有普遍的借鉴意义。从普通百姓出发,我理解智者的总结:我只是一个普通人,没有过人的才华,所以我从来不敢有什么奢望,能够拥有自由下的安定,足矣。但是现在看来,就连这么卑微的期待,都已经很难实现了。我又何尝不知,出去不仅不等于是到了天堂,更是有很多困扰。2007 年访美期间,我接触过一些留美学生,他们都是国内名校出身,都是精英,但他们无论事业上多么优秀,无论经济上多么富足,我觉得他们其实并不怎么幸福。哪里有自由哪里就有祖国,话是这么说,但实际上问题并非如此简单,祖国不仅包含自由这一元素,更包含着认同的元素、关怀的元素。缺乏后面两个元素,纵使自由且富足又能如何? 仍旧无法逃脱边缘化的命运,仍旧无法逃脱孤独和寂寞的命运,仍旧无法建立强大的自信和自尊。

祖国不是站在你背后,不是那个可以傲视全球的物质意义上的祖国;祖国是在心中,是那个能够让人感动、让人温暖的精神意义上的祖国、文化意义上的祖国。出去的最大危机,就是告别故土的同时,也失落了心中的

祖国。生你养你的土地离你已远，而在你脚下展开的新的土地再怎么如诗
如画，也是别人的土地。无论你怎么努力融入，你也不可能跟他们完全一
样，也很难完全融入那片土地。①

　　翻阅学院派的《中国移民史》让我感受到，如何补修现代海外漂流的中
国血魂，恐怕已是学术研究的历史选择。作为体验过了移民美国的万般不
易、又愿与开始着手远游的后来者们分享经历与往事的笔者，我预祝这个
特殊人群，事先反思应触及灵魂，继而行动该动如脱兔，从而一路顺风。

　　感谢蓝狮子财经出版中心的出版人吴晓波先生和编辑卓巧丽女士，他
们的诚挚邀请和万般鼓动，尤其是围绕在他们周围的财经读者，正是我愿
意分享本书内容的特定人群。上海交通大学海外教育学院的张广义主任
和戴明朝博士的热心联络和关注，也是本书写作得以启动的动因之一。当
然，如果不是我的太太和女儿愿意放下手头工作，重温和回顾我们一道走
来的点点滴滴，我也是无力再次串联起书中所记载的记忆碎片和程序细节
的。我的父母作为本书草稿的第一读者，努力在老花镜下逐字细读，使我
再次体会了本书渴望表达的主题：人生和文明代代传承的不易以及其中的
深刻含义。

---

　　① 笑蜀：《我的梦想：在自己的故土上找到祖国》，《南方周末》2008 年 12 月 2 日。详见
http：//xiaoshu．z．infzm．com/2008/12/02。

第一章 **1**
CHAPER
当代华人移民美国概况

引子：
数字胜于口舌

你会移民吗？

2011 年 4 月 21 日，面对《经济观察报》直奔主题的读者调查，统计发现：384 名主动参加问卷的读者中，360 位读者选择了肯定会移民，占了 93.75％；14 名读者表示坚决不会移民，占 3.65％；另有 2.60％的读者，即 10 位表示自己一时还说不清。至于选择移民最主要的原因如下：考虑财产安全占 30.29％；子女教育占 18.80％；享受养老福利占 16.71％；为了护照便利占 3.66％；享受更先进的医疗服务占 1.57％；其他各类答复占 28.98％。[①] 我想这中间很有深意，值得跟踪分析。

最近一段时间，汇丰银行的一份财富分析报告在大众媒体间广泛流传。中国已成为全球高端财富增长最快的市场，2011 年，中国私人财富市场仍将保持增长势头，高净值人群将达到 59 万人，基于种种经济现实和政策环境，该人群对直接购买内地住宅的投资热情下降，但对海外投资移民意愿强烈。受访者中约 60％正考虑投资移民，27％的亿万富翁已完成投资移民。如何看待这种现象？

[①] 详见经济观察网 2011 年 4 月 21 日读者调查结果。http://home. eeo. com. cn/bbs/thread－425331－1－1. html。

一个不争的数据是,相对上述假设性的虚拟调查,事实上,每年都
有数以万计的中国公民成功移民美国。

来自 2010 年美国官方
的统计数据

2011 年 4 月 7 日,美国国土安全部(DHS)宣布:在 2010 财政年度中,共有 33 969 名 18 岁以上的中国大陆公民加入美国籍,成为归化美国公民。[①] 按照所有入籍公民总数统计,2010 年中国大陆归化公民总量,在各国中排名第四。当然,这个数量不包括出生在美国,自然成为美国公民的下一代华裔美国人。中国血统和中国文化融入北美大地,这是我乐于见到的现象。比较种种说法,如蒙古人种

图 1-1 美国护照封面

通过白令海峡跨入北美,或者三宝太监(郑和)的远洋船队可能到过北美大陆,这些仅仅属于人类学和历史学研究的推测。而这一波东西方融合,无论在文化、社会还是血统上,都是最可靠的一次记录,是人类文

---

① 有关美国国土安全部下属的美国公民与移民服务局(USCIS)的新闻和年度统计报表,可以在公开的政府网站上查询。详见 http://www.uscis.gov/USCIS/Web%20Policies/Webstats%202011/CSWP_MonthlyMetrics_March2011.pdf。

明的进步。

　　尽管 2010 年度的大陆归化公民已经比 2009 年度减少近 3 200 人，比 2008 年峰值时减少 6 000 多人，但中国大陆归化美国公民的人数还是相当可观的。比较过去 10 年数据，2010 财政年度的约 3.4 万归化华裔公民数，排在历年中国公民入籍美国年度统计的第五位，可能接近中位数。这样估计的话，10 年里共有 34 万华裔新一代美国公民产生。按照美国法律，入籍美国公民之前，先要获得美国永久居留权至少 5 年，即成为通俗称为的"绿卡"（美国永久居民卡，见图 1-3）拥有者。因此，可以预计的是，构成 34 万华裔新公民的持有绿卡人数，基底庞大，中国公民通过各种合法途径移民美国，每年获得绿卡的人数保持在 7 万左右，从而可以推断，若继续维持当下水平，今后几年中，每年入籍人数仍将保持在 3 万人以上的水平。

图 1-2　美国护照（由威
严的蓝色基调构成）

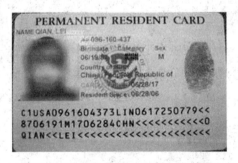

图 1-3　美国绿卡（其实是粉红色基调）

6

美国签证分两大类：
移民签证与非移民签证

　　签证是国家主权的表现形式，通过对他国公民颁发批准文书的形式展开。我们可以通过美国国务院国土安全部公民与移民服务局的官方网站获得全面准确的信息。

　　20世纪以来，美国对外发放的签证从公函形式到20世纪中叶的防伪图章形式，到目前已经成为可以联网查询的电子标签形式。但是，美国的签证分类基本上没有大的变化，只是依据国家利益，对于签证的审批条件，在不同的历史阶段

图1-4　B1/B2签证（赴美观光、商务人士的签证）

有着重要的战略性改变。其中非移民签证分商务 B1、旅游探亲 B2、高级公务 E1、学生 F1、交换学者 J1、工作 H1 和金融 K1 等。①

　　这些年来，对于中国公民而言，美国对华签证政策日趋宽松，无论是 B1/B2 旅游观光签证（图1-4），还是 F1/F2 学生签证和学生配偶签证（图1-5、图1-6），相比过去，都可以非常顺利地获得。亲属关系移

---

　　①　具体官方内容见 http://www.uscis.gov/portal/site/uscis。

民,特别是投资移民,申请效率和成功比例,也是有增无减。所有这些,都是各种人实现美国梦的基本前提。2010 年全世界共有 62 万人入籍美国,入籍人数是近 5 年来最少的。2008 年外国人入籍美国曾经创下 105 万人的历史纪录。归化美国人数最多的国家是墨西哥,有 6.7 万;其次是印度 6.1 万,菲律宾 3.55 万,中国(不含香港、澳门、台湾地区)、越南、哥伦比亚、多米尼加、古巴分列第四至第八位。2010 年外国移民由绿卡到入籍的

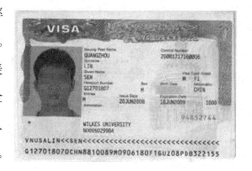

图 1-5　F1 签证(赴美留学生的专项签证)

图 1-6　F2 签证(留学生配偶的陪读签证)

平均等待时间缩短至 6 年,是 40 多年来最短的。其中亚裔申请人平均等待时间为 5 年,已基本达到由绿卡到入籍的最低年限要求。外国人入籍最多的州为加利福尼亚、纽约、佛罗里达、得克萨斯、新泽西等,入籍人数最多的大都会则是纽约、洛杉矶、迈阿密、芝加哥、华盛顿等,中国移民在这些地区居住与工作的比例也最高。新移民们选择这些地方,与当地提供的生活环境和工作机会,有着相当紧密的关系。

从感受美国到移民美国：
合理的过程

当然，移民美国的原因和方式有许多，在这里，我们主要介绍较为集中的情况，基本可以理解为走向美国的三个步骤。首先，作为一名中国公民，通过获得美国签证，亲历美国的生活和学习来了解美国，如果你对美国确有好感，或者其他种种因素，促使你产生长期生活在美国的愿望，那么，按照美国法律，你可以有许多途径获得美国长期合法居留的绿卡，比如投奔直系亲属、建立国际婚姻关系、赴美留学后作为引进人才居留，以及最近逐步为人所知的投资移民方案。其次，在美国生活若干年后，一般家庭与个人会反复比较中美两国的各种因素与自己的关系。最后选择是否加入美国国籍。笔者将上述这些数据和移民框架作为开场白，预示了本书的基本内容和观念。我想这确定会招来一些非议，有人会说你这是在为美国说好话，为那些向往美国的国人提供公开的信息，为打算移民美国的富有国人出谋划策。其实这些问题的解答，无法用一个书名和一个开头穷尽，需要深入详细阐述。根据招商银行 2011 年发布财富报告，中国内地千万富翁（指资产净值，不包括自住房等）中，六成有意投资移民，而资产净值亿元以上者有 27％ 已完成移民。① 不过，这条信息并没有普遍意义。值得我们关注的是，千百万中产人士的迁徙和移民现实。

---

① 引自招商银行 2011 年中国私人财富报告。详见 http://images.cmbchina.com/cmbcms/201104/8e0597fb－dd78－4a49－a128－99aa80c4ef0e.pdf。

在我看来，普通移民只是选择一种更加简单、舒适和安全的生活方式而已。据相关统计，改革开放以来，中国内地自费去美国留学的学生中，有九成结束学业后选择了留在美国工作，比印度的 80% 比例还高。在一个年薪 4 万美元和月工资 5 000 元人民币，猪肉和青菜的价格几乎相等的现实面前，很多人选择前者，完全可以理解。事实上，很多移民者的企业和资产都在国内，本人也长期在国内生活和工作，只是一部分家人在海外生活罢了。其实，这就和一个小城镇里的企业家，用自己个人资产的很小一部分在大城市里买了一幢房子，顺便上了一个大城市户口的概念差不多，实在不值得大惊小怪。许多家庭的现实选择是，仅仅将后人送往海外深造，自己却继续在这片土地上寻找一块得以放妥自我灵魂的墓园。

或许是因年轻时代接受了正统的医学教育，放大了悲天悯人，以拯救生灵为己任的人性"弱点"，我无法本能地从民族大义角度出发来做宏大叙事，思考重大命题。我习惯从最有利于个人和家庭的视角，发现有助生命健康完善的最佳方案。在我看来，人性的自由健康高于主义的泾渭分明，从人类文明史出发，世上本无高低与否，"神马"纷争，都是源于所谓精英的自以为是。基于生物和生命的本质，我们都是非洲"夏娃"的后代，理应消融冲突，回归人类和谐的"伊甸园"。

体验移民乐园里的
购物天堂

　　那么,有伊甸园吗?假如把美国称为伊甸园,立马就有板砖拍来。但把纽约称为购物的伊甸园,希望手握板砖者,稍息片刻为妙。也就是说,你不妨直接向美国驻华领事馆官员说,我要利用"黄金周"去纽约著名的伍德伯里奥特莱斯(Woodbury Common Premium Outlets)爽快地购物一次,相信这几年,签证官员面对你提供的机票行程、酒店预定、收入证明、资产证明等,立马就给你一个 B1/B2 签证,鼓励富有的国人过去消费,支援美国国内零售市场的复苏和发展。

　　笔者在纽约生活了 20 年,离市中心 90 分钟车程的伍德伯里奥特莱斯,被称为购物伊甸园,完全是经过游客的双手双脚投票后,获得的美誉。特别是近年来,每当有朋自国内来,我带领他们前往这所购物乐园,成了一个经典项目。既然这个地方已经在国内出了名,那么下决心移民美国以前,一定得先去美国体验一番,笔者不妨就先将伍德伯里奥特莱斯作为生活指南的一部分,先介绍起来。

图 1-7 伍德伯里奥特莱斯外景图

奥特莱斯（Premium Outlets）名牌折扣中心，在美国大城市附近几乎都有。纽约的伍德伯里奥特莱斯是美国 Premium Outlets 旗下拥有的 41 家名牌折扣中心中最著名的一家，地址是 498 Red Apple Court，Central Valley，NY。伍德伯里奥特莱斯的成名，来源于它的营业规模，以及繁多的来自世界各地的游客。最近几年，我不时闲荡在游乐迷宫般的商场中，顾盼来来回回血拼购物的亚裔面孔，聆听广播声中不时传来的普通话服务内容，往往恍惚起来，时空错位，以为漫步在北京或者上海的涉外购物市场里。国内游客喜爱的品牌，如巴宝莉（Burberry）、寇驰（Coach）、迪奥（Dior）、乔治·阿玛尼（Giorgio Armani）、古驰（Gucci）、鳄鱼（Lacoste）、耐克（Nike）、拉夫·劳伦（Ralph Lauren）、普拉达（Prada）和萨克斯第五大道精品百货店（Saks Fifth Avenue）等，共计 220 家专卖店。这里通常提供 25%～40%的商品折扣，到了感恩节、圣诞节和母亲节等促销季节，75%的甩卖折扣外加 30%的回报折扣，顾客往往不知不觉地真以为是白捡了心爱之物。举例来说，寇驰手袋 15～30 美元就可买到；Clinic 等名牌香水，10～20 美元够用一年；至于服装，几美元的清仓货里大有漏检，只要你有足够的时间和体力，这 200

多家专卖店足够你来回穿梭折腾的了。所以,在人民币和美元兑换比价日日上升,到了 6.54∶1,还在向往 5.54∶1 的生活场景中,纽约伍德伯里奥特莱斯确实是名副其实的购物伊甸园,够折腾,够爽快。

图 1-8 纽约伍德伯里奥特莱斯内醒目的汉语广告牌

　　花钱少,还是其次。眼下,对于中国游客,他们最关心的不是捡到了便宜,而是会不会花了大把的时间精力,却在异国他乡,买回去一箱 Made in China(中国制造)的商品。这些"中国制造",确实成为许多大折扣商品的主流,但是,客观地讲,花同样的价钱,你根本无法在国内的商场里找出同样质量价格性能比的商品。现在已有越来越多的美国品牌,逐步模糊商标上的中国制造标记,同时呈现设计公司、专利公司、监制公司、承销公司和分销公司的名字。而事实也确如此,品牌的建立,离不开整个网络的任何环节,生产制造只是其中一个环节。所以,当你面对一个成品的时候,它的背后不仅有中国制造,还有生活在美国上百万华裔公民和几百万华侨同胞的共同贡献,即包括了海内外炎黄子孙的创意、设计、资本、专利和流通。也就是说，由中国国土和中国文化输出的，不光是劳动力密集型产品，还有大量的技术成本，以及维持这种技术的大量各类人才。这样我们就回到了本书所关心的主题，他们是如何成群地来到北美这块大陆，并且生存下来的。而你是否也可能来到这块土地，按照自己的意愿，生存繁衍呢？

第二章

CHAPER 2

**非移民签证的基本
程序**

DS－160 非移民签证申请表必须在线填写提交

　　B1/B2 属于非移民签证，在位于北京、沈阳、成都、上海和广州的美国大使馆与总领事馆均可以办理。由于技术的提升和签证要求的提高，2010 年 3 月开始，所有的非移民签证申请人，都要统一在美国驻中国大使馆或者总领事馆处，填写一份非移民签证的 DS－160 签证申请表，而且必须在线填写提交。所以，在这里笔者只能附上签证申请表样本以供参考，另外美国驻华大使馆的汉语辅导非常有助于我们理解其中细节。

　　签证表格共计 4 页，一旦完成，立即生成一个特定的扫描密码，未来该申请人的所有新旧信息，全部归类在同一个文件中，现代电脑技术不难做到这一点，所以填表者来不得半点虚假，否则后果只能自负。我们在表格后，及时附上了由美国驻华大使馆制作的填表汉语辅导，这些官方信息值得信赖。

U.S. DEPARTMENT of STATE
CONSULAR ELECTRONIC APPLICATION CENTER

Nonimmigrant Visa Application

Application - *Sensitive But Unclassified(SBU)*

Photo Provided:

SAMPLE - IMMIHELP.COM

Confirmation Number:

A A 0 0 0 0 T I L X

Personal, Address, Phone, and Passport Information

Name Provided:	GUPTA , RAMESH
Full Name in Native Language:	DOES NOT APPLY
▲ Other Names Used:	YES
Other Name (1) :	NONE , RAMESHBHAI
Sex:	MALE
Marital Status:	MARRIED
Date of Birth:	01 JANUARY 1945
Place of Birth:	MUMBAI , MAHARASHTRA , INDIA
Nationality:	INDIA
Other Nationalities:	NO
National Identification Number:	DOES NOT APPLY
U.S. Social Security Number:	DOES NOT APPLY
U.S. Taxpayer ID Number:	DOES NOT APPLY
Home Address:	34 SHANKAR LANE
City:	BORIVALI
State/Province:	MAHARASHTRA
Postal Zone/ZIP Code:	400034
Country:	INDIA
Same Mailing Address?	YES
Home Phone Number:	91-22-5555-1111
Work Phone Number:	91-22-5555-1111
Work Fax Number:	91-22-5555-1111
Mobile/Cell Phone Number:	91-22-5555-1111
Email Address:	suresh@yahoo.com
Passport Number:	A9783434
Passport Book Number:	DOES NOT APPLY
Country/Authority that Issued Passport:	INDIA
City Where Issued:	MUMBAI
State/Province Where Issued:	MAHARASHTRA
Country Where Issued:	INDIA
Issuance Date:	10 JANUARY 2009
Expiration Date:	28 JANUARY 2019
Have you ever lost a passport or had one stolen?	NO

Travel Information

图 2-1　DS-160 非移民签证申请表 I

Principal Applicant?	YES
▲ Purpose of Your Trip to U.S.	
Purpose (1) :	TOURIST/PERSONAL TRAVEL VISITOR (B2)
Intended Date of Arrival:	29 JUNE 2010
Intended Length of Stay in U.S.:	6 MONTH(S)
Address where you will stay in the U.S:	123 PARK AVENUE
	EDISON, NEW JERSEY 08817
Person/Entity Paying for Your Trip:	OTHER PERSON
Name of Person Paying for Your Trip:	GUPTA , RAHUL
Telephone:	732-555-1212
Email Address:	rahul@yahoo.com
Relationship to You:	CHILD
Is the address of the party paying for your trip the same as your Home or Mailing Address?	NO
Paying Address:	123 PARK AVENUE
City:	EDISON
State/Province:	NJ
Postal Zone/ZIP Code:	08817
Country:	UNITED STATES OF AMERICA
▲ Other Persons Traveling with You:	YES
Are you traveling as part of a group or organization?	NO
Persons Traveling with You:	
Name (1) :	GUPTA , RAMILA
Relationship to You:	SPOUSE
Have you ever been in the U.S.?	NO
Have you ever been issued a U.S. visa?	NO
Have you ever been refused a U.S. Visa, been refused admission to the United States, or withdrawn your application for admission at the point of entry?	NO

U.S. Contact Information

Contact Person Name in the U.S.:	GUPTA, RAHUL
Organization Name in the U.S.:	DO NOT KNOW
Relationship to You:	RELATIVE
U.S. Contact Address:	123 PARK AVENUE
	EDISON, NEW JERSEY 08817
Phone Number:	(732)555-1212
Email Address:	rahul@yahoo.com

Family Information

Father's Surnames:	GUPTA
Father's Given Names:	AMRIT
Father's Date of Birth:	10 JANUARY 1933
Is your father in the U.S.?	NO
Mother's Surnames:	GUPTA
Mother's Given Names:	SAVITA
Mother's Date of Birth:	10 FEBRUARY 1934
Is your mother in the U.S.?	NO
▲ Do you have any immediate relatives, not including parents in the U.S.?	YES
Relative Name (1) :	GUPTA , RAHUL
Relationship to you:	CHILD
Status:	U.S. CITIZEN
Spouse's Full Name:	GUPTA , RAMILA
Spouse's Date of Birth:	29 MARCH 1947
Spouse's Nationality:	INDIA
Spouse's City of Birth:	DELHI

图 2 - 2　DS - 160 非移民签证申请表 II

Spouse's Country of Birth:	INDIA
Spouse's Address:	SAME AS HOME ADDRESS

Work / Education / Training Information

Primary Occupation:	BUSINESS
Present Employer or School Name:	STAR BAZAAR
Address:	2345 KHAR LANE
City:	MUMBAI
State/Province:	MAHARASHTRA
Postal Zone/Zip Code:	400011
Country:	INDIA
Month Salary in Local Currency:	45,000
Briefly Describe your Duties:	SALESMAN

Security and Background Information

Do you have a communicable disease of public health significance such as tuberculosis (TB)?	NO
Do you have a mental or physical disorder that poses or is likely to pose a threat to the safety or welfare of yourself or others?	NO
Are you or have you ever been a drug abuser or addict?	NO
Have you ever been arrested or convicted for any offense or crime, even though subject of a pardon, amnesty, or other similar action?	NO
Have you ever violated, or engaged in a conspiracy to violate, any law relating to controlled substances?	NO
Are you coming to the United States to engage in prostitution or unlawful commercialized vice or have you been engaged in prostitution or procuring prostitutes within the past 10 years?	NO
Have you ever been involved in, or do you seek to engage in, money laundering?	NO
Do you seek to engage in espionage, sabotage, export control violations, or any other illegal activity while in the United States?	NO
Do you seek to engage in terrorist activities while in the United States or have you ever engaged in terrorist activities?	NO
Have you ever or do you intend to provide financial assistance or other support to terrorists or terrorist organizations?	NO
Are you a member or representative of a terrorist organization?	NO
Have you ever ordered, incited, committed, assisted, or otherwise participated in genocide?	NO
Have you ever committed, ordered, incited, assisted, or otherwise participated in torture?	NO
Have you committed, ordered, incited, assisted, or otherwise participated in extrajudicial killings, political killings, or other acts of violence?	NO
Have you, while serving as a government official, been responsible for or directly carried out, at any time, particularly severe violations of religious freedom?	NO
Have you ever sought to obtain or assist others to obtain a visa, entry into the United States, or any other United States immigration benefit by fraud or willful misrepresentation or other unlawful means?	NO
Have you ever withheld custody of a U.S. citizen child outside the United States from a person granted legal custody by a U.S. court?	NO
Have you voted in the United States in violation of	NO

图 2 - 3 DS - 160 非移民签证申请表 Ⅲ

any law or regulation?

Have you ever renounced United States
citizenship for the purpose of avoiding taxation?   NO

Location Information

Current Location: MUMBAI, INDIA

Preparer of Application:

Did anyone assist you in filling out this
application?   NO

图 2 - 4　DS - 160 非移民签证申请表 Ⅳ

　　据美国国务院统计,2010 年,美国共对中国发出 80 万份各类签证,包括非移民签证和移民签证,签证成功率达 85％以上,这是一个前所未有的中美交流时代,无论移民还是非移民,均赶上了一个好时机。为此,美国国土安全局专门针对中国签证申请人出台了一个方案,用于提高服务质量,所有签证申请人在第二次申请同样类别的签证时,可以通过邮寄方式作业,只要该申请人没有不良记录,基本不用担心拒签。美国驻中国大使馆还特意制作了申请签证的网上步骤,助你逐一填写,一次通过。美国国务院的官方指导网站具备了最权威的解释,如果网络畅通无阻的话,建议申请者以此为据。①

---

　　① 美国国务院 DS－160 非移民签证申请,在线填表指导。http://travel. state. gov/visa/forms/forms_4230. html。

正确填写 DS－160 非移民签证申请表：
美国驻华大使馆的汉语辅导

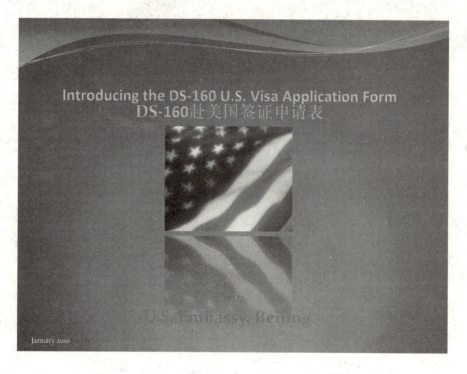

图 2－5　DS－160 非移民签证申请表填写汉语辅导图 I

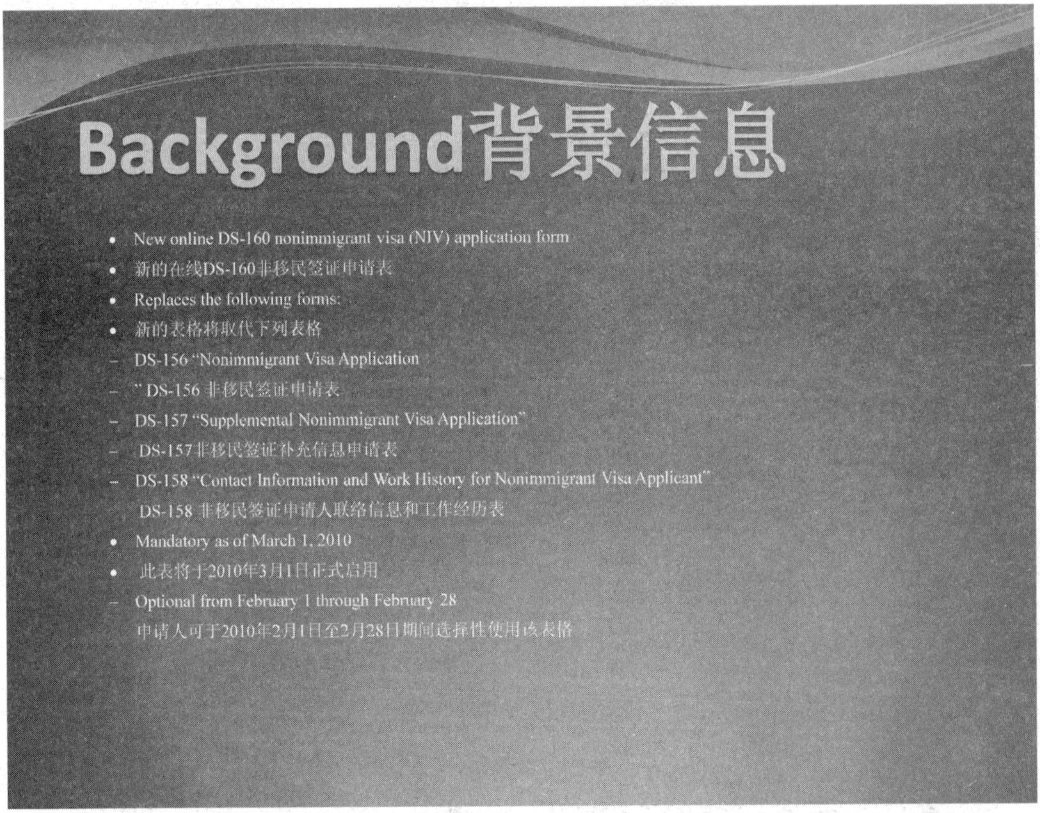

图 2 - 6 **DS - 160** 非移民签证申请表填写汉语辅导图Ⅱ

Advantages to Applicants
该表可为申请人提供以下便利:

- One form instead of three 一表取代以前三个表格
- Completely online – nothing to fill out by hand
  在线完成申请—无需手填
- Family and group feature – no need to fill in identical data more than once
  家庭和团组申请人—无需二次填写相同信息
- Save feature – don't need to complete all at once
  保存功能—不需要一次完成所有信息的填写
- Frequent applicants can save application for reuse
  频繁赴美申请人可保存申请信息以便重复使用
- Print only a single confirmation page
  只需打印单张申请信息确认页

图 2-7 DS-160 非移民签证申请表填写汉语辅导图 Ⅲ

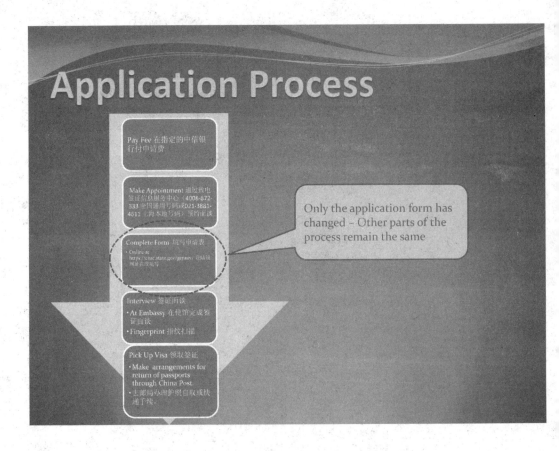

图 2 - 8 DS - 160 非移民签证申请表填写汉语辅导图 Ⅳ

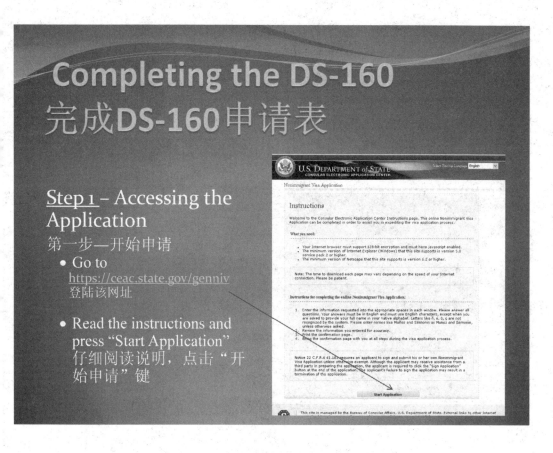

图 2-9　DS-160 非移民签证申请表填写汉语辅导图 V

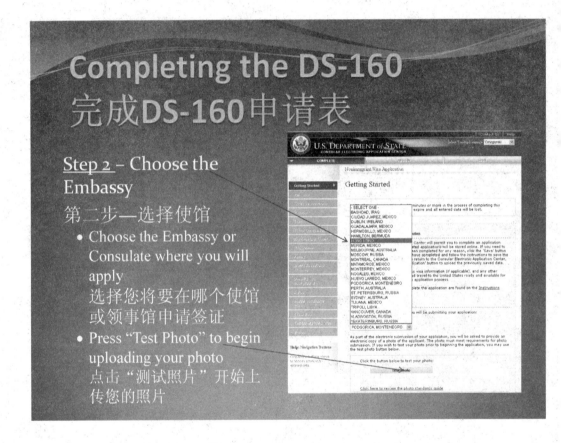

图 2-10 DS-160 非移民签证申请表填写汉语辅导图 Ⅵ

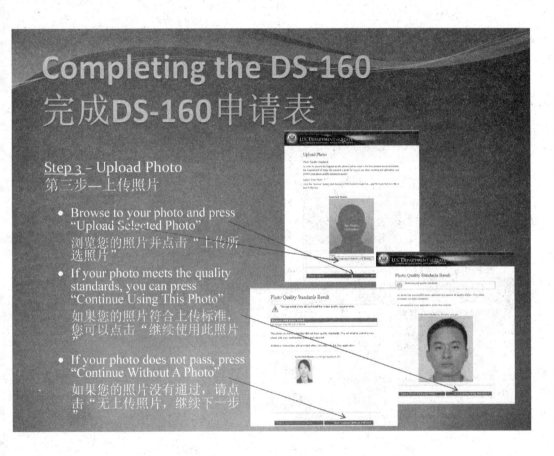

图 2-11 DS-160 非移民签证申请表填写汉语辅导图 Ⅶ

图 2－12　DS－160 非移民签证申请表填写汉语辅导图Ⅷ

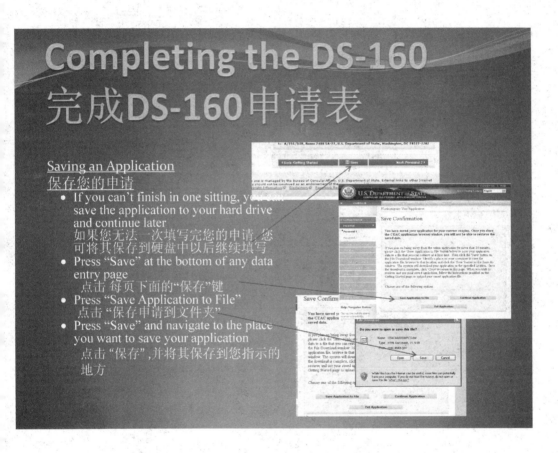

图 2 - 13　DS - 160 非移民签证申请表填写汉语辅导图 Ⅸ

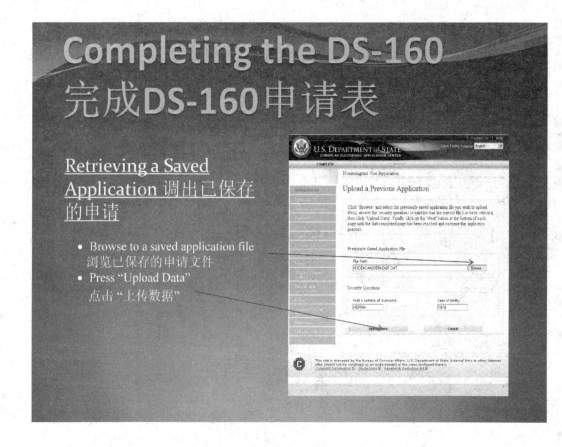

图 2 - 14 DS - 160 非移民签证申请表填写汉语辅导图 X

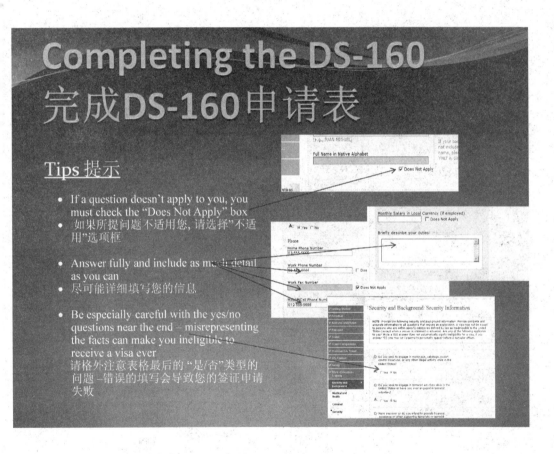

图 2 - 15　DS - 160 非移民签证申请表填写汉语辅导图 XI

Completing the DS-160
完成DS-160申请表

Step 5 – Reviewing Your Application
第5步 – 检查您的申请

- You have an opportunity to review and edit all your answers before submitting your application
  在递交申请前，您有机会检查并修改您的表格
- Check carefully that everything is correct – it's impossible to make changes later
  认真检查以确保所有信息都正确 – 之后您不能做任何的修改

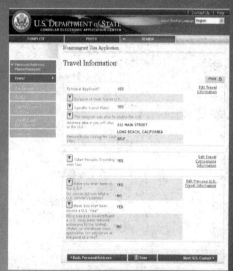

图 2 – 16 DS – 160 非移民签证申请表填写汉语辅导图 ⅩⅡ

Completing the DS-160
完成DS-160申请表

Step 6 – Submitting Your Application
第6步 – 递交您的申请

- Once you submit your application, you can't change it
  一旦您递交了申请，则不能再修改

- Pressing "Sign and Submit Application" constitutes your electronic signature, certifying that all the answers on the application are true
  点击"签字并递交申请"会构成您的电子签名，以此证明你所有回答均属实

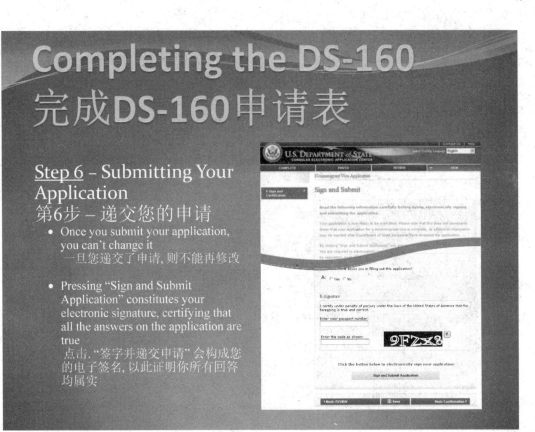

图 2 - 17　DS - 160 非移民签证申请表填写汉语辅导图ⅩⅢ

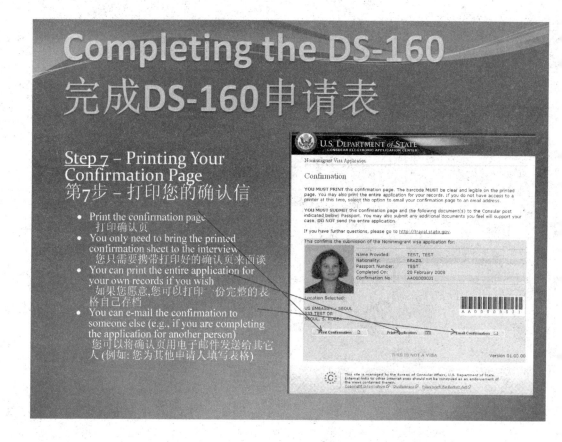

图 2 – 18　DS – 160 非移民签证申请表填写汉语辅导图 XIV

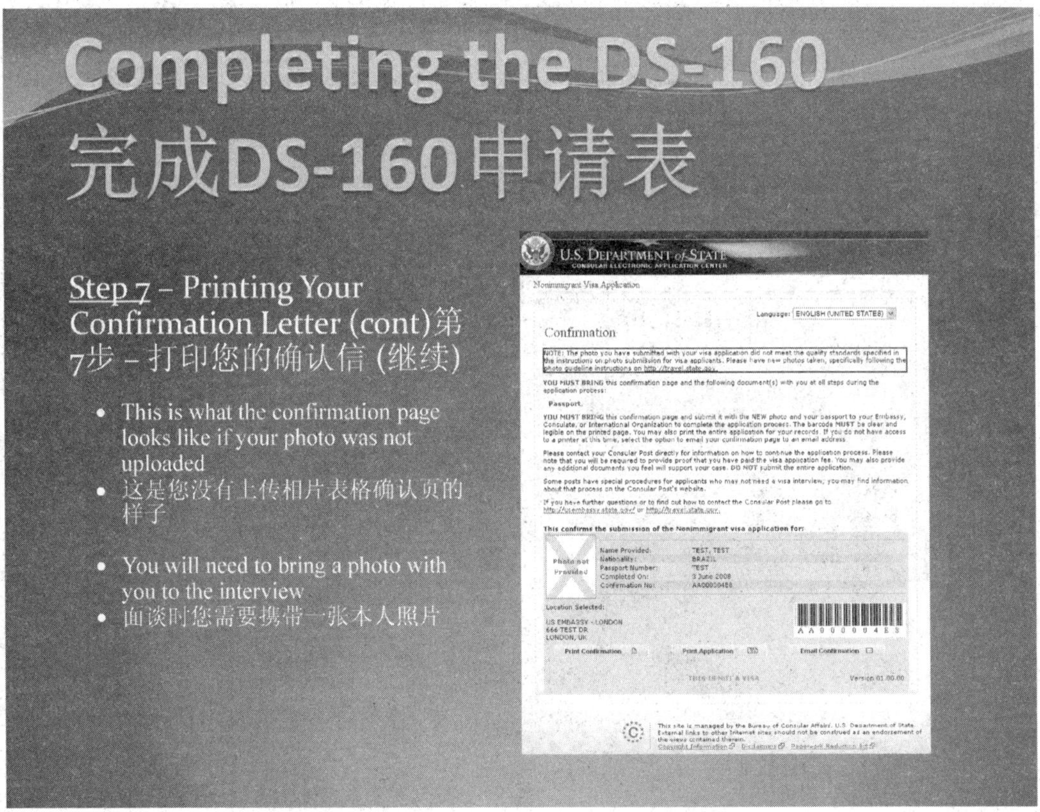
Completing the DS-160
完成DS-160申请表
Step 7 – Printing Your Confirmation Letter (cont)第7步 – 打印您的确认信 (继续)
This is what the confirmation page looks like if your photo was not uploaded
这是您没有上传相片表格确认页的样子
You will need to bring a photo with you to the interview
面谈时您需要携带一张本人照片
U.S. DEPARTMENT of STATE
Nonimmigrant Visa Application
Confirmation
Passport.
This confirms the submission of the Nonimmigrant visa application for:
Photo not Provided
Location Selected:
Print Confirmation
Print Application
Email Confirmation

图 2-19 DS-160 非移民签证申请表填写汉语辅导图XV

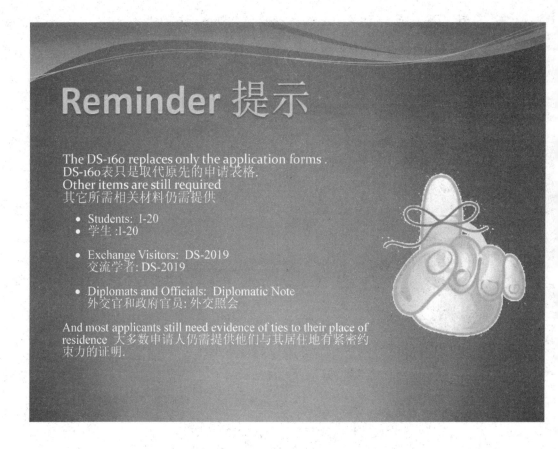

图 2 - 20 DS - 160 非移民签证申请表填写汉语辅导图 XVI

图 2 - 21　DS - 160 非移民签证申请表填写汉语辅导图 XⅦ

Contacts 联络方式

Consular Section: 领事处
Website: 网址: http://beijing.usembassy-china.org.cn/niv_info.html
Blog: 博客   http://blog.sina.com.cn/usembassyvisa
Phone: 电话   010-8531-3000
Fax: 传真   010-8531-3333
Address: No. 55 An Jia Lou Road, Chaoyang District
        Beijing 100600
地址: 北京市朝阳区安家楼路55号
邮编: 100600

(Slideshow created by Embassy Kuala Lumpur and Translated by Embassy Beijing CIU Team Han Yan, Li Ang, and Guo Xiaoli)

图 2 - 22　DS - 160 非移民签证申请表填写汉语辅导图XⅧ

签证面谈时可以准备一些
辅助性文件材料

　　上节内容,详细解答了如何填写 DS-160 非移民签证申请表的细节,这份中英文对照的解释,来自美国国务院和驻华大使馆,是公开的权威性官方指南。各位申请赴美签证之前,务必仔细阅读,精心体会。即使你有签证咨询中介机构为你服务,这些关键细节也值得你反复品味,毕竟,没有人可以替代你与移民官员面对面谈话。除此以外,在非移民签证面谈时,建议申请者最好备妥以下文件,以便移民官员询问时,作为证据出示。这些文件包括,但不限于下列数项:

　　• 必须在美国以外拥有一处您不会遗弃的住所的证明;

　　• 在美国仅作限定的短期停留的依据;

　　• 在逗留结束之后会离开美国的理由;

　　• 有充足的资金支付此行所需费用的证据;

　　• 美国公司或个人发出的邀请函、银行存折、户口簿、以往出国旅游的照片、房产证、工作和收入证明。

　　与移民官员面谈时,最好带上你拥有的所有老护照,特别是曾经贴有美国签证的护照,那些还未联网时期的文字信息,最能说明你的非移民倾向。值得重申的是,提供上述材料并不能保证您获得签证,但它们对您个人情况的陈述会有所帮助。

赴美探望子女的父母,在申请 B1/B2 签证时,应该准备好在面谈时证明您和您孩子的关系。您可以带上任何您希望可以证明你与子女之间亲属关系的材料,包括但不限于:亲属关系公证书、近期和以往您与子女的合照、子女出生证明、往来信件、子女的签证和(或者)绿卡等。

根据申请人的背景和经验,特别是在高科技、尖端商务等敏感领域工作的访客,领事馆会对一些 B1/B2 签证申请人进行额外的安全审核。为了让这个额外的步骤尽量迅速顺利地进行,建议您在面谈时带好以下英文材料:

• 您的简历,包括所有发表过的科研论文清单;

• 一份详细的行程,包括您在美期间的联系方式;

• 由您要访问的美国公司出具一份将要进行的业务讨论内容的明确说明;

• 如果您去参加培训,您需要提供一份详细的每日培训计划,包括所有涉及课题的描述,以及培训师的姓名。

基于我们之前的描述,目前在美国驻华各领事馆的签证数量庞大,因此都是通过电话预约签证日期的方式。即使到了面试的那天,还是有些值得申请人注意的问题。

第一,安静排队。许多申请人是首次办理赴美签证,兴奋异常,往往在排队的过程中,就耐不住寂寞,前后搭讪,或是掩盖焦虑的自我,或是展示自信的自我。其实,这两种现场表现都是不必要的,既不会增加你的签证率,反倒是在狭小的签证办公空间中,陡增了不和谐的噪音。

理论上说,美国领事馆属于美国官方领地,办公场所安静是第一位的。若吵闹过了头,签证官员完全可能以任何理由拒绝麻烦制造者入境。

第二,有问有答。事实上,签证官员来到面试你的窗口前,DS－160表格中显示的内容已经基本让他有了初步决定,大部分的问话都是证实性的。基于签证申请人的焦虑与记忆误差,千万不要主动陈述自以为得体的内容,不要答非所问,不要临时耍小聪明,要实事求是,言简意赅地依据 DS－160 表格上所填写的内容,有问才有答,这是以不变应万变的法则。

第三,携带老幼。一般来说,排队过程确实很长,使馆人员会做些人性化的调整,高龄老人的家属,也可以主动向工作人员提出帮助的请求,要求增加座椅或者适当减少排队时间。带儿童一起签证的申请人,需要教会儿童基本的文明礼仪,此外,儿童的童趣与可爱往往会缓解枯燥的签证面试过程,使签证官紧绷的神经得到放松,一念之间,或许你的签证申请就通过了。

以上简单介绍了非移民签证的程序和内容,它可以作为本书重点内容移民事务和留学事务介绍的前奏,理由很简单,假如你没有到过美国,如何下得了决心移民美国,或者将子女送往一个陌生的国度,留学数年?"梨子咬上一口,酸甜自然分晓",好像是某位老人的名言,曾经家喻户晓。

第三章
CHAPER 3
**投资移民：中产家
庭的再次抉择**

赴美投资移民
并不那么难

　　大约是 2000 年，就在我立足美国 10 年左右，我自以为有了一些资本和经验积累，开始筹划回国创业。这时我发现，许多国人早已发达起来，华人街上出现了越来越多的高消费人士，我的房客文先生，就是这样的一位令我诧异的同胞。

　　文先生来自北方一座中等城市，原本在中学教数学。由于他是家族里唯一可以使用一些简单英语的读书人，所以被派往常驻美国，为家族企业办事。说白了，也就是在美国各地收购废旧金属和塑料，输送回国后在家族企业中加工电线电缆，或者直接将废旧原料高价转手卖给第三方，倒腾赢利。

　　某日，文先生从刊登华人租售房屋信息最广的《世界日报》上，读到了我的二房一厅出租广告，与我通话后，立即过来看房。他开着一辆崭新的日产千里马（Nissan Maxima），令我吃惊的是，这样的房车主人本不该属于我的这套出租房房客的范围，因为这款高档房车车型在中国大陆很少见，是专门为北美市场打造的，即使是美国房东，也不一定舍得以此作为座驾。文先生在我出租的二房一厅里逛了不到两分钟，就下了订金："我最满意的是，你还提供私家车位。"几天后，文先生请家具公司搬来全套的崭新家具，完全没有我们当初移民美国的寒酸相：租房砍价，家具拼凑。

文先生的邮件特别多,而且来头重要,大部分是联邦国税局、纽约州国税局、公民与移民服务局和大牌律师事务所的公函。慢慢地我了解到,文氏家庭正在办理投资移民事宜,此时我已在美国居住了近10年,对此类移民事务却一无所知。文氏移民事务的发展走向,果然如数学教师出身的文总所料:不到两年,他就搬出了我的二房一厅公寓,在靠近纽约长岛的高档住宅区,购买了一栋独立的花园洋房。文先生的家族生意并非高不可企,但他的成功移民案例却让我刮目相看:只要有能力在美国做份小生意的华人,真的可以完成身份的转换,移民不在话下。

事实也真的获得印证。此后不久,我的几位朋友合资在西部城市郊外购地,建造一栋规模不大的小型商务楼,然后招商引资,从事相应的物业服务。为此,其中几位中国大陆合伙人也如愿获得移民投资绿卡。在美国投资移民法律看来,无论收废品,还是造房改建,都是实打实的生意,既有资金投入,又创造了当地的就业机会。

和所有美国城乡结合部的办公商务建筑一样,往往一个路边加油站,就是未来商务中心的选项,有眼光的小型房地产开发商或者房地产开发个人,一般就是将地图打开,沿着公路延伸,在十字路口占地立足。先开加油站,这是投资最小、生意最固定的买卖。坚持若干年后,周边商业环境一旦符合继续投资的标准,那就开始琢磨将加油站改建为小型购物中心或者综合办公楼宇,这样每月就有10~20份商业租金的收入,房产本身的价值在上升,自营的物业管理公司也细水长流,小本产业也算是从个体经营升级到了小企业化运作。

图 3-1 乌鸡变凤凰——小型商业改造项目

三十年后立足河东：
国人真的很有钱

　　21世纪伊始，投资移民这种方式在华人中逐步扩展开来。这种移民途径，在华人移民美国的历程中，完全是个全新的模式。撇开清末移民潮中的华人劳工历史不谈，20世纪70年代后期，中国改革开放开启的第一波赴美移民，基本上是设法找个沾亲带故的远房亲戚，将自己带进美国，电视剧《北京人在纽约》就基本上记录了那个时代的移民途径。之后大学生日益增多，年轻人努力用功，考了托福考美国研究生入学考试(GRE)，好不容易在美国大学拿了学位，再将学生签证转成 H-1B 签证①。只要肯坚持为老板廉价工作几年，最终确实会获得长期居留的绿卡。也有条件特别优异的留学生，申请特殊杰出人才移民，一步到位。但这种案例毕竟只属于少数精英，没有太大的普遍推广意义。

　　如今，国人中家族开办几家企业，或者城市中产家庭在大中城市拥有几套商品房的极多。相对来说，美国投资移民要求 50 万～100 万美元的投资标准，确实不算太高。所以，捧着大把的现钱，被美国法律规范地请进美国定居，正是历史上从来也没有出现过的好时机，我们正走在光明正大的移民路上。

----

　　①　H-1B签证是签发给在美国工作的人士的美国签证，属于非移民签证。这种签证必须由雇主出面为申请人申请，且申请人的雇用申请书需要美国公民与移民服务局的批准。——编者注

　　仅从对投资移民的资金要求上，比较几个国家或地区的投资移民门槛及要求，美国的优势一目了然。

表 3-1　五大热点移民国家或地区投资移民门槛及要求对比表

国家（地区）	投资金额门槛	投资项目要求
美国	50 万美元 （约合 325 万元人民币）	移民局①批准的项目；5 年
加拿大	80 万加元 （约合 547 万元人民币）	政府指定并担保的基金；5 年
澳大利亚	约 50 万澳元 （约合 349 万元人民币）	政府指定债券、企业等； 一般为期 4 年
新加坡	250 万新元 （约合 1 314 万元人民币）	政府批准基金，资产至少 1 000 万新元
中国香港	1 000 万港元 （约合 836 万元人民币）	2010 年 10 月刚取消 房地产投资类别

---

　　① 美国移民局在 2003 年 1 月 1 日前是指美国移民归化局（Immigration and Naturalization Service，缩写为"INS"），隶属于美国司法部。移民局的职能现已为美国国土安全局接收，其绝大部分功能被分配到国土安全局属下的三个单位。即公民与移民服务局（U. S. Citizenship and Immigration Services）、移民与海关执法局（Immigration and Customs Enforcement）和海关与边境巡查局（Customs and Border Patrol）。

只争朝夕快行动：
目前美国投资移民的机遇

　　美国移民局有关投资移民 EB-5[①] 报告书中指出：1991—2000 年，由于各种原因，投资移民没有获得预期的广受欢迎，每年 1 万个名额都有剩余。从 1996 年起，美国企业加强了吸引外国投资力度，移民局对申请投资移民的企业聘用美国籍员工的人数要求也稍加放松，此后投资移民申请有逐渐上升的趋势，但漏洞随之而来。移民局放松了不少条件以吸引更多投资者，如调整投资的方式、计算聘用工人的方式等，投资者开始透过美国现有的投资基金申请投资移民，在美国境内借款申请投资移民，从而减少真正投资的数额等。移民局发现，申请门槛稍微宽松后，就有投资移民申请者将资本投入基金，结果在美国的新创企业，所聘员工是原来即存在的员工，根本没有达到以投资移民创造就业机会的目的。不过这些陈年把戏，现在已经无法复制。东方经济复苏后事过境迁，真正的投资移民规模，开始向上攀升。

　　1998 年 8 月 31 日，移民局依据四个投资移民判例，向审理投资移

---

　　① 美国 EB-5 投资移民方案是美国移民法中针对海外投资移民所设立的移民签证类别，简称"EB-5"，它是美国所有移民类别中，申请核准时间最短、资格条件限制最少的一条便捷通道。可根据以下任一项取得 EB-5 资格：一，在美国任何地方投资 100 万美元并至少雇请 10 位雇员；二，在国家认可的低就业地区投资 50 万美元并至少雇请 10 位雇员；三，在经政府批准的"区域中心"（Regional Center）投资 50 万美元。——编者著

民的分局及移民律师协会,通报了有关投资移民的新规则及定义,主要包括:一,投资资金不能以"信托"方式处理,因为移民局认为信托不具创业的特性;二,移民局禁止投资移民在取得居留权后,把投资资本转手给企业的原始持有人;三,移民局不认为初步投资后,随后以分期付款的方式达到投资全额是合适的投资方法;四,投资者应明确说明投资款的来源细节。

上述四个投资移民判例分别是 Soffci、Izuumi、Ho 及 Hsiung 四人的投资案,可以视作经验教训的案例。这样,移民局对资金的来源、数额、贷款及分期和投资的回收有了不同的解释及规定,但是并没有完全阻绝以部分投资方式,投资以其他保证回收或财务安排,进行投资移民。因此,聘用专家为申请人依据投资地点与项目作个案处理,随机应变,这是值得推荐的方法,可以作为自己阅读法律文本和参考书籍的互相印证。

美国仿效加拿大,设置投资移民,源于加拿大投资移民法案,它确实带来了资金和经营人才。美国的投资移民设计,也是以吸引中国香港的资金和商业人才为主要目的,希望 1997 年中国香港的回归,会将有关的转移资金流到美国,据此而设置一条移民和投资的通道。不料投资移民演变至今 20 余年,结果却是中国内地的投资移民数量最大。投资移民提供给外籍投资者美国的居留权,提供现有或新设企业的经商机会,以此交换移民申请人的资本以及实际经营投资,条件不算苛刻。

投资移民是资金直接投入与企业实际经营的综合行为。但是移民局允许投资者能证明在投资的企业投入相当的时间,也可以算作符合

53

条件,这样就避免了所谓蹲"移民监"①的个人流动性问题,比如投资者海外旅行的时间,因为投资人的旅行与企业发展往往有很大的关联性,很难以投资不作为来界定。美国投资移民与加拿大投资移民不同之处在于,美国企业投资人不能投入资金后,完全不管所投项目。但是目前的特区项目还是考虑了非经营管理人才投资美国的现实问题,不必在企业管理上亲力亲为。投资者不需要有任何经营的经验或教育背景,唯一的条件就是要有足够的资金。此外申请的必要文件,包括申请书、个人的财务资料、经商计划、投资地区说明及其他的辅助证明。对于现有特区移民投资计划,一般已将统一的标准格式文件备妥,申请过程的复杂性大大降低。综合比较下来,目前投资移民的成功比率大约有五成。

合格的投资者,先获得两年的"有条件"永久居民的临时绿卡,权益与美国永久居民完全相似,"有条件"永久居民在美国的移民绿卡中不是特例,并非有意刁难申请者。只是在两年到期之前,要更换正式绿卡,其程序与通过合法婚姻程序的配偶移民类同。通过与美国公民建立合法婚姻关系的移民类别,也要求度过两年的"有条件"永久居民的临时绿卡阶段,届时,移民官员亲自考核婚姻真假。由于家庭生活没有投资经营这样书面化的证据,临时出现矛盾的状况经常发生,著名的电影《绿卡》,就是这类题材的艺术化反映。两年大限将至,为了更换为正式的永久居民身份,投资者要证明投资情况与当初在申请投资移民时类似,例如聘用的 10 个美国员工正常得到工资,投资项目仍旧属实,移

---

① "移民监"是个形象的比喻,比如要想移民就要坐监狱一样不能长期离开要移民的国家(短期可以),因为如果离开时间长了,就不能申请入籍或者会丧失移民身份。——编者注

民局就会按规矩允许申请人更换为正常的绿卡。

与加拿大投资移民的另一项比较不同的区别是，美国投资移民的申请人，应该以美国为主要居住地点，例如以该常住地址开设了个人的银行账户，办理了驾照，交纳了个人地方及联邦所得税，无论购买还是租赁，你要证明有自己的常住地址。投资人每年都应该在美国至少居住几个星期或几个月，以免移民局怀疑投资者"结构性地放弃美国的居住权"，即美国绿卡。由于种种原因，投资移民申请人一定要在美国以外滞留一年以上的话，最好向移民局申请"回美证（Re-entry Permit）"，这样可以比较安心地在外逗留。

在职业移民的种类中，有两个类别是和在美国投资设立公司并进行经营有直接的联系，就是企业家投资移民（职业移民第五优先，EB-5）和跨国公司经理主管移民（职业移民第一优先C类，EB－1C）。外国人如果想通过在美国投资的方式得到绿卡，可以根据各自的情况和条件选择其一。但这是两类完全不同的移民程序，千万不可混淆。

2011年年初，美国《侨报》报道了美国投资移民近两年越来越受到各国移民青睐的现状。据公民与移民服务局2010年第四季度发布的统计，在2010年财年中，来自中国大陆的投资移民申请居全世界之最，占全年发放的EB-5签证总数的41％，共计772人。

据公民与移民服务局的统计，2010年投资移民签证获得者的前五位来源地分别是中国大陆（772人，占41％）、韩国（295人，占16％）、英国（135人，占7％）、中国台湾（94人，占5％），以及印度（62人，占3％），其他国家和地区总共获得527份签证，占总数的28％。公民与移民服务局全年发放的EB-5签证为1 885件，而在2005年，这一数字仅为744件。这些有限的数字，也同时意味着目前的竞争较少，成功概率较高。

公民与移民服务局表示，目前 90％ 左右的投资移民都是以参与区域中心（Regional Centers）开发的方式来进行投资。这主要是区域中心相对于个体企业经营来说更稳定，在计算所创造的就业方面也更有优势。

过去两年里，由于美国经济不景气，全美各地涌现出许多以吸引投资移民为融资手段的区域开发项目，纽约市的布鲁克林海军船坞改造项目，是这些项目中最受青睐、最成功的几个项目之一。通常在这些被公民与移民服务局定义为"区域中心"的开发项目中，大部分是来自各国的有财力的移民人士，所谓近朱者赤，近墨者黑，项目中的申请人构成有时也会影响移民官员的判断，影响成功率。目前全美总共有 120 个被公民与移民服务局批准的"区域中心"。投资移民的批准率逐年上升，公民与移民服务局为此加大了这方面的移民官员的人力投入。

在 2005 年，投资移民最后一步 I-829 申请（临时绿卡转正式绿卡申请，即投资移民去除条件式申请）的批准率仅为 62％，2006 年至 2010 年，I-829 申请的批准率分别为 64％、69％、70％、86％ 和 83％，逐年提高。2010 年，新递交的 I-829 申请有 768 份，I-526 申请（投资移民申请）已达 1 955 份，创历史新高，不过相比其他移民申请，总数还是偏低，机会与挑战并存。目前投资移民每一步的申请处理时间平均为 5 个月左右，相当有序平稳。

美国投资移民
法案的基本要素

1991 年起,美国为了应对经济不景气,恢复经济活力,增加就业机会,各个州政府开始加大吸引资金力度,欢迎海外成功人士投资美国。为此,美国联邦政府设立投资移民项目,归属美国职业移民的第五类(简称"EB-5")。该项目每年有 1 万个名额,从设立至今,每年都有剩余名额。最近两年,了解 EB-5 的途径越来越多,不仅通过公开的网站,还有不少移民服务公司开设免费讲座,到处吸引申请人。问题是,这些信息可能是不完整的,有些主讲人可能连美国都没去过,兜售的是二手甚至三手的消息,当然,其中也不乏招摇撞骗的坏人。所以,笔者致力于将有关的美国移民机构的官方表格罗列在此,但这并不等于阅读此书,每位有志移民美国的人士,就有能力依样画葫芦,摆脱律师和中介公司,自己独立完成移民事务了。我只是倡导读者在决定进入投资移民程序时,不妨在掏出钱包支付移民公司服务费用以前,先期了解一下有关的初步内容,以便做到心中有数,避免花了冤枉钱,更主要的是,避免绕个大弯路,坐失良机。

近来美国的投资移民申请人数和批准人数大幅度增加,投资移民已成为当今的大热门。投资移民美国热的关键在于,美国的投资移民对申请人没有学历、语言、年龄和商业背景的要求,也没有限制申请自由旅行的要求。一旦申请成功,申请人的配偶和 21 岁以下的未婚子女均可同时获得绿卡,即美国永久居留资格。从此一家人可自由进出美国,享受美国社会福利。

美国 EB-5 投资移民方案有三种政策。

1. 一般政策。美国投资移民的一般政策是:(1)投资至少 100 万美元;(2)在两年内创造至少 10 个全职就业机会。

2. 优惠政策。在一些落后地区或者失业率高的地区,美国投资移民申请人可以享受优惠政策:在两年内仍然要创造至少 10 个全职就业机会,但是投资的金额降为 50 万美元。

3. 特区政策。无论是在一般政策下还是在优惠政策下,投资者都要创办投资实体,亲自进行管理,这对于大多数海外投资移民者不是很方便,所以美国国会推出了投资移民的特区政策——区域中心(Regional Center)项目。各州政府可以向联邦移民局申请成立区域中心,然后招商。外国投资者只要把 50 万美元投入获批准的某一个区域中心的项目,即可符合投资至少 50 万美元和在两年内创造至少 10 个全职就业机会这两个条件。这样的特区政策大大方便了大多数海外投资移民者。事实上,超过 90% 的申请人利用了这一特区政策。

比如,参与纽约市的区域中心项目就是值得推荐的一种方案。纽约州是美国经济发达的州之一,现在这个区域中心项目地处纽约市,靠近世界的金融中心,即纽约市政府对布鲁克林区海军船坞基地进行改造,利用投资移民的特区政策进行招商。纽约市区域中心的第一期项目已经在 2010 年夏天圆满完成,120 个指标已经用完。目前,第二期已经开始,共有 130 个指标。基本信息是:(1) 投资的 50 万美元存放在纽约市区域中心在花旗银行的托管账号,如果投资者的临时绿卡申请没有得到美国联邦移民局的批准,资金归还给投资者。(2) 投资者的临时绿卡申请得到美国联邦移民局的批准之后，投资的 50 万美元将借贷给公司。公司用其资产进行担保，投资者拥有对这些公司资产的最优先权。（3）纽约市区域中心承诺五年后归还本金，此外每年可能有 1%～2% 的分红。（4）纽约市政府和美国联邦政府也有资金投入。

　　总而言之，投资 50 万美元，最快半年内拿美国临时绿卡，两年后拿正式绿卡，五年后收回成本。参照这样的项目标准，投资移民美国的其他方案，就可以举一反三，货比三家了。

　　投资移民于 1991 年生效实施，是美国新移民法中职业移民项的第五类优先移民。新移民法规定投资移民的投资金额为 100 万美元，用于设立一个新的商业性公司，合资和购买，以及扩展现有的企业，并雇用至少 10 名美籍或有资格在美国工作的外籍全职员工。新移民法对于能投资 100 万美元以及能创造 10 个以上美国人工作机会的外国投资人，每年给予 1 万个具有永久居留权的移民名额。其中，至少 3 000 个投资名额保留给在郊区或高失业率区的投资者，并规定放宽限制，其投资金额为 50 万美元。

　　所谓"郊区"，指大都会或人口总数达两万人的城市以外的城市。所谓"高失业率区"，指失业率高于全国平均比率 1.5 倍的地方。施行细则并规定，即使在大都会或人口总数在两万名以上的城市，因某种地理或政治的特殊情况，也可符合高失业率区的条件。所以纽约等大城市，也可成为投资移民的特殊地区。

　　投资的资本包括现金、设备、存货或其他实质财产，定期存款、政府公债及其他容易变成现金的证券以及货款。但投资的资金来源，不得以非法手段取得，申请人应以经商记录、个人及公司报税税单，及其他文件来证明其资金来源均属合法，该资金来自哪个国家或地区不是关键因素,来自老爸的馈赠,也是合理的途径,只要老爸的资金来源经得住移民审核部门的询问即可。资金的合法来源包括薪资、分红、继承、投资收益、出售资产或者是贷款,当然贷款要经过专家设计,否则不一定通得过移民局的挑剔询问。

申请人必须创立一个新的商业性企业,所谓新的商业性企业,包括下列三种:

(1) 创设一个全新生意。

(2) 收买陷于困境的企业,加以整顿或重组,并保留原有员工。

(3) 买卖已存在的生意,并加以扩充。所谓扩充,指增加原生意资产净值40%以上,或增加原生意所雇员工数达40%以上。采取扩充方式申请移民者,也必须符合资金及雇用10名员工的基本要求。新的商业性公司可由一个人投资,也可由两个人以上的投资者联合投资。

投资移民的立法精神,在于创造就业机会。新的商业性企业必须雇用全职员工至少10名,员工指提供劳务而换取薪水的人,投资移民申请人及其配偶和子女不包括在内。美国法律规定的全职岗位指每周工作35小时以上。若同一职位由两人共同负责,而达上列时数标准,也可算为一个全职员工。

美国移民法中的投资移民雇用10名全职员工的施行细则,有一项很宽松的规定,即投资移民申请人可以先提出计划,表明公司要在两年之内需雇用至少10名全职员工,这样就可以将移民申请提前展开。

美国新移民法对投资移民的投资限制是两年。即投资移民申请人和配偶及子女可先取得有条件居留身份,两年之后如果移民局认定投资人确实履行有关规定,投资人和配偶及子女可成为美国的永久居民。一个得以落实的技术性空间是,投资者可在投资限定的两年之内的最后一天雇用 10 名员工。投资者本人及亲属已取得绿卡之后，如果工作不需要，可不再雇用员工。但投资者必须在两年内维持新企业的经营和雇用条件，维持企业的生存，以保证两年后仍能保持投资移民义务的履行，否则，仍无法永久居留美国。

申请投资移民的基本
程序与表格资料

　　申请人须填写 I–526 表格，连同各项证明，向投资企业所属的移民局提出申请。申请案若被批准，则投资人和其配偶及未满 21 岁的未婚子女，将先取得有条件的合法居留身份。当然，也不排除有人经过深思熟虑后，决定放弃进一步落实投资移民的申请。这时，你必须在取得有条件的合法居留身份满两年期限前的 90 天之内，填写 I–826 表格，向移民局提出解除投资移民的申请。一般来讲，如移民局认定投资人确实符合条件，投资人及家属可正式成为合法永久居民。由于投资移民只要求所投资的事业至少必须存在两年，若申请人取得正式绿卡后，卖掉生意，解雇员工，并不会影响申请人的永久居留权。

　　必须认清的是，美国法律规定了所有永久居民的纳税义务。在美国投资和申请永久居留身份后，该投资者在世界上其他地方的收入也必须在美国纳税，这是美国法律对享受本国福利的民众的基本要求，丝毫来不得含糊。

　　投资人不能先申请移民签证而后投资，而是在确实进行了投资之后才能申请签证。即使移民局很快批准了其投资移民的申请，也只是一个有条件限制的临时绿卡。两年之后，移民局对其投资项目进行考查，合格者方能将临时绿卡转为永久绿卡，倘若投资人在这两年中投资失败，投资人不仅会丧失大笔资金，而且还可能丧失永久居留权。

自 20 世纪 90 年代美国开放投资移民以来，投资移民以亚洲投资者占绝大多数，有 81％的投资移民来自亚洲，9％为欧洲投资者，5％从南美洲来，其余来自世界其他各地。虽然，当初制定投资移民法案，假想目标是涌出的中国香港资金，但是来自亚洲的投资移民者却以中国内地的"投资者"为多。

重要的是，让我们一起来认识这份 I-526 表格，这样无论你是否聘用律师或者其他专业人士为你提供移民服务，你都可以做到心中有数。填写"投资移民申请表"（I-526 表）不是一种走过场的形式。美国确实是由文件堆积、表格无数的管理系统构成，尽管效率很低，当事人急得要命，但美国不做表面文章，尤其是在电子化时代，任何信息都会联网记录在案。这一点申请人要格外小心，那里没有人情可以松动，每个公务人员都深晓渎职的严重后果，为了保住自己的饭碗，来不得半点虚假。

对于投资移民，美国政府对投入的资金来源审查极其严格，申请人仅仅出示资金证明是不足以说服移民官员的，你必须同时出具文件来说明资金的来龙去脉，保证资金的合法性。其中，合法的纳税证明是华人投资者最值得进行自我评估的关键环节。当然，美国政府的人性化处理也尽在案例中体现，它没有要求申请者本人挣来投资金额，也就是说，如果申请人超过 21 岁，无法跟随父母一起投资移民获得永久居留权，但父母可以把钱送给该申请人，由他自己单独出面申请投资移民，前提是，父母必须证明资金的来龙去脉，保证资金的合法性。目前，投资移民的临时绿卡申请大约需要 4 个月的时间。

投资移民 I－526 申请表的形式与内容

投资移民 I－526 申请表共有三张，具体如下。

Department of Homeland Security
U.S. Citizenship and Immigration Services

OMB No. 1615-0026; Exp. 01/31/2012
Form I-526, Immigrant Petition by Alien Entrepreneur

Do Not Write in This Block - For USCIS Use Only (Except G-28 Block Below)

Classification	**Action Block**	Fee Receipt
Priority Date		**To be completed by Attorney or Representative, if any** ☐ G-28 is attached Attorney's State License No.
Remarks:		

START HERE - Type or print in black ink.

Part 1. Information About You

Family Name ____ Given Name ____ Middle Name ____

In care of Street Number and Name: ____

Address: ____ Apt. Number ____

City ____ State or Province ____ Country ____ Zip/Postal Code ____

Date of Birth (mm/dd/yyyy) ____ Country of Birth ____ Social Security # (if any) ____ A # (if any) ____

If you are in the United States, provide the following information: Date of Arrival (mm/dd/yyyy) ____ I-94 # ____

Current Nonimmigrant Status ____ Date Current Status Expires (mm/dd/yyyy) ____ Daytime Phone # with Area Code ____

Part 2. Application Type ***(Check one)***

a. ☐ This petition is based on an investment in a commercial enterprise in a targeted employment area for which the required amount of capital invested has been adjusted downward.

b. ☐ This petition is based on an investment in a commercial enterprise in an area for which the required amount of capital invested has been adjusted upward.

c. ☐ This petition is based on an investment in a commercial enterprise that is not in either a targeted area or in an upward adjustment area.

Part 3. Information About Your Investment

Name of commercial enterprise in which funds are invested ____

Street Address ____

Phone # with Area Code ____ Business organized as (corporation, partnership, etc.) ____

Kind of business (e.g. furniture manufacturer) ____ Date established (mm/dd/yyyy) ____ IRS Tax # ____

RECEIVED: ____ RESUBMITTED: ____ RELOCATED: SENT ____ REC'D ____

Form I-526 (Rev. 11/23/10)Y

图 3－2 投资移民 I－526 申请表 I：姓名、地址等个人信息

Part 3. Information About Your Investment *(Continued)*

Date of your initial
investment (mm/dd/yyyy)

Amount of your
initial investment $

Your total capital investment
in the enterprise to date $

Percentage of the
enterprise you own

If you are not the sole investor in the new commercial enterprise, list on separate paper the names of all other parties (natural and non-natural) who hold a percentage share of ownership of the new enterprise and indicate whether any of these parties is seeking classification as an alien entrepreneur. Include the name, percentage of ownership, and whether or not the person is seeking classification under section 203(b)(5). **NOTE:** A "natural" party would be an individual person, and a "non-natural" party would be an entity such as a corporation, consortium, investment group, partnership, etc.

If you indicated in **Part 2** that the enterprise is in a targeted employment area
or in an upward adjustment area, name the county and State: County   State

Part 4. Additional Information About the Enterprise

Type of Enterprise (check one):

☐ New commercial enterprise resulting from the creation of a new business.

☐ New commercial enterprise resulting from the purchase of an existing business.

☐ New commercial enterprise resulting from a capital investment in an existing business.

Composition of the Petitioner's Investment:

Total amount in U.S. bank account .... $

Total value of all assets purchased for use in the enterprise................................. $

Total value of all property transferred from abroad to the new enterprise.......................... $

Total of all debt financing.. $

Total stock purchases.. $

Other (explain on separate paper)... $

Total $

Income:

When you made the investment......... Gross $ Net $

Now................................... Gross $ Net $

Net worth:

When you made investment.............. Gross $ Now $

图 3-3 投资移民 I-526 申请表 Ⅱ：投资总额、投资组成、资金来源等信息

Part 5. Employment Creation Information

Number of full-time employees in the enterprise in U.S. (excluding you, your spouse, sons, and daughters)

When you made your initial investment? [   ] Now [   ] Difference [   ]

How many of these new jobs were created by your investment? [   ] How many additional new jobs will be created by your additional investment? [   ]

What is your position, office, or title with the new commercial enterprise?

[   ]

Briefly describe your duties, activities, and responsibilities.

[   ]

What is your salary? $ [   ]   What is the cost of your benefits? $ [   ]

Part 6. Processing Information

Check One:

[ ] The person named in **Part 1** is now in the United States, and an application to adjust status to permanent resident will be filed if this petition is approved.

[ ] If the petition is approved and the person named in **Part 1** wishes to apply for an immigrant visa abroad, complete the following for that person:

Country of nationality: [   ]

Country of current residence or, if now in the United States, last permanent residence abroad: [   ]

If you provided a United States address in **Part 1**, print the person's foreign address:

[   ]

If the person's native alphabet is other than Roman letters, write the foreign address in the native alphabet:

[   ]

Are you in deportation or removal proceedings?   [ ] Yes (Explain on separate paper)   [ ] No

Have you ever worked in the United States without permission?   [ ] Yes (Explain on separate paper)   [ ] No

Part 7. Signature   *Read the information on penalties in the instructions before completing this section.*

I certify, under penalty of perjury under the laws of the United States of America, that this petition and the evidence submitted with it is all true and correct. I authorize the release of any information from my records that U.S. Citizenship and Immigration Services needs to determine eligibility for the benefit I am seeking.

Signature [   ]   Date [   ]

NOTE: *If you do not completely fill out this form or fail to the submit the required documents listed in the instructions, you may not be found eligible for the immigration benefit you are seeking and this petition may be denied.*

Part 8. Signature of Person Preparing Form, If Other Than Above (Sign below)

I declare that I prepared this application at the request of the above person, and it is based on all information of which I have knowledge.

Signature [   ]   Print Your Name [   ]   Date [   ]

Firm Name [   ]   Daytime phone # with area code [   ]

Address [   ]

Form I-526 (Rev. 11/23/10)Y Page

图 3-4 投资移民 I-526 申请表Ⅲ：雇员情况、申请时间和签名等信息

下面我们来大致分析投资移民 I-526 申请表的填写要求。

第一部分有关个人信息。你最好保证正确填写内容，姓名的姓（Family Name）和名（Given Name），千万不要搞错，否则，会与其他的资料无法吻合，给你带来无穷的麻烦。最多的例子是，写错一笔，这辈子就要改用假名，将错就错了。至于你没有的信息，如中间名，也要填上 N/A（Not Applicable，意为不适用），以示此栏不适用于你。对于大部分中国投资移民来讲，基本不会拥有社会安全号（Social Security）、绿卡号（A♯）等，所以此处以填 N/A 为妥。

第二部分涉及投资类别。一般来说，投资移民申请人已经与有关专业人员深入探讨过这个问题，已经在我们上述简介的三种投资方案中选出了一项。目前以选择工业园区，投资 50 万美元的案例居多。

第三部分主要是针对自办企业的投资移民。必须注意罗列所有企业股东的细节。而对于政府项目，只要写上投资地点与投资数额即可。

第四部分有关你所投资的企业财务状况。首先确认你所投资的企业是新设企业，全资购买，还是对已有企业的追加投资。然后逐一汇报目前的财务状况。

第五部分涉及企业的雇员状况。真实汇报你的正式雇员状况可以表明该企业对当地发展的意义。所谓正式雇员，也就是你在当地税务机关登记过的雇员名单，包括你自己。在美国，正式员工都要填写一份 W-2 表格，有资格申请 W-2 正式职位的申请人首先需要有社会安全号码，就像中国的身份证号。

为了帮助英文水平很好的读者自己慢慢琢磨投资移民 I-526 申请表的细节，我们将有关此表的英文填写指南附在下面，以便查阅。

Instructions

Read these instructions carefully to properly complete this form. If you need more space to complete an answer, use a separate sheet of paper. Write your name and Alien Registration Number (A-Number), if any, at the top of each sheet of paper and indicate the section and number of the item to which the answer refers.

NOTE: The filing fee is $1,500. Refer to "What Is the Fee?" on Page 3.

What Is the Purpose of Form I-526?

Form is used by an entrepreneur to petition U.S. Citizenship and Immigration Services (USCIS) for status as an immigrant to the United States under section 203(b)(5) of the Immigration and Nationality Act, as amended. That section of the law pertains to immigrant visas for an investor in a new commercial enterprise.

Who May File Form I-526?

You may file this petition for yourself if you have established a new commercial enterprise:

1. In which you will engage in a managerial or policy-making capacity;

2. In which you have invested or are actively in the process of investing the amount required for the area in which the enterprise is located;

3. Which will benefit the U.S. economy; and

4. Which will create full-time employment in the United States for at least 10 U.S. citizens, permanent residents, or other immigrants authorized to be employed, other than yourself, your spouse, your sons or daughters, or any nonimmigrant aliens.

The establishment of a new commercial enterprise may include:

1. Creation of a new business;

2. Purchase of an existing business with simultaneous or subsequent restructuring or reorganization resulting in a new commercial enterprise; or

3. Expansion of an existing business through investment of the amount required, so that a substantial change (at least 40 percent) in either the net worth, number of employees, or both, results.

The amount of investment required in a particular area is set by regulation. Unless adjusted downward for targeted areas or upward for areas of high employment, the amount of investment shall be **$1 million.** You may obtain additional information from our Web site at **www.uscis.gov,** or a U.S. Embassy or consulate abroad.

General Instructions

Fill Out Form I-526

1. Type or print legibly in black ink.

2. If extra space is needed to complete any item, attach a continuation sheet, indicate the item number, and date and sign each sheet.

3. Answer all questions fully and accurately. State that an item is not applicable with "N/A." If the answer is none, write "None."

Initial Evidence Requirements

The following evidence must be filed with your petition:

1. Evidence that you have established a lawful business entity under the laws of the jurisdiction in the United States in which it is located, or, if you have made an investment in an existing business, evidence that your investment has caused a substantial (at least 40 percent) increase in the net worth of the business, the number of employees, or both.

   Such evidence shall consist of copies of articles of incorporation, certificate of merger or consolidation, partnership agreement, certificate of limited partnership, joint venture agreement, business trust agreement, or other similar organizational document; a certificate evidencing authority to do business in a State or municipality, or if such is not required, a statement to that effect; or evidence that the required amount of capital was transferred to an existing business resulting in a substantial increase in the net worth or number of employees, or both.

图 3-5 投资移民 I-526 申请表填写指南 I：
表格填写目的、对象以及填表内容的依据

This evidence must be in the form of stock purchase agreements, investment agreements, certified financial reports, payroll records, or other similar instruments, agreements, or documents evidencing the investment and the resulting substantial change.

Evidence, if applicable, that your enterprise has been established in a targeted employment area. A targeted employment area is defined as a rural area or an area that has experienced high unemployment of at least 150 percent of the national average rate. A rural area is an area not within a metropolitan statistical area or not within the outer boundary of any city or town having a population of 20,000 or more.

Evidence that you have invested or are actively in the process of investing the amount required for the area in which the business is located.

Such evidence may include, but need not be limited to, copies of bank statements, evidence of assets that have been purchased for use in the enterprise, evidence of property transferred from abroad for use in the enterprise, evidence of monies transferred or committed to be transferred to the new commercial enterprise in exchange for shares of stock, any loan or mortgage, promissory note, security agreement, or other evidence of borrowing that is secured by assets of the petitioner.

Evidence that capital is obtained through lawful means. The petition must be accompanied, as applicable, by: foreign business registration records, tax returns of any kind filed within the last 5 years in or outside the United States, evidence of other sources of capital, or certified copies of any judgment, pending governmental civil or criminal actions, or private civil actions against the petitioner from any court in or outside the United States within the past 15 years.

Evidence that the enterprise will create at least 10 full-time positions for U.S. citizens, permanent residents, or aliens lawfully authorized to be employed (except yourself, your spouse, sons or daughters, and any nonimmigrant aliens). Such evidence may consist of copies of relevant tax records, Form I-9s, or other similar documents, if the employees have already been hired, or a business plan showing when such employees will be hired within the next 2 years.

6. Evidence that you are or will be engaged in the management of the enterprise, either through the exercise of day-to-day managerial control or through policy formulation. Such evidence may include a statement of your position title and a complete description of your duties, evidence that you are a corporate officer or hold a seat on the board of directors, or, if the new enterprise is a partnership, evidence that you are engaged in either direct management or policy-making activities.

Translations. Any document containing a foreign language submitted to USCIS must be accompanied by a full English language translation that the translator has certified as complete and accurate, and by the translator's certification that he or she is competent to translate from the foreign language into English.

Copies. Unless specifically required that an original document be filed with an application or petition, an ordinary legible photocopy may be submitted. Original documents submitted when not required will remain a part of the record, even if the submission was not required.

Where To File?

Updated Filing Address Information

The filing addresses provided on this form reflect the most current information as of the date this form was last revised. If you are filing Form I-526 more than 30 days after the latest edition date shown in the lower right corner, visit our Web site at www.uscis.gov before you file, and check the "FORMS" page to confirm the correct filing address and version currently in use. Check the edition date located in the lower right corner of the form.

If the edition date on your Form I-526 matches the edition date listed for Form I-526 on the online "FORMS" page, your version is current. If the edition date on the online version is later, download a copy and use it.

If you do not have Internet access, call the National Customer Service Center at 1-800-375-5283 to verify the current filing address and edition date.

Please read the filing instructions below carefully, to assure you file your application at the correct location.

Improperly filed forms will be rejected, and the fee returned, with instructions to resubmit the entire filing using the current form instructions.

图 3 - 6　投资移民 I - 526 申请表填写指南 Ⅱ :填表内容的依据
　　　　以及递交表格的程序和地方

Regardless of the location of the new commercial enterprise, file Form I-526 with all initial evidence requirements at the **USCIS Dallas Lockbox** facility.

For U.S. Postal Service:

> **USCIS**
> **P.O. Box 660168**
> **Dallas, TX 75266**

For Express mail or courier deliveries:

> **USCIS**
> **Attn: I-526**
> **2501 S. State Highway, 121 Business**
> **Suite 400**
> **Lewisville, TX 75067**

E-Notification

By filing your Form I-526 at a USCIS Lockbox facility, you may elect to receive an e-mail and/or text message notifying you that your application has been accepted. You must complete Form G-1145, E-Notification of Application/Petition Acceptance, and clip it to the first page of your application. To download a copy of Form G-1145, including the instructions, click on the link www.uscis.gov **"FORMS."**

What Is the Fee?

The filing fee for Form I-526 is **$1,500.**

Use the following guidelines when you prepare your check or money order for Form I-526:

1. The check or money order must be drawn on a bank or other financial institution located in the United States and must be payable in U.S. currency; and

2. Make the check or money order payable to **U.S. Department of Homeland Security**, unless:

   A. If you live in Guam, make it payable to **Treasurer, Guam**.

   B. If you live in the U.S. Virgin Islands, make it payable to **Commissioner of Finance of the Virgin Islands**.

   C. If you live outside the United States, Guam, the Commonwealth of Northern Mariana Islands or the U.S. Virgin Islands, contact the nearest U.S. Embassy or consulate for instructions on the method of payment.

NOTE: Spell out U.S. Department of Homeland Security; do not use the initials "USDHS" or "DHS."

How to Check If the Fees Are Correct

The form fee on this form is current as of the edition date appearing in the lower right corner of this page. However, because USCIS fees change periodically, you can verify if th fees are correct by following one of the steps below:

1. Visit our Web site at www.uscis.gov, select "FORMS," a check the appropriate fee;

2. Review the Fee Schedule included in your form package, you called us to request the form; or

3. Telephone our National Customer Service Center at **1-800-375-5283** and ask for the fee information.

Address Changes

If you change your address and you have an application or petition pending with USCIS, you may change your address online at www.uscis.gov, click "Online Change of Address," and follow the prompts, or you may complete and mail Form AR-11, Alien's Change of Address Card, to:

> **U.S. Citizenship and Immigration Services**
> **Change of Address**
> **P.O. Box 7134**
> **London, KY 40742-7134**

For commercial overnight or fast freight services only, mail

> **U.S. Citizenship and Immigration Services**
> **Change of Address**
> **1084-I South Laurel Road**
> **London, KY 40744**

Processing Information

Acceptance

Any petition that is not signed or accompanied by the correc fee will be rejected with a notice that it is deficient. You ma correct the deficiency and resubmit the petition. However, a petition is not considered properly filed until accepted by USCIS.

图 3 - 7　投资移民 **I** - 526 申请表填写

指南 Ⅲ：申请费用、联系方法等

Initial Processing

Once Form I-526 has been accepted, it will be checked for completeness, including submission of the required initial evidence. If you do not completely fill out the form or file it without required initial evidence, you will not establish a basis for eligibility, and we may deny your Form I-526.

Request for More Information or Interview

We may request more information or evidence, or we may request that you appear at a USCIS office for an interview. We may also request that you submit the originals of any copy. We will return these originals when they are no longer required.

Decision

The decision on Form I-526 involves a determination of whether you have established eligibility for the requested benefit. You will be notified of the decision in writing.

Approval

If you have established that you qualify for investor status, the petition will be approved. If you have requested that the petition be forwarded to a U.S. Embassy or consulate abroad, the petition will be sent there unless that consulate does not issue immigrant visas. If you are in the United States and state that you will apply for adjustment of status, and the evidence indicates you are not eligible for adjustment, the petition will be sent to a U.S. Embassy or consulate abroad. You will be notified in writing of the approval of the petition and where it has been sent, and the reason for sending it to a place other than the one requested, if applicable.

Meaning of Petition Approval

Approval of a petition shows only that you have established that you have made a qualifying investment. It does not guarantee that the U.S. Embassy or consulate will issue the immigrant visa. There are other requirements that must be met before a visa can be issued. The U.S. Embassy or consulate will notify you of those requirements. Immigrant status granted based on this petition will be conditional. Two years after entry, you will have to apply for the removal of conditions based on the ongoing nature of the investment.

Denial

If you have not established that you qualify for the benefit sought, the petition will be denied. You will be notified in writing of the reasons for the denial.

USCIS Forms and Information

To order USCIS forms, call our toll-free number at **1-800-870-3676.** You can also get USCIS forms and information on immigration laws, regulations, and procedures by telephoning our National Customer Service Center at **1-800-375-5283** or visiting our Internet Web site at **www.uscis.gov.**

As an alternative to waiting in line for assistance at your local USCIS office, you can now schedule an appointment through our Internet-based system, **InfoPass.** To access the system, visit our Web site. Use the **InfoPass** appointment scheduler and follow the screen prompts to set up your appointment. **InfoPass** generates an electronic appointment notice that appears on the screen.

Penalties

If you knowingly and willfully falsify or conceal a material fact or submit a false document with this request, we will deny your Form I-526 and may deny any other immigration benefit.

In addition, you will face severe penalties provided by law, and may be subject to criminal prosecution.

Privacy Act Notice

We ask for the information on this form, and associated evidence, to determine if you have established eligibility for the immigration benefit for which you are filing. Our legal right to ask for this information can be found in the Immigration and Nationality Act, as amended. We may provide this information to other government agencies. Failure to provide this information, and any requested evidence, may delay a final decision or result in denial of your Form I-526.

USCIS Compliance Review and Monitoring

By signing this form, you have stated under penalty of perjury (28 U.S.C.1746) that all information and documentation submitted with this form is true and correct. You also have authorized the release of any information from your records that USCIS may need to determine eligibility for the benefit you are seeking and consented to USCIS verification of such information.

图 3 - 8　投资移民 I - 526 申请表填写指南 Ⅳ：申请
程序、伪证惩罚和相关内容保密声明

The Department of Homeland Security has the right to verify any information you submit to establish eligibility for the immigration benefit you are seeking <u>at any time</u>. Our legal right to verify this information is in 8 U.S.C. 1103, 1155, 1184, and 8 CFR parts 103, 204, 205, and 214. To ensure compliance with applicable laws and authorities, USCIS may verify information before or after your case has been decided. Agency verification methods may include, but are not limited to: review of public records and information; contact via written correspondence, the Internet, facsimile or other electronic transmission, or telephone; unannounced physical site inspections of residences and places of employment; and interviews. Information obtained through verification will be used to assess your compliance with the laws and to determine your eligibility for the benefit sought.

Subject to the restrictions under 8 CFR part 103.2(b)(16), you will be provided an opportunity to address any adverse or derogatory information that may result from a USCIS compliance review, verification, or site visit after a formal decision is made on your case or after the agency has initiated an adverse action that may result in revocation or termination of an approval.

Paperwork Reduction Act

An agency may not conduct or sponsor an information collection and a person is not required to respond to a collection of information unless it displays a currently valid OMB control number. The public reporting burden for this collection of information is estimated at 1 hour and 15 minutes per response, including the time for reviewing instructions and completing and submitting the form. Send comments regarding this burden estimate or any other aspect of this collection of information, including suggestions for reducing this burden, to: U.S. Citizenship and Immigration Services, Regulatory Products Division, Office of the Executive Secretariat, 20 Massachusetts Ave., N.W., Washington, DC 20529-2020. OMB No. 1615-0026. **Do not mail your application to this address.**

图 3-9 投资移民 I-526 申请表填写
指南 V:法律依据和操作依据

完整的 I-526 申请表及其附件递交大约 4 个月之后,合格的申请人一般就会获得批准文件,这就意味着,你开始进入申请临时绿卡的阶段。

作为中国公民,如果申请人在美国境外,一旦美国移民局批准 I-526 申请表之后,批准书最后会转到美国驻广州领事馆。领事馆会在 3 个月左右通知申请人及其配偶和子女到领事馆领取赴美签证。一旦进入美国,每人都可以获得临时绿卡。如果申请人及其配偶和子女已经通过旅游签证进入美国,那么他们将通过 I-485 申请表,在美国境内调整身份,也就是申请绿卡。

恭喜填写 I–485 申请表：
开始拥有绿卡

有资格填写 I–485 申请表，意味着你已顺利获得临时绿卡，但它的有效期是两年，是有附带条件的。所以要想拥有永久绿卡，你可以提出去除附带条件的 I–829 申请。申请人必须在临时绿卡的两年有效期到期前的 90 天内提出去除条件的 I–829 申请。移民局要审核申请人在过去的两年内是否真正满足了投资移民的两个要求，即资金要求和雇员要求。如果 I–829 申请被批准，临时绿卡就变为永久绿卡。这样，你的人生就开始了新的轨迹。

OMB No. 1615-0023; Expires 12/31/2010

Department of Homeland Security
U.S. Citizenship and Immigration Services

Form I-485, Application to Register Permanent Residence or Adjust Status

START HERE - Type or Print (Use black ink)

	For USCIS Use Only

Part 1. Information About You

Family Name (*Last Name*)   Given Name (*First Name*)   Middle Name

Address - Street Number and Name   Apt. #

C/O (*in care of*)

City   State   Zip Code

Date of Birth (*mm/dd/yyyy*)   Country of Birth

Country of Citizenship/Nationality   U.S. Social Security # (*if any*)   A # (*if any*)

Date of Last Arrival (*mm/dd/yyyy*)   I-94 #

Current USCIS Status   Expires on (*mm/dd/yyyy*)

For USCIS Use Only

Returned	Receipt
Resubmitted	
Reloc Sent	
Reloc Rec'd	
Applicant Interviewed	

Part 2. Application Type (*Check one*)

I am applying for an adjustment to permanent resident status because:

a. ☐ An immigrant petition giving me an immediately available immigrant visa number that has been approved. (Attach a copy of the approval notice, or a relative, special immigrant juvenile, or special immigrant military visa petition filed with this application that will give you an immediately available visa number, if approved.)

b. ☐ My spouse or parent applied for adjustment of status or was granted lawful permanent residence in an immigrant visa category that allows derivative status for spouses and children.

c. ☐ I entered as a K-1 fiancé(e) of a U.S. citizen whom I married within 90 days of entry, or I am the K-2 child of such a fiancé(e). (Attach a copy of the fiancé(e) petition approval notice and the marriage certificate.)

d. ☐ I was granted asylum or derivative asylum status as the spouse or child of a person granted asylum and am eligible for adjustment.

e. ☐ I am a native or citizen of Cuba admitted or paroled into the United States after January 1, 1959, and thereafter have been physically present in the United States for at least 1 year.

f. ☐ I am the husband, wife, or minor unmarried child of a Cuban described above in **(e)**, and I am residing with that person, and was admitted or paroled into the United States after January 1, 1959, and thereafter have been physically present in the United States for at least 1 year.

g. ☐ I have continuously resided in the United States since before January 1, 1972.

h. ☐ Other basis of eligibility. Explain (for example, I was admitted as a refugee, my status has not been terminated, and I have been physically present in the United States for 1 year after admission). If additional space is needed, see **Page 2** of the instructions.

I am already a permanent resident and am applying to have the date I was granted permanent residence adjusted to the date I originally arrived in the United States as a nonimmigrant or parolee, or as of May 2, 1964, whichever date is later, and: (*Check one*)

i. ☐ I am a native or citizen of Cuba and meet the description in **(e)** above.

j. ☐ I am the husband, wife, or minor unmarried child of a Cuban and meet the description in **(f)** above.

Section of Law
☐ Sec. 209(a), INA
☐ Sec. 209(b), INA
☐ Sec. 13, Act of 9/11/57
☐ Sec. 245, INA
☐ Sec. 249, INA
☐ Sec. 1 Act of 11/2/66
☐ Sec. 2 Act of 11/2/66
☐ Other _____

Country Chargeable

Eligibility Under Sec. 245
☐ Approved Visa Petition
☐ Dependent of Principal Alien
☐ Special Immigrant
☐ Other _____

Preference

Action Block

To be Completed by
Attorney or Representative, if any
☐ Fill in box if Form G-28 is attached to represent the applicant.
VOLAG # _____
ATTY State License # _____

图 3 - 10 I - 485 申请表 I : 个人基本信息与申请类别

Part 3. Processing Information

A. City/Town/Village of Birth

Current Occupation

Your Mother's First Name

Your Father's First Name

Give your name exactly as it appears on your Form I-94, Arrival-Departure Record

Place of Last Entry Into the United States
(City/State)

In what status did you last enter? *(Visitor, student, exchange visitor, crewman, temporary worker, without inspection, etc.)*

Were you inspected by a U.S. Immigration Officer? Yes ☐   No ☐

Nonimmigrant Visa Number

Consulate Where Visa Was Issued

Date Visa Issued *(mm/dd/yyyy)*   Gender ☐ Male ☐ Female

Marital Status ☐ Married ☐ Single ☐ Divorced ☐ Widowed

Have you ever applied for permanent resident status in the U.S.?   ☐ Yes *(If "Yes" give date and place of filing and final disposition.)*   ☐ No

B. List your present spouse and all of your children (include adult sons and daughters). (If you have none, write "None." If additional space is needed, see **Page 2** of the instructions.)

Family Name *(Last Name)*	Given Name *(First Name)*		Middle Initial	Date of Birth *(mm/dd/yyyy)*
Country of Birth	Relationship	A # *(if any)*	Applying with you? Yes ☐ No ☐	
Family Name *(Last Name)*	Given Name *(First Name)*		Middle Initial	Date of Birth *(mm/dd/yyyy)*
Country of Birth	Relationship	A # *(if any)*	Applying with you? Yes ☐ No ☐	
Family Name *(Last Name)*	Given Name *(First Name)*		Middle Initial	Date of Birth *(mm/dd/yyyy)*
Country of Birth	Relationship	A # *(if any)*	Applying with you? Yes ☐ No ☐	
Family Name *(Last Name)*	Given Name *(First Name)*		Middle Initial	Date of Birth *(mm/dd/yyyy)*
Country of Birth	Relationship	A # *(if any)*	Applying with you? Yes ☐ No ☐	
Family Name *(Last Name)*	Given Name *(First Name)*		Middle Initial	Date of Birth *(mm/dd/yyyy)*
Country of Birth	Relationship	A # *(if any)*	Applying with you? Yes ☐ No ☐	

图 3 - 11 I - 485 申请表 Ⅱ：移民申请信息与
符合同时获得移民资格的家庭成员

. List your present and past membership in or affiliation with every organization, association, fund, foundation, party, club, society, or similar group in the United States or in other places since your 16th birthday. Include **any military service** in this part. If none, write "None." Include the name of each organization, location, nature, and dates of membership. If additional space is needed, attach a separate sheet of paper. Continuation pages must be submitted according to the guidelines provided on **Page 2** of the instructions under "What Are the General Filing Instructions?"

Name of Organization	Location and Nature	Date of Membership From	Date of Membership To

Answer the following questions. (If your answer is **"Yes"** to any question, explain on a separate piece of paper. Continuation pages must be submitted according to the guidelines provided on **Page 2** of the instructions under "What Are the General Filing Instructions?" Information about documentation that must be include with your application is also provide in this section.) Answering "Yes" does not necessarily mean that you are not entitled to adjust status or register for permanent residence.

. Have you **EVER**, in or outside the United States:

   a. Knowingly committed any crime of moral turpitude or a drug-related offense for which you have not been arrested?   Yes ☐ No ☐

   b. Been arrested, cited, charged, indicted, convicted, fined, or imprisoned for breaking or violating any law or ordinance, excluding traffic violations?   Yes ☐ No ☐

   c. Been the beneficiary of a pardon, amnesty, rehabilitation decree, other act of clemency, or similar action?   Yes ☐ No ☐

   d. Exercised diplomatic immunity to avoid prosecution for a criminal offense in the United States?   Yes ☐ No ☐

. Have you received public assistance in the United States from any source, including the U.S. Government or any State, county, city, or municipality (other than emergency medical treatment), or are you likely to receive public assistance in the future?   Yes ☐ No ☐

. Have you **EVER**:

   a. Within the past 10 years been a prostitute or procured anyone for prostitution, or intend to engage in such activities in the future?   Yes ☐ No ☐

   b. Engaged in any unlawful commercialized vice, including, but not limited to, illegal gambling?   Yes ☐ No ☐

   c. Knowingly encouraged, induced, assisted, abetted, or aided any alien to try to enter the United States illegally?   Yes ☐ No ☐

   d. Illicitly trafficked in any controlled substance, or knowingly assisted, abetted, or colluded in the illicit trafficking of any controlled substance?   Yes ☐ No ☐

. Have you **EVER** engaged in, conspired to engage in, or do you intend to engage in, or have you ever solicited membership or funds for, or have you through any means ever assisted or provided any type of material support to any person or organization that has ever engaged or conspired to engage in sabotage, kidnapping, political assassination, hijacking, or any other form of terrorist activity?   Yes ☐ No ☐

图 3 - 12 I - 485 申请表Ⅲ:个人社会、
政党背景与犯罪经历

Part 3.   Processing Information *(Continued)*

5. Do you intend to engage in the United States in:

    a. Espionage?   Yes ☐   No ☐

    b. Any activity a purpose of which is opposition to, or the control or overthrow of, the Government of the United States, by force, violence, or other unlawful means?   Yes ☐   No ☐

    c. Any activity to violate or evade any law prohibiting the export from the United States of goods, technology, or sensitive information?   Yes ☐   No ☐

6. Have you **EVER** been a member of, or in any way affiliated with, the Communist Party or any other totalitarian party?   Yes ☐   No ☐

7. Did you, during the period from March 23, 1933, to May 8, 1945, in association with either the Nazi Government of Germany or any organization or government associated or allied with the Nazi Government of Germany, ever order, incite, assist, or otherwise participate in the persecution of any person because of race, religion, national origin, or political opinion?   Yes ☐   No ☐

8. Have you **EVER** been deported from the United States, or removed from the United States at government expense, excluded within the past year, or are you now in exclusion, deportation, removal, or rescission proceedings?   Yes ☐   No ☐

9. Are you under a final order of civil penalty for violating section 274C of the Immigration and Nationality Act for use of fraudulent documents or have you, by fraud or willful misrepresentation of a material fact, ever sought to procure, or procured, a visa, other documentation, entry into the United States, or any immigration benefit?   Yes ☐   No ☐

10. Have you **EVER** left the United States to avoid being drafted into the U.S. Armed Forces?   Yes ☐   No ☐

11. Have you **EVER** been a J nonimmigrant exchange visitor who was subject to the 2-year foreign residence requirement and have not yet complied with that requirement or obtained a waiver?   Yes ☐   No ☐

12. Are you now withholding custody of a U.S. citizen child outside the United States from a person granted custody of the child?   Yes ☐   No ☐

13. Do you plan to practice polygamy in the United States?   Yes ☐   No ☐

14. Have you **EVER** ordered, incited, called for, committed, assisted, helped with, or otherwise participated in any of the following:

    a. Acts involving torture or genocide?   Yes ☐   No ☐

    b. Killing any person?   Yes ☐   No ☐

    c. Intentionally and severely injuring any person?   Yes ☐   No ☐

    d. Engaging in any kind of sexual contact or relations with any person who was being forced or threatened?   Yes ☐   No ☐

    e. Limiting or denying any person's ability to exercise religious beliefs?   Yes ☐   No ☐

15. Have you **EVER**:

    a. Served in, been a member of, assisted in, or participated in any military unit, paramilitary unit, police unit, self-defense unit, vigilante unit, rebel group, guerrilla group, militia, or insurgent organization?   Yes ☐   No ☐

    b. Served in any prison, jail, prison camp, detention facility, labor camp, or any other situation that involved detaining persons?   Yes ☐   No ☐

16. Have you **EVER** been a member of, assisted in, or participated in any group, unit, or organization of any kind in which you or other persons used any type of weapon against any person or threatened to do so?   Yes ☐   No ☐

图 3-13 I-485 申请表 IV：个人社
会履历详情调查

Part 3. Processing Information *(Continued)*

7. Have you **EVER** assisted or participated in selling or providing weapons to any person who to your knowledge used them against another person, or in transporting weapons to any person who to your knowledge used them against another person? Yes ☐ No ☐

8. Have you **EVER** received any type of military, paramilitary, or weapons training? Yes ☐ No ☐

Part 4. Accommodations for Individuals With Disabilities and/or Impairments *(See **Page 10** of the instructions before completing this section.)*

Are you requesting an accommodation because of your disability(ies) and/or impairment(s)? Yes ☐ No ☐

If you answered "Yes," check any applicable box:

☐ **a.** I am deaf or hard of hearing and request the following accommodation(s) (if requesting a sign-language interpreter, indicate which language (e.g., American Sign Language)):

☐ **b.** I am blind or sight-impaired and request the following accommodation(s):

☐ **c.** I have another type of disability and/or impairment (describe the nature of your disability(ies) and/or impairment(s) and accommodation(s) you are requesting):

Part 5. Signature *(Read the information on penalties on **Page 10** of the instructions before completing this section. You must file this application while in the United States.)*

Your Registration With U.S. Citizenship and Immigration Services

I understand and acknowledge that, under section 262 of the Immigration and Nationality Act (INA), as an alien who has been or will be in the United States for more than 30 days, I am required to register with U.S. Citizenship and Immigration Services (USCIS). I understand and acknowledge that, under section 265 of the INA, I am required to provide USCIS with my current address and written notice of any change of address within **10** days of the change. I understand and acknowledge that USCIS will use the most recent address that I provide to USCIS, on any form containing these acknowledgements, for all purposes, including the service of a Notice to Appear should it be necessary for USCIS to initiate removal proceedings against me. I understand and acknowledge that if I change my address without providing written notice to USCIS, I will be held responsible for any communications sent to me at the most recent address that I provided to USCIS. I further understand and acknowledge that, if removal proceedings are initiated against me and I fail to attend any hearing, including an initial hearing based on service of the Notice to Appear at the most recent address that I provided to USCIS or as otherwise provided by law, I may be ordered removed in my absence, arrested, and removed from the United States."

Selective Service Registration

The following applies to you if you are a male at least 18 years of age, but not yet 26 years of age, who is required to register with the Selective Service System: "I understand that my filing Form I-485 with U.S. Citizenship and Immigration Services (USCIS) authorizes USCIS to provide certain registration information to the Selective Service System in accordance with the Military Selective Service Act. Upon USCIS acceptance of my application, I authorize USCIS to transmit to the Selective Service System my name, current address, Social Security Number, date of birth, and the date I filed the application for the purpose of recording my Selective Service registration as of the filing date. If, however, USCIS does not accept my application, I further understand that, if so required, I am responsible for registering with the Selective Service by other means, provided I have not yet reached 26 years of age."

图 3 - 14 I - 485 申请表 V：
健康状况和签名

Part 5. Signature *(Continued)*

Applicant's Statement *(Check one)*

☐ I can read and understand English, and I have read and understand each and every question and instruction on this form, as well as my answer to each question.

☐ Each and every question and instruction on this form, as well as my answer to each question, has been read to me in the _____ language, a language in which I am fluent, by the person named in **Interpreter's Statement and Signature**. I understand each and every question and instruction on this form, as well as my answer to each question.

I certify, under penalty of perjury under the laws of the United States of America, that the information provided with this application all true and correct. I certify also that I have not withheld any information that would affect the outcome of this application.

I authorize the release of any information from my records that U.S. Citizenship and Immigration Services (USCIS) needs to determine eligibility for the benefit I am seeking.

Signature *(Applicant)*	Print Your Full Name	Date *(mm/dd/yyyy)*	Daytime Phone Number *(include area code)*

NOTE: *If you do not completely fill out this form or fail to submit required documents listed in the instructions, you may not be foun eligible for the requested benefit, and this application may be denied.*

Interpreter's Statement and Signature

I certify that I am fluent in English and the below-mentioned language.

Language Used *(language in which applicant is fluent)*

I further certify that I have read each and every question and instruction on this form, as well as the answer to each question, to this applicant in the above-mentioned language, and the applicant has understood each and every instruction and question on the form, as well as the answer to each question.

Signature *(Interpreter)*	Print Your Full Name	Date *(mm/dd/yyyy)*	Phone Number *(include area code)*

Part 6. Signature of Person Preparing Form, If Other Than Above

I declare that I prepared this application at the request of the above applicant, and it is based on all information of which I have knowledge.

Signature	Print Your Full Name	Date *(mm/dd/yyyy)*	Phone Number *(include area code)*

Firm Name and Address

E-Mail Address *(if any)*

图 3 - 15 I - 485 申请表 Ⅵ : 填表
声明和代填人士声明

临时绿卡升级永久绿卡

OMB No. 1615-0045; Expires 04/30/2011

I-829, Petition by Entrepreneur to Remove Conditions

Department of Homeland Security
U.S. Citizenship and Immigration Services

Do not write in this block - For USCIS use only (Except G-28 Block Below)		
☐ Applicant Interviewed	**Action Block**	Fee Receipt
		To be completed by Attorney or Representative, if any ☐ G-28 is attached Attorney's State License No.
Remarks:		

START HERE - Type or print in black ink.

Part 1.   Information About You

A # (if any) [   ]   Form I-526 Receipt Number [   ]

Family Name [   ]   Given Name [   ]   Middle Name [   ]

Address:

In care of [   ]

Number and Street [   ]   Apt. # [   ]

City [   ]   State or Province [   ]

Country [   ]   Zip/Postal Code [   ]   Daytime Phone # [   ]

Date of Birth (mm/dd/yyyy) [   ]   Country of Birth [   ]   U.S. Social Security # (if any) [   ]

Since becoming a conditional permanent resident, have you ever been arrested, cited, charged, indicted, convicted, fined, or imprisoned for breaking or violating any law or ordinance (excluding traffic regulations), or committed any crime for which you were not arrested?

☐ Yes   ☐ No   (If yes, explain on separate sheet(s) of paper, including disposition, if any.)

Part 2. Basis for Petition *(Check one)*

a. ☐ My conditional permanent residence is based on an investment in a commercial enterprise.
b. ☐ Reserved.
c. ☐ Reserved.
d. ☐ I am a conditional permanent resident spouse or child of an entrepreneur, and I am unable to be included in a Petition by Entrepreneur to Remove Conditions (Form I-829) filed by my conditional resident spouse or parent.
e. ☐ I am a conditional permanent resident spouse or child of an entrepreneur who is deceased.

Part 3. Information About Your Husband or Wife

Family Name [   ]   Given Name [   ]   Middle Name [   ]

Gender ☐ Male ☐ Female   Date of Birth (mm/dd/yyyy) [   ]   Date of Marriage (mm/dd/yyyy) [   ]

Other names used (including maiden name or aliases) [   ]

A# (If any) [   ]   Current Immigration Status [   ]   Is your current immigration status based on the petitioner's current status? ☐ Yes ☐ No

RECEIVED: _____ RESUBMITTED: _____ RELOCATED: SENT _____ REC'D _____

Form I-829 (Rev. 11/23/10) Y

图 3 - 16   I - 829 申请表 I : 个人与
配偶基本信息

Part 4. Children *(List all your children. Attach another sheet(s) of paper, if necessary.)*

Family Name		Given Name		Middle Name		
A# (if any)		Current Immigration Status		Date of Birth (mm/dd/yyyy)		Living with you? ☐ Yes ☐ No

Family Name		Given Name		Middle Name		
A# (if any)		Current Immigration Status		Date of Birth (mm/dd/yyyy)		Living with you? ☐ Yes ☐ No

Family Name		Given Name		Middle Name		
A# (if any)		Current Immigration Status		Date of Birth (mm/dd/yyyy)		Living with you? ☐ Yes ☐ No

Family Name		Given Name		Middle Name		
A# (if any)		Current Immigration Status		Date of Birth (mm/dd/yyyy)		Living with you? ☐ Yes ☐ No

Family Name		Given Name		Middle Name		
A# (if any)		Current Immigration Status		Date of Birth (mm/dd/yyyy)		Living with you? ☐ Yes ☐ No

Family Name		Given Name		Middle Name		
A# (if any)		Current Immigration Status		Date of Birth (mm/dd/yyyy)		Living with you? ☐ Yes ☐ No

Part 5. Information About Your Commercial Enterprise

Type of Enterprise *(Check one)*:

☐ New commercial enterprise resulting from the creation of a new business.

☐ New commercial enterprise resulting from the reorganization of an existing business.

☐ New commercial enterprise resulting from a capital investment in an existing business.

Kind of Business *(Be as specific as possible)*:

Date Business Established *(mm/dd/yyyy)*   Amount of Initial Investment

Date of Initial Investment *(mm/dd/yyyy)*   % of Enterprise You Own

Number of full-time employees in enterprise in United States (excluding you, your spouse, sons, and daughters):

At the time of your initial investment: Presently: Difference:

How many of these new jobs were created by your investment?

Form I-829 (Rev. 11/23/10) Y Pag

图 3 – 17 I – 829 申请表 Ⅱ：子女信息与
投资企业信息

Part 5. Information About Your Commercial Enterprise   (continued)

Subsequent Investment in the Enterprise:

Date of Investment	Amount of Investment	Type of Investment

Provide the gross and net incomes generated annually by the commercial enterprise since your initial investment. Include all income generated up to date during the present year.

Year	Gross Income	Net Income

Has your commercial enterprise filed for bankruptcy, ceased business operations, or have any changes in its business organization or ownership occurred since the date of your initial investment? ☐ Yes (Explain on separate sheet) ☐ No

Has your commercial enterprise sold any corporate assets, shares, property, or had any capital withdrawn since the date of your initial investment? ☐ Yes (Explain on separate sheet) ☐ No

Part 6. Signature (Read the information on penalties in the instructions before completing this section.)

I certify, under penalty of perjury under the laws of the United States of America, that this petition and the evidence submitted with it is all true and correct. I further certify that the investment was made in accordance with the laws of the United States and was not for the purpose of evading United States immigration laws. I also authorize the release of any information from my records that the U.S. Citizenship and Immigration Services needs to determine eligibility for the benefit being sought.

Signature of Applicant	Print Name	Date

NOTE: If you do not completely fill out this form or fail to submit any required documents listed in the instructions, you may not be found eligible for the requested benefit and this petition may be denied.

Part 7. Signature of Person Preparing Form, If Other Than Above

I declare that I prepared this petition at the request of the above person and it is based on all information of which I have knowledge.

Signature	Print Name	Date

Firm Name and Address (Include Telephone Number with Area Code and E-Mail Address.)

图 3 – 18 I – 829 申请表Ⅲ:投资规模、
运营现况以及签名

出入境记录 I－94 表格：
小卡片大作用

对于大部分投资移民申请人而言，开始作出正式申请决定之前，可能已经作为访客去美国短期旅游或者商务考察过。所有以往的出入境信息，此刻对你的移民申请，有着相当重要的影响，它体现了出入境者的守法程度和信用程度。所以出入境登记表（卡）I－94 是一项极为重要的移民资料，千万不要因为这张小小的白色卡片影响了你的良好记录。对于投资移民申请人来讲，基本都有至少一次到过美国旅游、考察或学习的经历，否则，你无论如何也不愿将大笔的资金投资到一个自己对其一无所知的国度。进入美国时，在飞机等交通载体上你就得开始填写白色的 I－94 表格，过移民关卡的时候，移民官员会在你的表格上盖上图章，写上签证类别。请千万保管好这张名片大小的卡片，在离开美国时，如领取飞机登机牌的时候，主动交给边防登记处。这样，最后在移民局会有一份你完整的出入境记录，否则，就会被误认为你滞留美国，违反了签证规定，将后患无穷。

DEPARTMENT OF HOMELAND SECURITY
U.S. Customs and Border Protection

OMB No. 1651-0111

Admission Number

Welcome to the United States

└┴┴┃┴┴┴┴┴┴┴┴┘

I-94 Arrival/Departure Record - Instructions

This form must be completed by all persons except U.S. Citizens, returning resident aliens, aliens with immigrant visas, and Canadian Citizens visiting or in transit.

Type or print legibly with pen in ALL CAPITAL LETTERS. Use English. Do not write on the back of this form.

This form is in two parts. Please complete both the Arrival Record (Items 1 through 13) and the Departure Record (Items 14 through 17).

When all items are completed, present this form to the CBP Officer.

Item 7 - If you are entering the United States by land, enter **LAND** in this space. If you are entering the United States by ship, enter **SEA** in this space.

CBP Form I-94 (10/04)

Admission Number

OMB No. 1651-0111

└┴┴┃┴┴┴┴┴┴┴┴┘

Arrival Record

1. Family Name	
2. First (Given) Name	3. Birth Date (Day/Mo/Yr)
4. Country of Citizenship	5. Sex (Male or Female)
6. Passport Number	7. Airline and Flight Number
8. Country Where You Live	9. City Where You Boarded
10. City Where Visa was Issued	11. Date Issued (Day/Mo/Yr)
12. Address While in the United States (Number and Street)	
13. City and State	

CBP Form I-94 (10/04)

Departure Number

OMB No. 1651-0111

└┴┴┃┴┴┴┴┴┴┴┴┘

I-94
Departure Record

14. Family Name	
15. First (Given) Name	16. Birth Date (Day/Mo/Yr)
17. Country of Citizenship	

CBP Form I-94 (10/04)

See Other Side   **STAPLE HERE**

图 3 – 19 I – 94 表格标准格式 I

This Side For Government Use Only
Primary Inspection

Applicant's
Name _____

Date
Referred _____ Time _____ Insp. # _____

Reason Referred

☐ 212A ☐ ☐ ☐ PP ☐ Visa ☐ Parole ☐ SLB ☐ TWOV

☐ Other _____

_____

_____

Secondary Inspection

End Secondary
Time _____ Insp. # _____

Disposition _____

---

18. Occupation	19. Waivers
20. CIS A Number **A -**	21. CIS FCO
22. Petition Number	23. Program Number
24. ☐ Bond	25. ☐ Prospective Student

26. Itinerary/Comments

_____

_____

_____

_____

_____

27. TWOV Ticket Number

| | | | | | | | | | | | | | | |

Warning A nonimmigrant who accepts unauthorized employment is subject to deportation.
Important - Retain this permit in your possession; *you must surrender it when you leave the U.S.* Failure to do so may delay your entry into the U.S. in the future. You are authorized to stay in the U.S. only until the date written on this form. To remain past this date, without permission from Department of Homeland Security authorities, is a violation of the law.
Surrender this permit when you leave the U.S.:
  - By sea or air, to the transportation line;
  - Across the Canadian border, to a Canadian Official;
  - Across the Mexican border, to a U.S. Official.
Students planning to reenter the U.S. within 30 days to return to the same school, see "Arrival-Departure" on page 2 of Form 1-20 **prior to surrendering this permit.**
Record of Changes

_____

_____

_____

_____

Port: **Departure Record**

Date:

Carrier:

Flight # / Ship Name:

_____

图 3-20 I-94 表格标准格式 II

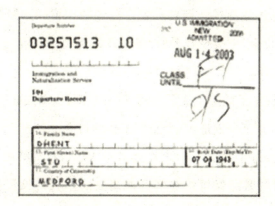

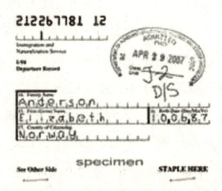

图 3-21　I-94 表格经过移民官员审核过的真实样本

美国投资移民相关
知识归纳

投资移民是美国新移民法中职业移民项的第五类优先移民,编号 EB-5。投资移民以提供外籍投资者在美国的居留权和"现有或新成立的企业"经商机会,交换投资者的"投资及实际经营投资"。投资移民申请条件要求如下。

1. 投资数额不低于 100 万美元,或者在郊区、高失业率区投资不低于 50 万美元,并至少创造 10 个全职工作的机会。

EB-5 项目每年给予 10 000 个具有永久居留权的移民名额,其中至少 3 000 个投资名额保留给在郊区或高失业率区的投资者。所谓"郊区",指大都会或人口总数达 2 万人的城市之外的城市;所谓"高失业率区",指失业率高于全国比率 1.5 倍的地方。新移民法施行细则规定,即使在大都会或人口总数在两万名以上的城市,因某种地理或政治的特殊情况,也可符合高失业率区的条件。

投资移民的立法精神,在于创造就业机会。投资的新商业性企业必须雇用全职员工至少 10 名,员工指提供劳务而换取薪水的人,承揽人不包括在内。所谓全职,指一周工作 35 小时以上。若同一职位由两人共同负责,而达上列时数标准,也可算为一个全职员工。合格的受雇人,包括美国公民、有永久居留权的外国人及有合法工作许可的外国人,投资人及其配偶和子女不包括在内。新移民法中关于雇用 10 名全职员工有项很宽松的实施细则，即投资签证申请人不必在公司最初建立时即雇用 10 人，可以先提出计划，表明企业要在两年之内需雇用至少 10 名。投资者可在投资限定的两年之内的最后一天雇用 10 名员工。当投资者本人及亲属已取得绿卡之后，如果工作不需要，可不再雇用员工。

2. 投资指提供资本。资本包括现金、设备、存货，或其他实质财产，定期存款、政府公债及其他容易变成现金的证券以及货款，都可视为资本。

3. 投资的资金不得以非法手段取得。施行细则规定，申请人应以外国经商记录、个人及公司报税税单，及其他文件，证明所投资金的获得均属合法，但不必证明该项资金来自国外。投资者不一定必须有任何经营的经验或教育程度，唯一的条件就是"有足够的资金"。资金的来源要"合法"，可以从薪资、花红、继承、投资收益、出售资产或者是"贷款"中提取。贷款最好经过设计，否则不一定能通过移民局的审查。

4. 申请人必须创立一个新的商业性企业。纯粹的房地产投资，指买土地或住宅，坐等升值，这种投资不符合规定。新的商业性公司可由一个人投资，也可两个人以上的投资者联合投资。

所谓新的商业性企业，包括以下三种。

(1)"新企业"投资，包括创新企业或重组旧企业。

(2) 收买陷于困境的"困难企业"，加以整顿或重组，并保留原有员工，所谓"困难企业"指企业在被注资之前的 12～14 个月，损失了资产价值的 1/5。

(3) 投资或注资已存在的生意，并加以扩充。所谓扩充，指增加原生意资产净值 40% 以上，或增加原生意所雇员工数达 40% 以上。采取扩充方式申请移民者，也必须符合资金及雇用 10 名员工的基本要求。

美国投资移民
项目介绍

一、布鲁克林海军工业园（BNY）

　　纽约市是美国最大城市及第一大港,位于美国大西洋海岸的东北部、纽约州东南部。一个多世纪以来,纽约市一直是世界上最重要的商业和金融中心。纽约市是一座全球化的大都市,也是世界级城市,直接影响着全球的媒体、政治、教育、娱乐以及时尚。纽约与英国伦敦、日本东京并称为世界三大国际都会。纽约市坐落在世界上最大的都会区——大纽约都会区的心脏地带,是国际级的经济、金融、交通、艺术及传媒中心,更被视为都市文明的代表。此外由于联合国总部设于该市,因此被世人誉为"世界之都"。

　　在这个 IT(信息技术)世界,我们通过网络,无论在世界的哪个角落,都可以基本掌握相同的框架性信息,比如纽约市区域中心(NYCRC)开发的投资移民项目,即布鲁克林海军工业园(BNY)开发项目,已经有大量的网络信息。

　　该工业园由纽约市政府拥有并管理。第一期的投资移民项目将融资6 000万美元招募 120 个投资人,其内容为工业园内规模最大的一幢建筑(128 号建筑)的重新翻新,由原来的造船车间改为绿色能源加工及办公基地(以下简称"128 项目")。这一项目具有以下特点。

第一，它位于美国经济实力最强，也是高度受人关注的区域——纽约市，该市极具经济活力和实力；

第二，该项目与一直顺利推广发展的费城 EB-5 项目在结构上极为相似；

第三，该项目的主要负责人均为纽约有经验、有实力的房地产开发商及律师。

由于美国经济发达、科技领先、教育资源丰富，退休福利良好等原因，很多追求事业发展并重视子女教育的成功人士，始终将美国列为移民的首选之地。随着美国政府对移民政策逐步放松，"美国热"吸引了越来越多投资者的眼球。

该项目的申请流程包括以下步骤。

(1) 免费评估；

(2) 建立委托关系；

(3) 签订投资代理合同；

(4) 客户提供个人信息和企业信息；

(5) 咨询顾问/移民律师讨论并制订申请方案；

(6) 资产/经营状况评估；

(7) 资深顾问及移民专家准备完整的申请文件；

(8) 申请人核准申请文件；

(9) 移民律师核准申请文件。

"128 项目"是纽约市投资移民特区推出的第一个项目，可靠性是其特点，工程得到政府的全力支持，而且此项目的投资移民中介服务也相对完善。

布鲁克林海军工业园区位于 EB-5 移民投资项目的指定范围内。纽约区域中心的主要目标是引入移民投资,创造就业机会,改善社区环境。布鲁克林海军工业园区是纽约市经济的一个重要组成部分,扮演着布鲁克林区经济生活的重要角色,为增加纽约市的就业提供稳定的推动力。海军工业园区也是现任政府经济发展政策中的一个关键。海军工业园区已经被指定为纽约州的目标就业区域,因此,EB-5 项目在海军工业园区内得到能以 50 万美元作为最小投资单位的批准。

截至 2010 年,有超过 200 个商户要求入驻海军工业园区。这个园区之所以能够吸引商家,分析其原因如下:首先,海军工业园区将保留工业区域,让商户有信心扩展业务、投资设备;其次,海军工业园区归纽约市政府所有,没有房产税和营业税;再次,海军工业园区被指定为州和市的开发区和工业区,因其创造就业机会而得到较多的税收优惠;最后,海军工业园区的地理位置也是一个重要因素,它靠近布鲁克林区—皇后区的高速公路和威廉斯堡—曼哈顿大桥,从曼哈顿很容易乘短途火车到达。

区域中心项目适合那些不愿处理较多日常管理工作的投资者。这个项目取消了"雇用至少 10 名专职员工"的条款,取而代之的是,这个项目采取了一个较为宽松的基本要求"间接创造就业机会"。投资者不需要居住在投资地,他们可以自由选择美国任何一个州作为居住地。更重要的是,该项目的投资额只需 50 万美元。每一个区域中心项目都必须被美国移民局提前批准,以获得申请 EB-5 绿卡资格。

对于 EB-5 项目如何才能收回资金,保证资金安全?只有两个方法:一是寄望于所投资项目在未来的运作中能够做到稳健经营、不亏损;二是要考察所投资项目是否有抵押担保。因此,投资移民项目申请人在选择项目的时候,必须要先对自己的偏好进行思考——是追求低风险、低回报,还是追求高风险、高回报? 同时,请历史悠久和经验资深的专业移民中介机构帮助自己进行深入和全面的分析,开阔自己的视野,也是避免隐忧、降低风险、顺利移民的一种重要方式。

二、纽约大都会投资移民区域中心

以下这些内容在相关网页上均有详细介绍,但是因为纽约大都会投资移民(EB-5)区域中心(New York City Metropolitan Regional Center,简称 NYCMRC)是经过美国移民局批准,以纽约大都会地区为区域中心的投资移民项目,并不多见,所以还要重复强调。

为了满足越来越多的海外移民对美国大都会地区的投资热情,纽约大都会投资移民区域中心特地将全球金融文化中心——纽约大都会地区作为投资主体,成为美国少有的以大都会城市为区域中心的投资移民项目。

纽约大都会投资移民区域中心(NYCMRC)是以世界金融文化中心——纽约市为中心,涵盖周围纽约州和新泽西州多个郡县,被称为美国最富有、最繁华的大都会地区。纽约大都会投资移民区域中心涵盖地区主要有:纽约市的曼哈顿区、皇后区、布鲁克林区、布朗克斯区以及斯塔滕岛区 5 个行政区,纽约知名郡县长岛(纳苏郡和苏福克郡)和威彻斯特,以及环抱纽约市的新泽西 13 个郡县。

纽约市拥有享誉世界的高等学府,市内坐落着哥伦比亚大学和纽约大学等知名大学;曼哈顿下城的华尔街是全球金融中心,提供着最领先的金融信息;百老汇、林肯中心、大都会博物馆等吸引着世界各地的艺术家们来此表演、学习和欢聚;纽约市还有自由女神、中央公园等知名旅游胜地。

新泽西州是美国 24 家世界 500 强企业的总部所在地,人均收入高居全美第三,且拥有的豪宅比例为全美之首。其中很大的原因是新泽西北接纽约市,且两地交通便利,很多纽约人将家安在一河之隔的新泽西,每天乘车来曼哈顿上班。因此新泽西被戏称为曼哈顿人的"卧房"。

纽约大都会投资移民区域中心项目主要投资于办公大楼、零售店、居民与写字楼混合使用的商业建筑、公共停车场、宾馆以及商业贷款等项目。纽约大都会投资移民区域中心投资组合多元化,有利于减少投资风险。该区域中心项目由纽约大都会区域中心投资移民有限责任公司运营,投资模式为海外投资者和项目运营商组成合伙企业,公司负责商业房地产的购买、改建和项目运营。纽约大都会投资移民区域中心项目团队完全由长期投资于纽约地区的经验丰富、业界知名的房地产商、律师团、经济学家以及分析师等专业人才组成,拥有纽约地区专业的投资移民咨询和最准确的数据。公司通过有效的管理和风险控制实现合理投资、优化组合,借此投资黄金地段,以实现资产增值,获取投资收益;团队用真诚负责的态度运营项目,以实现投资的有效性和长期性,为投资者规避风险,顺利获得绿卡和投资收益;运用清晰合理的投资收尾战略计划,维护投资人的投资收益。

此外,纽约还有"威斯汀酒店及医疗中心项目"等,可以专项咨询有关专家。

除此之外,自 2005 年起,由于人民币相对美元的持续升值,对于真正有意投资移民的候选人而言,关注的还有资金的安全性和投资回报的可能性。这里介绍几个位于华人商业区的成功投资项目。

法拉盛地区是纽约新兴的华人商务区,也是皇后区的一个交通枢纽,地铁 7 号线的终点站就位于此地。2010 年,当地华商出售了久享盛名的皇朝连锁餐饮集团，进行资产重组，将空置了 10 年的交通要道上的原犹太购物中心全部改建成华人购物中心，成为一个集副食品龙头超市、美食中心和百货中心积聚的人气商务中心，既考虑到了华人的消费习惯，又满足了上班族一站式购物的时效要求。这样的商业投资项目，需要上亿的资金，分拆成上百个股权，雇用上百位员工，作为独立的投资移民申请个案，由会计师和律师统一办理。所以，该做法不知帮助多少美国当地和海外公民实现了"美国梦"。

这样的机会在华人社区几乎一直在默默产生。许多成功的 IT 人士、医生和律师，不断用高额的常规收入，去寻找另外行业的投资机会，比如收购或参股银行，收购小型物业改建成商业办公大楼，这样具有社会公信和物业保障的项目，投资移民的资金参与其中，确实具有保值升值和获得美国正式身份的双重效用。虽然投资额度起码 100 万美元起，方能达到投资移民的基本门槛，但这是双赢的投资回报、移民机会。

自己或者与他人合伙成立公司，投资美国商业机会，会计师可以提供全面的服务，你也可以进入州政府网站①，浏览所有细节。

---

① 纽约州政府网站地址：http://www.dos.state.ny.us/corps/。

第四章 4
CHAPER
这就是美国：移民
美国的切身经历与
感悟分享

自由化和未来生活方式的普及，也就是超工业社会生活方式的普及。

——阿尔文·托夫勒

说实在的，本书第三章的文本过于枯燥。这些内容，本来是应该由律师或者专业机构负责理解和实施的。但是，如果你有足够的耐心与责任感，也不妨尽可能了解，这样有助于你对今后的移民过程了如指掌，避免走弯路。笔者当年就是这样把握自己的移民路径的，现在，让我们转变一下思维方式，开始分享一些历史的真实场景吧。

细说起来，美国移民法律制订的移民途径多种多样，来到纽约自由女神像下，艾利斯岛上有血泪，那也是为了追求更好生活付出的成本。想要改变现状，但不付出努力空谈追求，只会虚构永远的乌托邦。美国法律针对不同的历史时期，根据自身的需要，一直都有一些移民特色项目政策，如果你对上述投资移民的介绍心存疑虑，不妨与笔者一起回顾自己走过的移民经历，那个时候的故事不可复制，但是这种把握机遇的能力，永远不能放弃，这就是移民的精神，也是在美国奋斗所必须具备的心理条件。

承认移民倾向，
移民改变人生

　　赴美的签证经历曾经是许多人的噩梦。20 世纪 90 年代，第一波出国浪潮高涨的时候，我才二十几岁，是上海交通大学的青年讲师。因为在校园里消息灵通，于是随波逐流，考试填表，采取广种薄收战术，最后如愿收到来自美国大学的录取通知。

　　上海交通大学距离美国驻上海总领事馆不远，骑自行车不过 10 分钟，是我上下班必经的路口。有个问题，在此之前我一直没弄明白，为何领事馆的大门外面，每天总是挤满了人。曾经有人这样记叙过这番场景：领事馆的门前排起彻夜的签证长队，人们带着暖壶和躺椅，就像购买春运火车票的架势。这样排队出国的阵势还被人利用，一位美籍华人及时印制了"拥有一方美国土地"的精美证书，没有具体方位地址，由全美各州的土地、空间集结成为一平方英寸的面积，这项虚拟世界，不亚于今日的网络世界创意。针对这个商业创意，市场上迅速形成神秘耳语：拥有此证，就拥有美国资产，该证正是获取赴美签证的有利材料。某晚，位于南京西路上海杂技场的证书销售处，人流似海，没有面值的购证预约券，当即炒至每张 5 000 元人民币，这个当年的绝对高价，开创了日后炒作从股票到房产预约券的纪录。

　　到了某日，我也加入等候签证的队伍，朝我挤过来不少懂行的市民，向我打听签证文件的细节内容，发表他们对我获得签证成功几率的个人见解，并且相互打赌。我恍然大悟：他们是在模拟用兵，实战练习，推演最易获得签证"黄道吉日"的技巧，用以提高自己签证成功的几率。

我有些不以为然。

轮到我站在了签证官面前，这位亚裔女士头也不抬，问道：担保书哪里来的？我真诚地解释，委托香港的表姐特意去律师楼办理了担保文件，还有火漆印为证。"啪!"，签证官盖上了她的橡皮图章："对不起，你有移民倾向。"前后不到两分钟，不容争辩，辩也白搭，队伍后面的申请人过来了，维持秩序的保安也过来了……

这就算是传闻中的"拒签"了，即没有获得赴美签证许可。

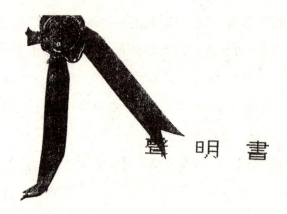

图 4-1　香港担保书封面

聲　明　書

　　我，~~黄~~ _____

止，現任 _____

謹以至誠聲明：

　　本人在交通銀行香港分行有儲蓄存款121,265.56港元（隨附上銀行証明）。

　　本人願意在經濟上負責供應我的表弟 _____

_____ ）（現任中國上海市 _____ 號202室）

　　　　求學期間的學費、膳宿費及一切生活費用。

　　本人謹根據香港一九七二年宣誓及聲明條例衷誠作此聲明，並確信其為真實無訛。

　　　　聲　明　人：

　　　　香港身份證號碼

　　此項聲明係於一九八九年七月廿四日在香港中環德輔道中四十五號永隆銀行大廈十一樓及在本人面前提出。

　　　　監　誓　人：
　　　　香港律師　　　PHILIP PAK-YIU YUEN

图 4 - 2　香港担保书（在 20 世纪 80 年代，中国内地居民较易获得香港
　　　　亲友的经济担保）

(Answer all items. Type or print in black ink.)

I, _____ residing at _____
      (Name)   (Street Number and Name)

_____ - _____
(City)   (State)   (Zip Code if in U.S.)   (Country)

certify under penalty of perjury under U.S. law, that:

1. I was born on _____ in _____
               (Date-*mm/dd/yyyy*)   (City)   (State)   (Country)

If you are not a U.S. citizen based on your birth in the United States, or a non-citizen U.S. national based on your birth in American Samoa (includ Swains Island), answer the following as appropriate:

    a. If a U.S.citizen through naturalization, give Certificate of Naturalization number _____

    b. If a U.S. citizen through parent(s) or marriage, give Certificate of Citizenship number _____

    c. If U.S. citizenship was derived by some other method, attach a statement of explanation.

    d. If a Lawful Permanent Resident of the United States, give A-Number _____

    e. If a lawfully admitted nonimmigrant, give Form I-94, Arrival-Departure Record, number _____

2. I am _____ years of age and have resided in the United States since _____
                                                   (Date-*mm/dd/yyyy*)

3. This affidavit is executed on behalf of the following person:

Name (Family Name)	(First Name)	(Middle Name)	Gender	Age

Citizen of (Country)	Marital Status	Relationship to Sponsor

Presently resides at (Street Number and Name)	(City)	(State)	(Country)

Name of spouse and children accompanying or following to join person:

Spouse	Gender	Age	Child	Gender	Age
Child	Gender	Age	Child	Gender	Age
Child	Gender	Age	Child	Gender	Age

4. This affidavit is made by me for the purpose of assuring the U.S. Government that the person(s) named in **item (3)** will not become a public charge in the United States.

5. I am willing and able to receive, maintain, and support the person(s) named in **item 3**. I am ready and willing to deposit a bond, if necessary, to guarantee that such person(s) will not become a public charge during his or her stay in the United States, or to guarantee that the above named person(s) will maintain his or her nonimmigrant status, if admitted temporarily, and will depart prior to the expiration of his or her authorized s in the United States.

6. I understand that:

    a. Form I-134 is an "undertaking" under section 213 of the Immigration and Nationality Act, and I may be sued if the person(s) named in **item** becomes a public charge after admission to the United States;

    b. Form I-134 may be made available to any Federal, State, or local agency that may receive an application from the person(s) named in **item** for Food Stamps, Supplemental Security Income, or Temporary Assistance to Needy Families; and

    c. If the person(s) named in **item 3** does apply for Food Stamps, Supplemental Security Income, or Temporary Assistance for Needy Families my own income and assets may be considered in deciding the person's application. How long my income and assets may be attributed to th person(s) named in **item 3** is determined under the statutes and rules governing each specific program.

图 4 - 3 Ⅰ - 134 表格 Ⅰ (经济担保书)

n employed as or engaged in the business of _____ with _____

(Type of Business)   (Name of Concern)

_____ -
(Street Number and Name)   (City)   (State)   (Zip Code)

...erive an annual income of: *(If self-employed, I have attached a copy of my last income tax return or ...port of commercial rating concern which I certify to be true and correct to the best of my knowledge ...d belief. See instructions for nature of evidence of net worth to be submitted.)* $ _____

...ave on deposit in savings banks in the United States: $ _____

...ave other personal property, the reasonable value of which is: $ _____

...ave stocks and bonds with the following market value, as indicated on the attached list, which I certify ...be true and correct to the best of my knowledge and belief: $ _____

...ave life insurance in the sum of: $ _____

...th a cash surrender value of: $ _____

...wn real estate valued at: $ _____

With mortgage(s) or other encumbrance(s) thereon amounting to: $ _____

Which is located at: _____ -

(Street Number and Name)   (City)   (State)   (Zip Code)

... following persons are dependent upon me for support: *(Check the box* in the appropriate column to indicate whether the person named is ...lly or *partially* dependent upon you for support.)

...me of Person	Wholly Dependent	Partially Dependent	Age	Relationship to Me
	☐	☐		
	☐	☐		
	☐	☐		

...ve previously submitted affidavit(s) of support for the following person(s). If none, state "None".

...me of Person	Date submitted

...ave submitted a visa petition(s) to U.S. Citizenship and Immigration Services on behalf of the following person(s). If none, state "None".

...me of Person	Relationship	Date submitted

☐ intend   ☐ do not intend to make specific contributions to the support of the person(s) named in **item 3**.

...you check "intend," indicate the exact nature and duration of the contributions. For example, if you intend to furnish room and board, state how long and, if money, state the amount in U.S. dollars and whether it is to be given in a lump sum, weekly or monthly, and for how long.

_____
_____
_____

Oath or Affirmation of Sponsor

...owledge that I have read "Sponsor and Alien Liability" on Page 2 of the instructions for this form, and am aware of my ...sibilities as a sponsor under the Social Security Act, as amended, and the Food Stamp Act, as amended. ...y under penalty of perjury under United States law that I know the contents of this affidavit signed by me and that the statements are ...d correct.

...ure of Sponsor _____   **Date** _____

图 4-4 I-134 表格 II (美国亲友出具的经济担保书比较直接有效，
但附上 1040 税表就更具说服力)

　　经济担保书的作用现在对中国公民的作用已经日减。当年我们一贫如洗,只有靠海外亲友的一纸承诺,来说服移民官员允许自己走通移民这条道,这种方式在华人移民的历史中维持了近百年。如今你出示的资产证明自然比其可信百倍,但对于老年人和幼儿等缺乏个人资产者申请赴美移民和旅游,I-134表格依然有其优势。I-134表格作为美国官方认可的经济担保文件,只要担保人如实填写个人财务状况,最主要是能够同时附上工资证明、存款证明、报税证明,经公证签名,移民官员基本还是认可担保人的承诺,从而简化了移民手续。

出国改变人生曾经是
我们的生存寄托

有人总结过，移民美国的总体实践战略是：跳下船逃进去，找亲人带进去，读好书考进去，捧上钱请进去。在笔者有能力追寻出国梦想的当年，唯有"读好书考进去"一种走向。

20 世纪 80 年代，全中国的大学校园笼罩在"造原子弹的，不如卖茶叶蛋"的典型经济窘境里。记得数学系的一位兄弟向我痛诉，上个月的一张出公差的电车票，居然还被教研室主任压着无法报销，理由是，经费亏空。

校园人就这样奋斗在穷则思变的自我激励中，好在此乃儒家学说认可的人性本能之一，不算大逆不道。1984 年，国家颁布关于自费留学生的新规定，敞开了具有工程师和大学讲师以上职称人员自费留学的大门。初步形成国家公派、单位公派和自费留学三种主要途径，自费出国留学成为主体，对象包括访问学者、研修生、进修生等。"出国潮"的强烈冲击和震撼，掀起了这样的心理波澜：走，还是不走？到哪里去？去干吗？校园是读书人集聚处，天真幼稚者众，所以本性流露亦更加率真。每日在校园里过道上见面，年轻教师间的问候语都发生了剧烈变化：不再是"吃了吧"的国问，代之以"还没出国呐"、"办得如何啦"。这里的潜台词是，年轻教师留校三年尚未出国赴美，肯定源于托福或成绩不佳，自感智商低人一等。生存压力之大，由此可见。

　　不久，单身教师宿舍里，流传了这样的消息：新加坡国立大学已经派出专人驻守校园，凡有本校单身教师愿意应聘，一律接受，待遇从优。每月2 500新币外加免费一室一厅；如果已婚，欢迎同行，配偶暂无一技之长者，每月另有1 500新币过渡；携儿带女者，每人每月再加1 500新币，住房待遇升级，免费配备二室一厅。据说，这是一项特殊的人种结构改良国策。有刚毕业留校的通信专业硕士小刘，决意后马先行，数周后居然真的飞走了。可见，消息的真实性不容怀疑。

　　这样一来，反倒是位居研究室主任一级的中层教师们，开始不安起来。他们属于"文化大革命"前的本科生，"文化大革命"后的研究生，既有出国留学的宏愿，又不想放弃已经在学院专业上占尽先机、大展宏图的好时光。想不到，新加坡的人才计划真是环环相扣，一丝不误，主意早就打到精英人士的下一代身上。我们主任尚在小学五年级的儿子，被只身保送新加坡，教育费用和生活费用一律全包。几年之后，功成名就的主任唯一的遗憾，就是儿子已经无法与其自然沟通，下一代算是为他国生育了。据统计，自清末洋务运动到1949年，总计留日学生4万，留美2万，留欧2万；1949—1978年，以留学苏联、东欧为主，共约1.2万人次；而自1978年以来，已经有超过50万人次的中国大陆留学生，分布于世界各地。

　　在这样的大环境下，我收到的第一份录取通知书来自美国费城，托马斯杰斐逊大学医学院。这所以开国元勋名字命名的大学，录用我深造，可谓你情我愿，但却面临"拒签"的局面。这段纠结花费了近20年，我才慢慢得以理解，美国是个竞争社会，不欢迎乞食者，也不讨厌争食者；那位签证官员的"心证"能力，确实一流。

　　你想，当年我们大学的财政状况，作为外交情报官员的签证领事，肯定略有所闻。事实也是如此，教师报销的出差车票尚且要拖，教师的生活水准一定拮据。像我这样一个年近三十的男人，却精瘦如青春少年，到了美国，不利用机会多赚外快，改善生活，完全不符合生物本能。"谁说我有移民倾向"，"我没有移民倾向"，这样的自我澄清，在签证官员面前，是毫无说服力的，事实明摆在当年的我们身上、脸上和文件上。时间到了 2010 年年初，几位在上海外资企业任职的年轻朋友，利用"黄金周"来美国度假购物。试想他们站在签证官员面前的那份自信，腆着中年男人的小肚子，依次递上个人资产证明、收入证明、房产证明，事实胜于雄辩。到了美国，就是用鞭子赶着，他也不会去与低收入者争饭碗，讨剩菜，即使他有移民倾向，也是投资性的，正好符合美国法律近年面向富裕人士推出的、欢迎鼓励的移民类型。

最为关键的是，"移民"一词，在我们当年从小学课本到大学教材里，出现频率极低，而且贬义居多，移民近似偷渡。《海霞》《小螺号》等启蒙电影里，悄悄移上岸来的全是坏蛋。我们从小被告知，世界上还有三分之二的人民，生活在水深火热之中，领导派你出国是拯救全人类。但自己想着移民出国，离开中国，理由一定不够光鲜。要是连美国人也认定你有穷人思富的"移民倾向"，担心你移民美国，平白无故多占一份社会福利。真是一桩两边不靠谱的事。所以，直到扎根美国后，生活才开始逐渐教会我们理解移民背后的真实深意。

穷学生爆炒律师鱿鱼：
办移民身份可以做成一桩私活

与所有坚持的故事一样，终于有一天，我开始了在纽约最著名的医学中心从事博士后研究的生涯。其实，外籍博士后是道坎，是种尴尬的临时工身份。他比学生多一些经验，但比员工少许多机会，关键是外籍博士后没有居留权，就等于没有一切，包括执业资格和优厚待遇。所以，无论是为了研究条件还是改善生活，我同时开始用心研究的，还有美国移民法律，一项称之为"杰出人才"（Outstanding Researcher）的移民条款，引起了我的极大关注。

说实话，20世纪90年代初期，大陆赴美留学的大部分学生，学位还没有拿到，学术造诣还不如我。被"拒签"后的我，踏踏实实在国内的一流大学内，做着本分的工作，成为一个有论文和专著在国内外发表，还获得一些奖励的年轻教师，现在只要把这几年积累的原始材料归归拢，看上去还真像杰出人才那么回事，一不小心倒成了交上好远的"失马塞翁"。可是，这样的自我评估纯粹属于"自恋型"的对号入座，周围并无先例可以借鉴，如何证实我的这项"研究"成果？

我反复研究了有关法律的各处细节，决意放手一搏。中文报纸上充满了各式移民服务的律师广告，我挑了一位看似老练的犹太移民律师，约好周末面谈。已经忘记了这位律师的大名，姑且称之约瑟夫，恐怕这位律师也是第一回遇见一位自说自话，要求指定移民种类的中国学者。

我说：依据我的材料，我只想通过"杰出人才"类，快速移民，不愿耗费几年的等待，就为一张绿卡。

约瑟夫：您的需要就是我的工作。我的移民服务收费3 000美元。首付800美元，如果您认可，我们正式开始。

我说，我是认真的。当场写给律师800美元支票，这几乎就是我的全部家当，本月老婆和女儿的生活费，只剩下最后80美元了。

约瑟夫律师职业性地点点头：好的，我正式接受您的委托。10分钟后，他从文件柜中整理出一套空白表格，极其细致地与我一项一项核实确认，最后他说：请您回去认真填写，并按要求附上书面证据，请您目前的雇主签名后，我们再见一次，请您准备好余额2 200美元。我们争取一次成功。

我心中狂喜，约瑟夫律师的详细讲解，证明了我以往的移民法研究成果是有效的，我的条件基本合格。我冷静地与他握手告别，郑重声明，我回去后逐项落实。一星期后，我将整理有序的移民申请材料直接寄往移民局，过了14个工作日，正如移民条例所明确的，我收到了移民局的收件通知，再过了14个工作日，好消息如期而至，经美国移民归化局评估，我与我的家庭成员被正式批准，纳入 I－485身份调整期。一年后，我们全家获得美国长期居留权。

办妥移民身份意味着工作和
生活开始美国化

第一次申请赴美签证,我真诚辩白自己没有移民倾向,结果踏上美国国土以后,环境逼迫人生,因而怀揣着极大的移民愿望,且这种愿望,经过努力,竟然可以在不到一年半的时间内如愿以偿。在此期间,约瑟夫律师不断打电话催我,还在惦记着我的余款,哪知我的这笔血汗钱,已经牢牢掌握在自己手中。约瑟夫律师提醒我抓紧办理书面证明材料,我以正在国内委托有关方面逐级办理为由,迟迟没有踏进他的事务所一步。

历史有时候就是这样出人意料。"知识就是力量"的口号,是我从小开始背诵的格言,事实上,却从来没有真正领会过。"知识就是力量"的真谛,是我们一家三口离开纽约市移民归化局大门后,倏然领会的。这种力量会助你脱离困境、落实身份、获得机会、创造财富、换取空间、赢得时间。

比如说,太太马上以美国居民的身份,在华尔街一流的美国公司中,相中一份合适的职位,其结果是,她决定暂时中止在纽约大学攻读的全额奖学金博士学位。这种美式选择,在深受"万般皆下品,唯有读书高"儒家文化熏染的家庭中,一般是很难痛下告别学位的决心的,可现在这个家庭安在纽约,现实环境比意识概念更具冲击力,看似美国社会提供了机会,其实也是压力下的机会。又比如说,对于我们这些具有医学学位背景的留学人员来说，美国居民的身份立马帮你省下了数十万美元的医学院学费，可以直接参加美国医师执照考试（USMLE），完成住院医生培训过程，成为职业医生，一步迈入主流阶层。

我们从东方的人情社会，来到法治的纽约，通过这次成功的身份转换经历，确实被它的这种现代化体制所折服。尽管它的抨击者，包括我们自己，对这种体制下的许多问题，还有种种的不满，但是，一个微小的家庭个案，真的能够在人地生疏、几乎倾家荡产的困境下，严格按照法规的细节，迎来"触底反弹，高位解套"的欢喜结局，任何一个理智的人，都无法否认，这里的法制规则和市场规则已经相当成熟。

图 4-5　纽约移民局大楼（联邦广场 26 号，雅各布 K.贾维茨联邦大厦，
是纽约移民局地址，与签证有涉的外国人几乎都要与其打交道）

新移民更要小心处世，
把握做人做事原则

　　我开始向周围的朋友传授"杰出人才"移民的技术路径，不断有成功的好消息向我反馈，于是也就有了热情友好的建议：你得抓紧机会，直接登报打广告，公开接受移民服务项目，收入肯定大大超过博士后研究，我拒绝了。

　　在我居住的这个华人街坊，正是人才辈出、黑白两道集聚的地域。曾有电视剧《北京人在纽约》，细致地描绘底层打工移民的生活，而我生活的留学人员圈内，故事也大都异类。比如，大导演李安，如今他已经家喻户晓，我曾经在世界华人圈内发行极广的《侨报》上开辟专栏，记载过这样的随笔：

　　……李安自纽约大学电影研究所第一名毕业后，因未得拍片机会而在家当了 6 年"家庭主夫"，妻子工作赚钱，他负责带小孩，并且擅长烹饪。直到 1991 年，台湾"中央电影公司"找他拍摄《推手》，一战成名。所以，在李导影片中，灶头功夫和餐饮细节，极具华人街坊生活气息。

　　李安潜伏在纽约市法拉盛街坊的这个时段，（中国）台湾地区移民和（中国）大陆移民刚刚开始向皇后区的这个小镇集聚。说它是个小镇，其实也是夸张，不过一条不足 300 米的大街而已。往北,过不了地铁 7 号线的终点站,有一家名为 BLUE STAR 的老外杂货铺,店主反应敏捷,逮住机会开始贩售华裔顾客喜爱的蔬菜、海鲜与水果,不过如今早已遁身匿迹,被更为土特产化的温州菜市所替代。往南,曾经有规模最大的金山超市,几乎囊括华人所需的日常生活用品,由第一代广东移民后裔经营,一向以货全、质好和价高著称。时至今日,却难敌农场种植、物流网络和最佳店面三位一体的福建移民集团。金山超市改变策略,伴随移民新军,向更为纵深的美国腹地,开拓汉式商铺去也。

那段时节,潜心为人夫父的李安,早上 8 点将太太送上 7 号地铁,她是一位生物医学博士,研究所的职位攸关全家生计,怠慢不得;好在孩子们的学校就在附近,公立的学校不仅将学费、书费免了,作为低收入的新移民李氏家庭,恐怕孩子的午餐和车费,也可以申请减免;接下来便是自由自在的李导一天的幸福生活,如果李导后来平凡一生,史家会说他赋闲养性;如今李导功成名就,也不妨认为他是做实了功课。我们可以跟随厨艺一流的李导去逛街买菜,虽说全家仅靠李嫂挣工资,但是也不必为油盐柴米操心,拜师灶王的李生尽可一展手艺。金山超市的走地鸡 69 美分/磅,游水鱼 59 美分/磅;素菜与水果同价,听上去稍贵些,小青菜与蛇果、樱桃和草莓一伙,49 美分/磅;芦笋和冬瓜好比进口的新鲜龙眼,69 美分/磅也可搞定;九层塔是制作台湾三杯鸡必备的配料,商家也会向附近某户擅长农活的后院自耕地订货,每磅 99 美分,周末来李家做客的游子便得以一解乡愁;至于牛肉、猪肉和鸡肉等东西方共享的食品,BLUE STAR 的橱窗上广告日日更新,傍晚还会惊喜打折,5 美元的食物,拎到你手疼。马路对面的人人小馆,打出标准的江浙小菜的招牌,特别是他家的周末早点,独家经营的烧饼油条,锅贴粢饭,简直就是垄断了整个街坊。李导历经法拉盛街坊的6年潜伏生涯,肯定也在此排队等位,心得无数。

所以,当我们再次跟随李导逛逛《喜宴》,玩玩《推手》,会会《饮食男女》时,已经完全不会被他所再现的生活技艺所惊吓到。影片建构的,就是"卧虎藏龙"的李安,潜伏在皇后区法拉盛街坊的生活缩影,东西语种混杂,南北方言交叉,色、香、味、形等灶上功夫一应俱全。只是那时节,在李导潜心体验生活的街坊里,上海话还没有流行起来。所以,风光以后的李安,即使精耕细作大片《色戒》,仔细听听电影里老上海的本地话,实在不敢恭维,讲得"奇出怪样",所以我推断,大导演好久不回社区了吧,"上海闲话"现在已经通行法拉盛街坊啦。

相对于李安,李舫舫等另一类纽约华人街坊中的大腕,熟悉的人就不多了。李舫舫在国内出版过纪实小说《我俩——北京玩主在纽约》、《我俩——一九九三》等作品,基本上就是混迹黑白两道之间的华人生存写照:"肆无忌惮的北京玩主,与盗窃国库的女阴谋家,交锋于世界上最大的狩猎场"。李舫舫来自北京,曾为国家级出版机构的编辑,聪明绝顶。发迹之前,他混迹于犹太居民居多的纽约市内公园里,靠下国际象棋赢钱为生,他的对手中,不乏苏联国家队的优秀选手。博弈长考之余,李舫舫还悟出一丝暴富商机:制作绿卡,贩卖身份。等到美国联邦调查局(FBI)有所察觉,他已挣得盆满钵满,洗手上岸了。在美国,人人都有能力拥有机动车,但李舫舫的代步工具,却借用了青少年的小轮自行车,骑在纽约华埠的大街上,千万别以为他在炫耀技巧,路人通常只会将他当做派送外卖的苦力，而这正是发财后的李舫舫想要追求的行事效果。李舫舫家所处的半条街坊，房产其实都归在他的名下，现在，他整天寻思着，不是棋局，也不是非法移民，而是瞒着房管局，设法改装房子，多弄出几间屋子，想着法子多收进些房租，也算是自食其力了。对他来讲，与房管局周旋，比起对付移民局和警察局，要容易多了。黑白两道之间，最不易的，还是赌场挣钱，李舫舫可以对付一个国际级象棋大师，实在无力对付整个赌场的打手系统，即使你手气如虹，脑袋还是会遭受威胁。

　　李舫舫事发之后，他有过一段真诚的感言："回想起来，做老绿（帮偷渡客搞绿卡），这事情一开始就包含着悲剧因素。人生的铁链就在这一环上断裂了。这些年来，我曾经疯狂地、病态地向社会索取所需，现在总算是有报应了。"有这样一个街坊邻居做参照，我自然决意放弃移民服务的创业机会，这是一桩走错一步，就是违法掉脑袋的生意，何况我连棋谱都记不住。至今，我还为自己当初的软弱犹豫和无能无财庆幸。

往事如烟，
并非无稽之谈

我们当时生活在世纪之交，所叙述的这些故事的时间，都是 20 世纪八九十年代，听上去都像在讲古代的故事，尤其是对我们的孩子们来说。21 世纪来临后，我的同辈朋友们大都在国内发了财，出国移民的夙愿，开始在下一代身上实现。这里的前提条件是，美国放开了留学签证的大门，几乎雪藏了借用"移民倾向"拒绝签证的橡皮图章。这是一个法制的政府，调整了法规后，一切都是合理合法的，这是一个尊重市场的政府，金融危机的压力，迫使它开放教育市场，增加国内市场规模。同样是留学生，却完全是一番新的移民气象。

家中接待过两位来自上海的留学生客人。白筠刚上旧金山大学一年级，天一已是芝加哥艺术学院的硕士生，快要毕业。对于她们来讲，来纽约拜访自由女神，感受大都会博物馆，溜达华尔街，体验百老汇真人秀，都是必需的留学经历。而上述游学内容，都会通过网络，第一时间将当天的实况与国内的亲朋好友分享。

通常，对于年轻访客，我不会自告奋勇充当翻译和导游，陪伴他们出游，这是极可疑的行为，好比他们父母派出的"海外督察"。我通常将公交一卡通和全球定位系统（GPS）教会他们用，其他的事情，只要确保手机畅通，就基本万无一失了。新新留学生的这些开支费用与活动内容，肯定不会出现在 20 世纪 80 年代留学生的计划栏中。

春节回国，返美途中，我的邻座正好是一位结束了回国度假，回美返校的上海女孩。其实，一眼望去，在我前后几排的旅伴中，这样"90后"学生模样的乘客，便有好几位。他们特征比较一致：行李不多，不像当年的我，一趟旅程，恨不得把整个家搬上，好省下几个用1：10汇率计算的美元；小留学生们几乎都挂着耳机，随时处于"工作"的状态，手上的电子产品不是iPhone，就是iTouch。

其实，本人出国时，在配置上，也算不惜投资，目的是为了上好英文课，无论如何，也要备妥一台随身听。比起我们当时的收入，一台随身听录放机的花费，可能占了我们一两个月的工资，而一部手机的使用寿命，对于"90后"，只有半年一年的时间，不是因为损毁了，而是因为功能更新了。有些90后的英语水平，恐怕比母语还好，出口自如，他们在飞机上交流，偶尔会嵌入几个汉语词汇，只是为了加深语言表达的感情色彩。

在我的书房里，陈列了一张100年前，中国赴美小留学生的集体照，这张著名照片的复印件，在网上很容易搜索到。比较起来，这批孩子们13～18岁不等，与现在的90后留学生年龄相仿，但是面目表情凝重，压力重重。这一代人名声如雷贯耳，人生却未必幸福。美国历史学家费侠莉教授，以我国地质科学与科学人文开创人丁文江教授为研究案例，结果从第三维度解读出了他们这一代留学生的历史感；20世纪初，在西方求学的中国留学生，即使用西方自然科学或者社会科学知识武装了自己，但他还是继续沿用孔儒的眼光，审视和要求自己的功名地位和家国责任，公众也以同样的眼光看待他，就像欣赏以往金榜题名举人的地位和责任一样。

第五章 5
CHAPER
留学打造移民：成
功家庭的二代工程

自费留学：
双赢机制下的新世纪移民模式

　　"90后"留学生们的出国目标，单纯明朗，不是为了追求先进技术，就是为了追求丰富人生，移民就是移民，不用遮遮掩掩，心态很阳光。概括起来，眼下赴美留学的中国学生，不光在时代上，还是在质量上，均属与前人不同的品种，可以分为以下几类。

一、高中大学都留学，一路获取奖学金

　　北京的殷钟睿同学，在哈佛大学读本科，同时兼任哈佛大学中国大陆留学生协会主席。2008年，他作为哈佛大学华裔华侨学生代表，参加"相约上海，共创未来"夏令营活动，讲述从小注重阅读培养的重要性，他属于中产家庭教育下一代的一个成功范例。

　　殷钟睿的父母都是大学毕业生。妈妈一直把孩子的教育放在自己的事业之上。她很早就意识到，孩子幼小的时候，培养其阅读兴趣比什么都重要。由于全家跟随爸爸到英国工作两年，出国回国，每次搬迁，都是对小钟睿的一次语言能力、知识结构和思维方式的全新挑战，于是全家齐心协力，最终将小学到初中的文化融合，转换成对小钟睿的能力培育。2003年，15岁的殷钟睿出版了他的英文纪实体作品《小小留学生》。

　　临近中考之际，殷钟睿在美国大使馆举办的一次活动中偶然获知，

123

可以通过美国中学入学考试(SSAT),获准去美国高中留学。凭着扎实的基础,他在离录取截止日期仅一个月的时间内,最终获得位于美国马萨诸塞州安多福的菲利普斯学院的全额奖学金,走进了这所著名的学府。1878 年,清政府派往美国的留美幼童,就有多位在这里就读,他们中间有人日后成为了为甲午海战壮烈殉国的民族英雄,也有杰出的外交家。200 多年来,这所美丽的小镇中学,先后走出 3 位诺贝尔奖获得者,6 位普利策奖获得者,5 位艾美奖获得者,1 位奥斯卡奖获得者,1 位奥运会金牌获得者。美国第一任总统乔治·华盛顿访问该校后,便将 1 个侄子和家族中的 8 个孙辈送到这里。美国总统大小布什,也先后都是这里的学生。

殷钟睿在菲利普斯学院不仅学业表现出色,而且刚到学校不久,他就从 30 多位新来的国际学生中脱颖而出,成功地竞选成为"国际学生会委员"。一年后,又竞选成为该会主席。随后在全美竞争最激烈的哈佛本科生申请中,顺利过关。其中的名校效应,完全符合美国的社会伦理和市场法则。

二、兴趣多多,机会也多多

毕业于上海市第三女子中学的方琳同学,现在已经从耶鲁大学完成学业。

当初,方琳获得耶鲁大学录取通知书的时候,同学们中间不免窃窃私语,就凭方琳在同学们中间并非突出的平时学习成绩,海外留学或可成功,但也不至于一下跳到耶鲁大学吧。按照一般中国教育体制的观念理解,考试成绩,就是一流大学录用的最高标准。可是,这可能就是中国式的标准。纽约最著名的史岱文森高中曾经发生的一则故事,是典型美国式标准的表述。杰米是个智力平平的男孩,毕业的时候,他向往进入哈佛大学深造,他在申请表中如实填写了自己的考核成绩和申请志愿,此外,他也在申请信中声情并茂地汇报了自己高中4年学习期间,如何承包管理了一个公共洗手间的卫生清洁,获得师生们的一致好评。此事在年级老师的推荐信中,同样也作为杰米的突出特点给予了肯定。最终,杰米如愿以偿,得以进入哈佛社会学专业就读。哈佛大学注重各类学生的特点,比如坚持、平实、热心公益活动,培养一个社区活动家与一个科学家,具有同等的重要意义。

方琳的耶鲁大学成功之路,其实就是中国版本的杰米哈佛之路,她作为中学辩论队队长,获得过全市比赛的冠军,这在注重民主竞选的美国大学眼中,就是具备了未来政治明星的潜质。同时,方琳从小学习手风琴,至今没有放弃,演奏技巧一流,旁证了她做事认真的特点,耶鲁大学就是需要接受各类璞玉,用于精雕细凿。

三、同一个世界,普世的价值

来自南京的闵婕同学,走的是另外一种赴美留学的路径。

她几乎没有像同班同学一样陷入中国大陆高考预备的奋斗中,却在另一种美国高考复习中,愉快地度过。美国大学学术能力评估测试(SAT),就像已被年轻人熟悉的"托福"考试一样,由全美教育考试中心统一考试,每年举办数次,在世界各地同时举行,最接近中国考生的考点有三个地方,中国的香港、台北和新加坡。

面对SAT测试,闵婕等中国考生之所以感到压力不大,大致有几个原因:(1)数学题目难度相当于中国高一年级水平;(2)不考听、说两项,使得中国学生的哑巴英语暂时蒙混过关;(3)作文评分规范,三段式的范文演绎基本可以拿个平均分数;(4)英语阅读的难点在于文史知识面的积累,而孩子们恰好处于最佳记忆年龄段。

虽说美国不评三好生,不鼓励学生参与政治活动,但是还是有一些全国性的大型组织活动,比如模拟联合国活动(MUN),如果你在该活动中积极参与,代表学校参加当地社区大会,直至全国性的年会。那么,学生个人的社会活动能力和全球政治地理的热点关注能力还是会得到大学录取主管的重视。

闵婕所在学校的老师具有全球眼光,组织了学生参加国际模拟联合国活动,既锻炼了他们的英语能力,也培养了公关能力。闵婕是这项活动中的突出表现者,自然就被美国各大名校看中。

四、"富二代"还是张扬的群体

混一种资历,或者混一个脸熟,可能就是不少像"有财"这样的"煤炭王子"或者"地产公主"的真实想法。

纽约市皇后区的中心区域法拉盛,一直是通行汉语的华人聚集区,周围大大小小的社区大学,包括二年制的"副学士"(Associate's Degree)学院内,注册了许多来自国内富有家庭、但是学业欠佳的学生。

"有财"们住在商业中心周围的高档公寓里,出国前就已盘算好购买的名牌汽车,不费吹灰之力,全都心想事成,嘴里中还往往感叹着两个字——便宜。

晚上,这群打扮自成一路,与当地同龄人很少交往或者不屑与之交往的学生,在中餐馆里三五成群,他们的鼻音或者翘舌音又响又亮,满桌的剩菜从来不像当地居民一样打包。事实上,晚餐的价格是他们自国内开始独立消费以来最便宜的一种消费。美中不足的是,他们不敢像在国内那样把盏酣饮，因为不满 21 岁，违法饮酒会招来警察，这点分寸拿捏得还是很准。"富二代"名扬海外，就是当地的黑帮孩子也不会与其交恶，说不定哪天还得要相互关照一把"生意"来"发财"。

读书做学问，不是他们对自己的主要社会定位，也不是他们家庭对他们的期许，这些孩子承担了更为重要的家族责任，子承父业。他们对当地房产、股票、市场的关注与熟悉程度超过了同龄学生的平均水准。事实上，他们利用父辈的资金，已经在法拉盛地区的华人资本市场上小试牛刀，小有斩获，自信心与自制力大增，构成一段成功的留学经历。

五、在走读高中当自立男孩

相对美国的大学本科，外国学生赴美就读高中的入学成功比例很高。在签证官员看来，这些孩子追求学业的真实程度更高。所以，对于许多学生家长来说，早日放出宝贝孩子独立学习生活的年龄逐年下降，这种环境压力下的出路是一种提高升学成功率却又无奈的选择。

外国学生基本与美国的公立高中无缘，有资格签发海外学生录取证书 I-20[①] 的私立高中有走读与住宿制两种。

凯文是另一类中产家庭的男孩，学业平平，名牌大学毕业的父母，望子成龙心切，委托在纽约华埠附近一所走读制公立高中任职的好友，为凯文办妥留学手续。

一夜间，这个 16 岁的"90 后"独生子，就要开始从"上海宝贝"到"海外游子"的人生转变。他独自租住在一间 10 平方米的卧室里，与另外

---

① I-20 表格是由美国政府承认的学校签发给国外的申请者用以证明其合法学生身份的文件。——编者注

一对夫妇和一个打工仔共享一套三居室的公寓,总面积可能还不及国内的住房大小,所有关于洗涮、烧煮、清理的家务,一切按合住原则办理,周围人各自负责。在家里,这些活通常是由钟点工代劳,凯文闻所未闻,见所未见,所以钟点工成为他出国预科的第一位老师。临行前三天,他还在反复背诵番茄炒鸡蛋的细节。凯文白天上学,回住处后与父母在网上讨论最近几天必须办妥的移民局手续步骤,而这些公文内容,即使神通广大的父母也是爱莫能助,学业难题尚未解决,16岁的少年就要额外面对一大堆法律难题。在这个无亲无友、周围人各自忙碌的少年世界中,放学后的时间如何度过? 交友、黑帮、毒品、色情,在这个缺乏自制力和塑造世界观的年龄阶段,父母二人经常被好莱坞青少年问题电影和夜半噩梦搞得惊魂不定,怀疑自己当初的决定与选择。

六、寄宿高中成就常春藤梦想

在 16 岁的花季,青岛姑娘可人就读了纽约长岛的石溪中学(The Stony Brook School)。长岛的美丽与富裕闻名于世,一如美丽的青岛,可人的父母当然不是给孩子来度假的。通过移民纽约多年的表姑,父母知道了美国寄宿制高中的优势。

原生态美国的寄宿制高中体制主要是为那些有特殊需求的美国家庭服务的。比如双亲太忙,无暇照顾孩子;孩子顽劣,家长无力教育孩子。在大部分美国孩子心目中,寄宿制学校是个可怕的去处,就好比不少中国家长吓唬小孩一样,不听话就送你去派出所。在崇尚个性自由的美国,寄宿制学校相对统一的生活节奏,相对严格的作息时间往往被夸大,而其相对成功的教育效果往往就被掩盖了。

针对华人家庭,比较各种赴美留学之路,寄宿制高中的优势还是明显的。

第一，由于其在各类大学的良好声誉，大学录取人员对其毕业生的质量有所青睐，因此，美国寄宿制高中为中国孩子进入美国一流大学提供了捷径。

第二，寄宿制学校相对严格的作息时间和校务管理，使得海外家长对其孩子的课余安全和生活保障有了一定的把握，毕竟，对于家长而言，安全是第一位的。

第三，寄宿制高中的每年花费总体上没有超出平均水平，更主要是限制了学生的课余社会空间，额外消费反而低于独立生活与学习在居民社区的走读制学校的小留学生。

七、行踪神秘的"官二代"

官员分几种，小官与大官，在位官员与下野官员。所以，"官二代"也就有了不同的旅美生涯。一般来讲，"官二代"在美国并不避讳自己的身份，事实上也无法回避这种与生俱来的特征，这是一个网络时代。好在美国的自由与民主，他人未必都重视你的学生身份，何况还有同学想与你较量一番呢。通常情况下，学生会有一个英文名，这样就自然回避了名字上的敏感程度。曾经有华人媒体大幅地报道了一位前高官的后代，母女俩在美国隐姓埋名 10 年方有出头之日，整个一部辛酸血泪史，但是文化背景颠倒了，美国不相信眼泪。我不知这是作者的意图还是故事主人的心愿，要把世上处处描写成陷阱密布，方能凸显主人公的杰出，血脉真有这么重要吗？柬埔寨首相洪森来纽约看望儿子，就下榻在华人街坊上的一间酒店，无非多定间房，热闹一天也就过去了，就像某位街坊举办了一个大的派对，过去了，也就忘记了。从历史的大处着眼,别说已故政客的后代,就是在位政要的直系血亲,在海外公开自由享受西方文化的多了去了,这个时代三十年风水轮流转,没人在乎你。"You are nothing!"这句话在美国代表藐视、自信和公平,谁都别把自己太当回事,尤其是在学生期间,理想主义的自由平等价值纯洁无瑕,撕开你的面具,或许还会多少赢来一些尊严。否则,哪位当官的没有一些丑事,全都由你的孩子承担去了。全球各地的"官二代"都在此地,规则如一。

八、留学生总体趋势

2009年6月3日,"中国之声"《央广新闻》19时15分报道:2009年高考在即,北京、上海一些高三的班级高考前就逐渐有学生缺席课堂,一个原本有着40多名同学组成的班级,坚持上完高三年级最后一堂课的竟然只剩下6位,这其中有一些学生已经彻底放弃了国内的高考,准备到国外去读大学。

汇丰银行财富管理调查:在受访的7个国家或地区中,中国家庭最重视子女教育。有82%的受访户打算送子女出国留学,在亚太地区中比例最高。另外,在未来的6个月中,他们将把31%的计划投资投入到子女教育上,这一比例与印度并列第一。

中国内地、马来西亚、印度的大部分富裕人士均计划送子女出国留学,比例分别为82%、75%和70%。中国台湾地区则为50%,新加坡为45%,约达半数水平。而日本和澳大利亚较低,分别只有17%和4%有此打算。

教育投入方面,7个国家或地区中,中国内地和印度达31%为最高,其次则为中国台湾地区,比例达22%。最低的仍是澳大利亚,受访者仅将 10％的投资计划放在子女教育上。至于每名子女所需的教育费总额，亚太地区受访者估计平均介于 4.3 万～15.6 万美元。

一位财经界的年轻作家写了一本《百万宝贝计划》的畅销指南，既与大伙分享了他初为人父的感受，又拿第一手资料计算了培养孩子的投入产出，实属难得。作为老爸，曾设身处地为上海老爸们计算过，细节如下：

老爸分两种，资深老爸与青涩老爸。前者基本无语，行动不便，儿女们尽管茶饭伺候便是，他已是兼具老爸与老爷级的人物了；后者刚被青春期的儿女们，从奶声奶气的爸爸或 Dady，唤成"老爸"，正在兴头上！儿女的事情最好都揽在身上，包括升学留学这档子事。

出国留学这回事，老爸当年也憧憬过，奋斗过，只是时运不济，无法如愿。如今与儿女一起从头来过，自然是勇猛与精明不减当年。

老爸是有智慧、有胆识的人物，不然如何娶了老妈，买了新房，炒股赚钱，下海功成。

但老爸的怜悯之心是最让儿女们动情的，眼看十五六岁的孩子，整天为升学与考试烦恼，心中最不是滋味。

孩子不是天才，能上清华北大、复旦交大，当然光宗耀祖。但是如今每年几百万人竞相争，这副架势下，小家碧玉能考上一个称心的"一本"，已经上上大吉了。孩子的辛苦，大家自然心知肚明。问题是，四年毕业以后，找来一份工作，收入一两千，那恰恰是老爸这辈子最不明智的决策和投资回报了，财务分析明摆着的嘛。

高中补习三年 3 万～6 万

四年大学学费 2 万～5 万

四年大学生活费 5 万～10 万

孩子打工收入 0～1 万

总计 10 万～20 万元人民币支出，大学毕业后工作 10 年，方有机会收回。

至今为止，老爸所有的投资回报，还没有这么慢过。还有新的决策方案吗？投资理财，是老爸最擅长的技术，老爸马上发现了决策新动向。手上还有一套小房型的二居室，市中心位置，目前市值 150 万元人民币，眼看人民币升值已达高峰，出手后折价 20 万～25 万美元，正好够孩子留学美国，拿个本科文凭的成本投入。如果孩子懂事，课外打个短工，饭票有了，能力也有了，毕业后在当地找个年薪 3 万～4 万美元的普通工作，积累一些海外工作履历，不但成本回收快，恐怕还有无量前途，真是不敢想下去了。

重点中学设置出国班
应对留学潮

2011 年出国留学的最新趋势在于去美国读名牌中学。中学生出国留学风气日盛，就连北京的名牌中学也纷纷在高一年级开办"出国班"，让学生做好升读美国等名牌大学的准备。这种特殊"出国班"每年学费高达 10 万元人民币，但名额还是供不应求。《北京晨报》报道，2011 年年初，人才辈出的北京四中的一场"中美课程班咨询会"，容纳四五百人的会场里，连通道上都挤满了学生家长，校方计划在 9 月入学的高一年级中美课程班招收 60 人，每年学费约为 9 万～10 万元人民币。

"出国班"入学门槛不低，录取学生的中考成绩最多只能低于该校正常录取线 10 分。三年后，该班毕业生不必参加高考，就可直接申请就读美国或加拿大等数十个国家及地区的名牌大学。目前，北京包括中国人民大学附属中学、北京市第四中学、北京市第十一中学、北京大学附属中学、首都师范大学附属中学、北京师范大学附属实验中学等多所名牌中学，都从高一起开设这类"出国班"，课程设置和培养模式不再严格依据中国教育部制定的教学大纲，而是根据国际标准，每年学费 8 万～10 万元不等。

从出国留学的角度来看，这样的课程设计有其优势。以往高三才开办"出国班"的经历，让一些优秀学生处于两难境地，学生不得不兼顾国内高考和国外高校录取，各种复习准备工作让他们应接不暇，这些优秀学生即使被外国高校录取，也不能迅速调整适应未来学习环境。因此，让有志出国的学生提前适应海外中学内容，与外国课程衔接，可以帮助其更好适应未来留学生活。

高一开始的"出国班"等同于让学生提早留学，各方褒贬不一。有家长认为，今后参与社会竞争的肯定是国际化人才，学生提前做准备很有必要。也有人担心，这会引发优秀中学生流失，公办教育资源流失，以北京四中为例，近年出国留学人数愈来愈多，这些出国学生成绩，基本都在年级前 100 名以内。其实，留还是不留，不必动则上升到民族大义的高度。归根到底，子女教育还是应该回归家庭。事业和出路，唯有家庭成员间的讨论，才有合情合理的决定。

可以想象，"出国班"主要以外国教学大纲而不是中国教学大纲为主，教学语言以英语为主。如果学生决定报考美国大学，准备 SAT 或者美国大学入学考试（ACT），势必成为一种主要学习内容。上述两类美国大学统考，比较适合中国学生的学习范式，主要基于两个特点：一个特点是数学和语法的要求，不会超越中国教学大纲高中二年级的水平；另一个特点是哑巴英语考试，即没有听力与演讲的要求。但是，由于全部是英语环境下的基础语言、数学和写作能力测试，学生在规定时间内的考题数量相对较多，考试时间为三个小时，所以，要求非英语母语的学生，具备快速阅读与理解题意的能力。从这个角度而言，生活中的英语环境要比教室里的英语环境，对学生考试能力的培育起着更大的影响力。"出国班"每年的 10 万元学费，不是一个便宜的数字，即使赴美国私立寄宿高中就学，3 万美元也基本可以满足一年的学习开销，对于一个有志考取一流美国名牌大学的家庭而言，笔者以为后者成功的几率更大，从近年人民币不断升值来看，事实上赴美就读高中，更具备性能价格优势，相关内容，我们还会在之后的章节中重点阐述。

二代工程,视角
眼光宜久远

做完美移民,需二代工程。现在,文字延伸到了我最珍视的部分,涉及孩子的成长、家庭的意识以及温暖的家风。这部分内容,我最乐意述说,但又不敢贸然动笔,记忆触及,唯恐落下显摆的痕迹,尽管许多细节,已经在不同的场合,与许多友人真诚分享过。如今闺女长大成人,时过境迁,重新回忆这部分家庭的私密、人生的乐趣,与新移民家庭分享欢乐与经历,也尝试着用文字的形式点滴收藏一小部分时光遗存。

就从"收藏"这个用词开始,它基本传递了生命中最值得珍爱的本能。

我恐怕是上海最早涉及艺术品收藏的"文化大革命"后大学生之一了,不是因为家底雄厚,仅仅因为校园的外面,就是上海最早自发形成的,肇家浜路街心花园邮票市场兼古玩市场,耳濡目染,读书人的优势和机会就到来了。

艺术品收藏基本上是一项知识型活动,成功的收藏是一项历史、人文、科学与金融素质的综合体现,而不是一掷千金的大款赌博行为,或者被电视鉴宝秀牵着鼻子走的投机行为。比如说,在当年人们鄙视"民国货"瓷器的时候,我就敏锐发现了"珠山八友"藏品的艺术价值和升值空间,所以20年后,我基本有了这样的底气,自己应该是业内戏称为"民国官窑"精品领域的主要收藏者之一。但对于大部分的收藏爱好者而言,无法超脱收藏的宿命,买进大于卖出,敝帚自珍,最终陷入一场没有结局的"噩梦"。在收藏界,唯一值得我们花时间深入探讨的哲学命题(无关商业营利)是,到底应该收藏物质,还是收藏人生?或者说,在物质的估值和人生的投入上,你更愿意倾向哪方?

出国前夕,女儿三岁,我决定携女共赴未来,这种行动,实在有违当时的通常做法。当年,大部分留学生家庭,采用保守的单独成行方案,等到夫妇俩在他乡基本立足,再将孩子接去共同生活。所以,在首批抵达美国的周围朋友中,我们一家三口,日子过得最像一个正常的家庭。不少小夫妻,好不容易在异国他乡团聚,工作生活两方面,已经压力重重。但空闲下来,自然就是思念不在身边的幼小孩子,搞得我们都不敢带孩子示人,以免惹得他人祥林嫂般,逢人就念叨孩子,想宝贝就掉眼泪,何等的凄惨。

我初步统计了一下,50%的家庭将孩子接去美国上初中,理由是先学好汉语,其实这个年龄段的孩子最叛逆,也是同龄孩子中相互作弄、打闹最无常的阶段,所以,中国大陆刚来美国的孩子免不了操一口带着外来口音的英语,美国的校园生活一开始就成为孩子在同学中郁闷烦恼的元素,更加增加了他与主流融合的障碍;30%的孩子,高中时抵达美国,由于SAT等准备仓促,结果失去了进入一流大学的最佳机会。在美国,本科大学决定了一个人今后的社交层面和事业范围,尽管还有硕士、博士阶段的学习调整,但其影响力大大低于一步跨入名校带来的进入社会推动力,所谓门派、渊源和血统是也,此观念不光中国有,看重清华北大、复旦交大等名牌大学,就是在海外也是如此,人以类聚,恐怕属于人类的文化天性,中外统一。

当年,赴美签证到手以后,我估计了一下,利用半年时间,在美国重建家园的开销，应该至少是几千美元，我的科研横向合作不少，每月收入已经属于偏上水平，但也不过每月300～400元人民币，所以，唯一可以动脑筋的，就是我的藏品。床底塞满了收藏的锅碗瓢盆，用我太太的话说，就是仅供做美梦的道具，于是，我决定"倾床而出"。这个时候，拍卖行刚在上海出现，我留下了"珠山八友"，将历年收藏的康熙青花瓶、宣德铜器、缂丝绣品、三代玉器，所有不成系列的藏品，哪怕名头再大包括著名老画家唐云、朱屺瞻、曹简楼的作品，全部出手，基本凑齐了美国重建小家的费用。现在的藏家可能会觉得可惜，不过几千美元，放在今天，上千万人民币都值，还去洋插队干吗？代价太大。

但是当年，收藏市场的行情和国民收入的底线就是如此，人类学家说，人是一种向未来开放的动物，幻想前景、依赖未来、敢于投资未来是一种人生极致的选择，也是一种藏家的品格。

我自认为自己很有艺术品投资眼光，不会不清楚这些艺术品的未来升值空间，但是，放在家庭与女儿的价值面前，取舍应该是无需讨论的。为此，我将这种选择定义为"二代工程"，这个想法在旅美20年后终于形成，已在本书的序言中，完整描述过。新移民由各种年龄段的家庭构成，因此随行的孩子也是年龄不一，我觉得有必要分享不同时段留美孩子的教育关键。

新移民家庭要坚定地 将孩子送到幼儿园

很多新移民小夫妻努力说服自己，工作太忙，收入太少，孩子送回国内，暂请家人领养，等到孩子到了上学的年龄，再接回美国，直接进入校园生活。这种安排的得失，是值得商榷的。

在我供职近 10 年的纽约西奈山医学中心，经常张贴着精神与神经科招募志愿者参与心理与精神分析研究的广告，这家美国最好的临床科室第一句话便是：欢迎母语不是英语的志愿者，但须 6 岁以前移民美国。这绝对不是种族歧视，而是出于科学实验的积累，6 岁以前来到英语世界的移民，未来成长过程中，其语言和文化不会显示出与英语作为母语的本地孩子的显著性差异。

我们来到美国的新居，女儿感到很新鲜，因为她还根本无法区别辞家去国的异样。我们租用的小屋，位于房东的后院，唯一的好处，就是开门见绿的草坪，那是上海老家没有的场面。休整一周后，我们告诉女儿，应该上幼儿园去了，那里有小朋友一起玩，这正中女儿的心思，一个人在草坪中玩了一周，够了，也够孤独的。

纽约的幼儿园，全部是收费经营。或者也可以在上学的前一个学期，申请小学的学前班。但那个免费的课程只有半天，只有具备全职家长或者专职保姆的家庭才能承受。核算一下时间成本和直接支出，总的花费可能比全日制幼儿园还贵，这个课程，基本上是为了培养那些在家散漫惯了的孩子，为他们预习上学的规矩。家长们基本上也是冲着那些声誉排名较好的学校，提前抢占名额去的。

女儿养育史上，需要面临的第一次重大决定，就是放弃她的母语。事实上，女儿开口说话很迟，这倒不打紧，我相信，这表明孩子的逻辑能力发育，可能超前了形象思维的发育，4岁的女儿用上海口音与我们交流不久，现在又要去适应另一种称为"国语"的汉语发音。这种放弃，对于一位上海父亲，还有另外一种痛苦，生活中少了一种文化上的亲近感。上海"嗲妹妹"是一种地方品牌，娶进门后的上海太太，基本不会再以"嗲妹妹"的模样展现在丈夫面前，这是历史规律，我早有心理准备。如今女儿一旦放弃了说"上海闲话"的能力，就意味着本男性今生再也无缘上海"嗲妹妹"了，但这时需要体现男人的牺牲精神。

街坊上最适合我们家庭的日托班，恐怕就是名为"纽约至善中文学校"的一家老牌幼稚园了。这是一家由台湾移民开设在一栋独立别墅里的幼儿园，每月收费485美元，含午餐，下午6点以前必须接走孩子，否则每小时加收5美元误时费。这对我们确是一项考验，5美元的额外潜在风险，意味着5加仑牛奶，是全家一个月的牛奶消耗量。但我看重的是，幼稚园的老板，或称校长，是一位年逾六旬的老先生，他曾任台湾某师范学院的校长，儒雅的传统国学教养，有一丝令人景仰，也或许可以影响办学的风气。尽管事实上，第一次预约见面，我们就对他的女助理心存不满，她的势利眼神明摆在一张半老的徐娘脸上：哼，大陆客！你们承担得起学费吗？这里还从未接收过大陆新移民的孩子呐。但我们别无选择。这就是20年前的一幅炎凉世态，政治和经济的差异，在海峡两岸华人中的生活中，表现得还是相当直白。

女儿乖巧、白皙，确是上海"嗲妹妹"的胚子。刚满18个月，就上了幼儿园，不哭不闹，成了几位自己还像小妹妹一般的歌舞老师的小宝贝，所以从她们那里学得身手，好歌好舞艺，也算是经历过排场的。小娃娃的这几招，一下就在纽约至善中文学校的学生中脱颖而出，夏天毕业的时候，已经成为毕业班领舞的小主角，盛典开始了，大家一起为孩子的成长欢呼。孩子生来就是人与人之间最好的润滑剂，不同文化背景下的移民之间，几个月相处下来，成见也就淡了。

小学开始，新移民面临文化危机

在纽约市，学区规定 5 岁的孩子就可以享受公立上学教育，入学年龄以 12 月 31 日前出生为限。这下，12 月出生的女儿，刚好轮到上学机会，与当年年初出生的孩子玩在一起，个子自然矮了一截。

9 月的纽约，天气还很炎热，放学后的女儿，在后院里尽情放肆玩耍，从自行车上摔倒，又不顾一切地爬上去再骑，直到膝盖上磨破了皮，出血无数，才想到回家。平时在学校，女孩儿爱追逐疯闹，所以胳膊大腿常常挂彩。我们见多不怪，习以为常，回家后贴上个邦迪护创膏，也就罢了。

谁料，一起民事案件却由此从天而降。

几周后，我们收到一封来自纽约州福利部青少年处的公函，文字不长，声称业已受理对我们夫妻俩的投诉，有人控告我们具有虐待子女的嫌疑。依据法律法规，有关人员将登门调查，核实该案细节。公函要求我们在 7 个工作日内主动回电，预约执法人员上门时间。公函上，案例登记号码、公章、官方签名，一应俱全。我们刚刚来自人治社会，哪里见过这等法律文书与程序。当天通宵无眠，可说是对我们夫妇俩最大的折磨，面对我们唯一的宝贝闺女，思绪却纠结在下列问题。

第一，到底是谁投诉、告发我们，邻居、警察，还是过路人？

第二，投诉立案的证据是？

第三，哪些渠道可以帮助我们？学校、朋友，还是律师？

第四，此事的结局是？最坏的结局是？

我们越想越害怕。当时不久前，纽约的中英文报纸反复报道过一则案例。哥伦比亚大学有一对中国大陆留学生小夫妻，宝宝出生刚满一岁，正依恋妈妈，可惜丈夫毕业后工作一直没有落实，只好靠太太的一份晚上的临时工作维持家计，明知学生签证规定不得打工，但是为了生存只能硬着头皮碰运气。小爸爸整晚整晚地搞不定宝宝，孩子的哭声惹恼了外籍邻居，一个电话打到市政府投诉，控告小夫妻虐待婴儿。执法人员上门调查的结果确认，小夫妻没有合法收入，家庭经济状况拮据，不利于婴儿生存，必须立即将孩子解救出来，暂时委托福利救济部门收养。

现在，事情已经提升到了保护女儿、争夺抚养权的原则高度。次日早上，我们立即奔赴女儿的学校，希望获得一丝指导，回复却令我们大吃一惊，原来投诉我们虐待孩子的，就是校方，班主任一连几天发现女儿身上出现淤血斑块，询问女儿，可她不发一言，老师越发觉得事情的严重性，殊不知，女儿此刻的英语程度，仅是我们上学前强化的两个单词："上厕所"与"要喝水"。老师再请同班的一位华裔孩子代为其翻译，询问细节，女儿同样不发一言，小男生的一口粤语，更像外国话。事情铁板钉钉了，老师立即上报校方，否则，事情进一步发展，就成了班主任的责任。以上所有细节，都是20年后才揭晓的，与女儿一起回忆童年，是我们的快乐时光，这些记忆片断，慢慢从她的口述中，被我们还原成当时的情景。

看来，我们只有一周的时间落实自救，我们必须清除所有可能因误会、推理，从而论证成为涉及虐待，或者无力正常抚育孩子的线索。首先要在附近马上租一套公寓，搬离现在居住的后院小屋，它看上去太不正规，远离美国人心目中一家三口的正常居住条件；然后要将厨房冰箱的空间，用各种食物和饮料填满，牛奶和面包，必须放在显著位置，以示基本口粮充足；接下来就是打扮新居了，一室一厅里的清洁卫生与温暖气氛，可以显示小家庭的生活品位。所有这些细节，都是几位最亲密的朋友，到处打听，悄悄商量后，加以改进落实的，以免再次留下不利证据，误导调查人员。

一周后，一位文静的非洲裔女性调查人员按响了我家门铃，我们热情地迎她入座，自信地介绍了我俩体面的就学专业和就业单位，这两个纽约大学旗下的部门肯定赢得了她的好感，然后我们谈移民的不易，谈子女的养育心得，谈女儿的异国好奇，我们努力暗示她参观一下我们的冰箱藏品，可是她还在兴致勃勃地记录谈话内容，最后留下一句：别担心，祝你们好运！调查前后共计花费了 20 分钟，公务期间，她没有喝过我们准备的茶水，也没有吃过一口水果，这些出于中国文化的待客礼仪，都被她以微笑婉拒了。我们祈祷这位不拿群众一针一线的"雷锋式"阿姨，将好人做到底。果然再过一周，公函又到了："本案业已注销。"

如果我们学会了客观地用美国式的思维审视全部过程，其实很值得借鉴推广，为每个孩子营造安全幸福的生长环境：老师及时发现了异常的情况，工作尽职；政府有效地审理了案件；20 分钟的正常调查时间内，公务员获得了她需要的所有细节；而家长确实为孩子尽了最大的努力保护孩子与家庭，而这正是法律法规希望获得的社会效果。在这里，政府与民众的关系是清晰的,也是我们从未体验过的,协调、管理替代了以往印象中的专政和教导,这就是社会差异,也是我们第一次在另一种文化社会中收获。

记忆中,有部叫《刮痧》的中国电影,其中用太多的中国视角表达文化差异,抨击异族伦理,展示文化自卑,电影本身再次渲染了文化冲突,有害无益。万事过了头,就不易修复裂痕。在这方面,如果拜读过援华抗日军事顾问史迪威将军的回忆录或相关史料,老一辈的智慧,不是当下的精英可以达到的高度。史迪威将军1911年首次来到中国,之后数次出任驻华公职。他在阎锡山治下的山西修路,却更欣赏这位西式管理军阀采用加州治理干旱的技术,引进美利奴羊种和谷物牧草优良品种,他甚至拜读了阎锡山制定的反对陋习、提倡新生活的山西公民守则;他在冯玉祥治下的陕西治军,并没有因为这位笃信基督的将军要求部队言必上帝、行必《圣经》的观念,使两人在文化上和宗教上更加接近,从而惺惺相惜,反而不断反对冯将军购买坦克飞机,鼓励他搞好基本建设,赞同他对士兵的职业培训和文化教育。当时中国民间底层的落后状况和政治混乱的现实状况,从来没有阻碍这样一位西方精英将家安在中国的愿望,他在东方看到了更多文化融合的美好侧面和未来希望。

给孩子选择
什么样的教育

因为搬迁了新居，我们有理由转入更接近住址的小学，改变孩子的上学环境是考虑原因之一，更重要的，是了解到了这个就近的公立小学，学生较少，经费相对充足，因此教育水准较高。举个例子来说，某日女儿带回一张通知，本周末，学校组织外出参加音乐会，邀请家长参加，但是名额有限，总共一辆校车的限额，所以先到先得。作为新移民，这是一场难得的免费高雅艺术活动，我们举家欣然前往。到了音乐会场，方才意识到，这可不是哄孩子玩的普通亲子活动，会场位于纽约市第七大道 881 号的卡耐基音乐厅，名声如雷贯耳，与维也纳音乐厅等齐名，世界各地的演奏家都以登上它们的舞台作为艺术生涯的里程碑。

手头正好有条 2011 年 1 月 25 号的报道，有人质疑"昂贵的科普"无助于提高国民科学素养，新闻源于广东科学中心开业三年半，票价太高，更无儿童优惠。科学中心 150 元的门票应该降价，甚至完全免费，才能真正起到推进科普的作用。按照中国式的高雅管理思路，让孩子们进入一流音乐厅的常规演奏会，会有影响艺术效果等诸如此类的托词。但是美国学区和校方的考虑是值得投入，卡耐基音乐厅也看得更高更远，对孩子来说，确实还没有掌握艺术技巧，但艺术的环境、艺术的氛围和艺术的投入，高于一切，或许从此改变一个人的一生，用一句流行的家庭教育术语：学琴的孩子不变坏。

　　果然，返程的校车上，女儿已经深受艺术的感染，她愿意放弃在校车上与其他孩子相互追逐的乐趣，放学回家多操练琴键上的技巧，尽管这个时候，我们还只有一架电子键盘供她练习。可是这一天是个转折点，半年后的学生汇报音乐会上，5 岁的"小不点"，在喜来登酒店的大厅内，努力爬上高高的琴凳，引来一场哄笑，而她最终第一次在 7 英尺长的三角钢琴上，用力敲完了所有的音符，而且节奏完整，迎接她的，就是掌声了。

　　我们所在的学区，也就是街道，有十几所小学。在办学条件最好的209 小学中，学区特别设置了一个约 25 位小朋友的阿尔法（α）课程班，作为学区教学试点、对外交流和展示教学成果的实验班。当然，教育是双向的，你也得招收一批特别好学的孩子，才能专门配合学区提供的特殊培养计划。等到我们在家长会上了解到这样的情况，当然已经满额。班主任是位华裔的老师，她理解我们的愿望，公事公办地说，可以为我们申请，排队在等候名额中，最终就看运气了。按照学校条例，家长的要求，全部要公平对待。只不过其他的家长，并非与我们一样觉得阿尔法课程有助孩子成长。做一个平常人，是大多数美国人民的骄傲理想，而我们不远万里来到纽约，必须承认是一个不甘平庸的家庭。

　　千万不要以为，华裔老师的做法带有人情取向。其实，作为华裔老师，她还特别注意自己，不要有种族倾向流露，以免惹上职业麻烦。我们可以感觉到，平时教学活动中，她还情愿更关照其他族裔的孩子，不过我们理解她的行为方式，每个人的生存都不易。学期期末有老师家长"一对一"见面的节目，我们按照传统的尊师礼节，特意带上了一份精致的真丝围巾，老师深表谢意后说："我最喜欢的礼物，是学生自己在课堂上做的圣诞贺卡，我已经拿到了，其他礼物请收回吧。"

　　到了下一个学期，班主任换成琼斯小姐，女儿已经开始知道如何与同学、老师相处，中国式乖乖女的性格，发生了很大的变化。琼斯小姐告诉我们，女儿最大的特点，是敢于举手发言，开始学习新词汇、新语句的时候，她就第一个大声地朗读起来了，自信得很。尽管老师知道女儿在家里还是以母语为主，但在尝试新词汇的发音上，她比英语家庭的孩子还要充满信心。之后女儿告诉我们，大家都是新学的，我就不害怕出错了。语言是人类交流的第一信号系统，对大脑和行为的发育极其关键，这一点上，天分可能是存在的。与女儿整日厮混在一起的是一群韩国裔女孩，从她们那里，女儿不仅学了一口韩国俚语，还缠着我们一起玩拍手游戏，也是韩语版本，结果全家都乱喊（韩）一气了。

　　现在，我们可以感觉到，女儿内心已经不再是一只中国式的温顺绵羊，这个环境暗示她，只有发出声音，才会让人注目。实践这个愿望的时机来了，四年级的时候，校长来信告知，209小学的阿尔法班名额空缺，已经轮到我们，如果继续愿意转学，现在就可以决定。之后女儿高调地宣布："我要开始竞选班长！"这是美式小学教会她的人生第一门技巧。

延伸阅读

纽约市唯一择优录取的公立初中

2011 年 5 月，新任美国最高法院大法官的艾琳娜·卡根 (Elena Kagan) 出现在公众视野，人们对她曾任哈佛大学法学院院长的专业水准，记忆犹新。可女儿对我说，"她不仅是我哈佛大学的校友，还是我亨特中学的校友"。

纽约市立大学亨特学院附属的亨特中学，都大纽约地区[①] 1 500 万人口中，唯一设立全市统考制度、每年录取 400 名六年级孩子的公立中学。一般来讲，除了家庭特别富裕，或者宗教信仰特别强烈的家庭，一般纽约新移民家庭的子女，均在公立的中小学读书。公立中学遍布全市五个行政区域的各个街道社区，当地居民收入有高低，所以政府的税收有差距，尽管各学区已经尽量平衡，但是公立学校的质量上下差距还是明显的，由此也不断推升了学区较好地段的房价和人口数量。可怜天下父母心，所以，纽约的许多家庭，对于亨特中学一年一度的招生制度和考试安排极度关注，极力争取自家子女被录取的机会。

---

① 大纽约地区以纽约市为中心，包括纽约州上州的 6 个郡与长岛的 2 个郡，新泽西州的 14 个郡，康涅狄格州的 3 个郡，以及宾夕法尼亚州东北部的 1 个郡所组成。是全美最大的都会区，也是全世界最大都会区之一。——编者注

20世纪90年代初期，亨特中学录取统计上，出现了亚裔学生特别是华裔孩子比例逐年上升的趋势，这种现象引起了其他族裔家庭的极度不满，他们认为，这是考试方法在鼓励死记硬背惹的祸，作为一家市立中学，它对市民的这种反应相当敏感。

华裔、日裔、韩裔和印度裔家庭的传统文化，都非常关注孩子的从小培养，家庭教育很严格，相比西方家庭的散养传统，有很大的区别。事实上，对于十一二岁的孩子，考试前突击准备一下，与临时匆忙上阵，结果肯定不同。更主要的是，东方家庭的孩子被认为死记硬背的特点更突出，这种学习方法可以获得一时的考试高分，却难以获得可持续的能力发展。对于这些评论，东西方家庭的争论当然很激烈，利用各种讨论平台，从人类的起源涵盖当前的政治经济发展，各自取证，激烈辩论，但类似的东西方文化争论，学者们早已延续了近一个世纪，毫无结果。所以，纽约市的这场"亨特门"博弈，最后还是演绎为一场利益之争，目标无非是为各方的孩子争取最大的录取机会，最后只能是政治解决，选票决定利益。校方宣布，除了保持一贯的统一考试制度，再增加一门命题作文。这样，考分的取舍不再是依据多选题那样的机械无误，作文评分的上下出入，微妙地成为亨特中学平衡各族裔录取比例的工具之一，也确实筛落了不少考分处在边缘地带的亚裔孩子。

世事总归难以十全十美。

女儿以接近满分的高分顺利进入亨特中学，录取书到手的那天，女儿还与她妈妈开了一场玩笑，声称遗憾落选，可电话里难以压抑的喜悦还是泄露了天机,妈妈与女儿间的血缘联系,本来就为第六感的沟通埋下了基因的种子。但亨特中学开学之后,女儿的日子,就不是每天都笑得出来了。

我们家位于长岛郊区和纽约市区的交界处,距离位于曼哈顿岛上中央大道和94街的亨特中学,就是开车,也起码有一个小时路程。纽约的学校,一般是早上8点开门迎客,对于远途的学生,基本只有三个选择,父母开车接送、校车接送和搭乘公交车。曼哈顿岛上交通拥挤,学校不在我们上班的途中,所以不予考虑自己接送;中学开始,校车接送是收费服务,而且一家一家的上门接人,你可能要提前几小时就上车,严重影响睡眠;唯有搭乘公交车是学校推荐的主要方法,而且每位学生都可以申请免费交通卡,既环保节能,又安全准时。但要做到几年全勤,也是一件值得自我嘉奖的事。

早上6点半,必须起床出门,先是在家门口搭乘公交汽车,然后转乘前往曼哈顿的地铁。通常,你要设法利用在地铁上的几十分钟打个盹,这样到达学校后,可以精神饱满一些。完成这些每天必需的交通,对于大部分功课必须午夜以后才能完成,而且分散在郊区各地的学生来说,并非易事。培养毅力,先于技艺。

寄宿制高中，中国留学生考取一流美国大学的跳板

在过去的 10 年中，已经有不少来自中国大陆的初中与高中学生，只身赴美；或者在家长的陪伴下，通过各类途径，在美国的各等中学里，开始了更为早期的留美学习生涯，被称为小留学生。

这些早期小留学生面临的问题是，由于对美国的教育体制认识不清，在普通中学走读，小小年纪同时面临了签证、法务、住房、交通和一日三餐等成人事物，既花费了不少钱，又在生活细节处理中，花费了本该用于学业的时间，以至留学效果不够理想。对于学生和家长而言，出国留学是一项兼具人才培育和投资理财一举两得的项目。痛下决心，让孩子少小离家的目的，一定是希望他们进入名校，大展宏图。美国教育的私立制度，确实保证了我们中国籍的孩子，具有进入名校的可能性，但这需要好好合计。

比如说，作为一个私立的董事会管理下的教育机构，学费和赞助是其经济来源的主要部分，像哈佛大学这样的众多一流大学，鼓励校友和社会人士捐赠，并在录取新生时，为校友家庭和社会巨额捐赠家庭的孩子网开一面，早就是一个公开的秘密。100 万美元的捐赠额，可以换来一个进入名校学习的机会，但不能保证换取该名校的毕业证书，这样也是一种良性互动的制度设计。许多著名的常春藤大学，与特定的高中保持了良好的互动关系，就是因为这些高中可以提供学业优良、家庭背

151

景和资助雄厚的学生资源。所以,在美国,进入一个声名良好的高中,就是踏入一流大学的前奏。富人集聚处的丰厚地产税养活了一所著名的高中,而著名高中的毕业生从一流大学毕业后,收入回报丰厚,再次养活了母校,无论高中还是大学,就是在这样的良性循环中,一代一代培育了后人。

所以,伴随中国经济的高速发展,一部分富裕家庭应该不仅将眼光放在国内一流高中的"出国班"中,更应将视线聚焦美国富裕地区的高中,尤其是寄宿制中学,理由如下所列。

第一,人民币升值使得支持小留学生的财务状况成为可能。对于一个每年有能力支付10万元人民币,决定让孩子放弃全国教学大纲,不再参加全国大学统一考试的家庭而言,支付2万～3万美元,也就是12万～18万元人民币,在一个真正的美式英语环境中,严格训练孩子的SAT或者ACT习题速度和精确性,其中的成功几率,基本是可以计算出的。

第二,寄宿制中学的严格管理一定程度上解除了家长的后顾之忧。对于美国孩子梦魇般可怕的寄宿学校,限制的是所谓人性自由,换取的是人性的自律。学校统一划一的军队式生活学习纪律,其实未必比国内的学校管理还严格,但是规范的住宿、餐饮和学习、生活,尤其是对外籍孩子的学籍护理,家长真的可以通过网络交流来"遥控"你的宝贝了。

第三,将进一所好高中作为考入著名大学的依托,投资回报概率很高。高中十一年级开始,不断有来自全国各地的著名大学来寄宿高中作招生宣传,孩子在老师的配合下,不仅可以完成优质的申请材料,而且可以与心仪的大学提早接洽,这些额外的优势,都是在北京、上海等"出国班"中无法获得的资源,也是国内学生最后不得不花大价钱,聘请中介机构从头来过的申请入学程序。而著名大学毕业的就职机会与工资回报，下文会集中介绍。

下面罗列了全美较好的寄宿制高中，可以作为小留学生的入学参考。但是，由于时效的动态性和统计单位的不同，可能信息会有出入，笔者将有关网址列出，以便读者可以随时查询（http://www.boardingschoolreview.com/toptwenty.php）。笔者相信还有更多好的高中不在其列；同时，大家在选择高中时，还要结合自身情况，咨询有关专家。

表5-1 美国寄宿制私立中学（女校排名）

排 名	学 校	类 型	所在州	平均SAT成绩
1	The Hockaday School 霍克黛女子中学	All-girls	得克萨斯州	1 992
2	The Madeira School 马德拉中学	All-girls	弗吉尼亚州	1 920
3	Emma Willard School 艾玛维拉德中学	All-girls	纽约州	1 892
4	Santa Catalina School 圣特凯特利那中学	All-girls	加利福尼亚州	1 886
5	Miss Porter's School 波特中学	All-girls	康涅狄格州	1 863
6	Dana Hall School 丹娜豪女子中学	All-girls	马萨诸塞州	1 854
7	Westover School 西部中学	All-girls	康涅狄格州	1 850
8	San Domenico School 圣多明尼哥中学	All-girls	加利福尼亚州	1 821
9	Miss Hall's School 米斯豪女子中学	All-girls	马萨诸塞州	1 806
10	Linden Hall 林顿豪女子中学	All-girls	宾夕法尼亚州	1 806

排 名	学 校	类 型	所在州	平均SAT 成绩
11	Annie Wright School 安妮怀特中学	All-girls	华盛顿州	1 800
12	Garrison Forest School 葛莉森林女子中学	All-girls	马里兰州	1 790
13	Salem Academy 塞伦中学	All-girls	北卡罗来纳州	1 787
14	Foxcroft School 福克斯克罗夫特女子中学	All-girls	弗吉尼亚州	1 774
15	Chatham Hall 查塔姆霍尔中学	All-girls	弗吉尼亚州	1 770
16	Saint Mary's School 圣玛丽中学	All-girls	北卡罗来纳州	1 750
17	The Ethel Walker School 埃尔沃克中学	All-girls	康涅狄格州	1 661
18	Stuart Hall School 霍尔高中	All-girls	弗吉尼亚州	1 661
19	St. Timothy's School 圣提矛斯中学	All-girls	马里兰州	1 550
20	Grier School 葛丽尔女子中学	All-girls	宾夕法尼亚州	1 540

表 5-2 美国寄宿制私立中学(男校排名)

排 名	学 校	类 型	所在州	平均SAT 成绩
1	Georgetown Preparatory School 乔治城预备中学	All-boys	马里兰州	1 950
2	McCallie School 迈克林中学	All-boys	田纳西州	1 823
3	Woodberry Forest School 伍德贝瑞森林中学	All-boys	弗吉尼亚州	1 814
4	Avon Old Farms School 埃文农场中学	All-boys	康涅狄格州	1 780

续 表

排 名	学 校	类 型	所在州	平均 SAT 成绩
5	Trinity Pawling School 圣三一珀林中学	All-boys	纽约州	1 750
6	CFS. The School at Church Farm 主教农场中学	All-boys	宾夕法尼亚州	1 730
7	Salisbury School 萨利士伯瑞男子中学	All-boys	康涅狄格州	1 730
8	Subiaco Academy 苏比亚可中学	All-boys	阿肯色州	1 710
9	Christian School 基督中学	All-boys	北卡罗来纳州	1 700
10	South Kent School 南肯特中学	All-boys	缅因州	1 680
11	Kiski School 柯士奇中学	All-boys	宾夕法尼亚州	1 584
12	Grand River Academy 格兰德河流中学	All-boys	俄亥俄州	1 550
13	Christchurch School 基督城中学	All-boys	弗吉尼亚州	1 546
14	Fishburne Military School 费什布尔军校	All-boys	弗吉尼亚州	1 535
15	St' John's Northwestern Military Academy 圣约翰西北军校	All-boys	威斯康星州	1 530
16	Fork Union Military Academy 福克联合军校	All-boys	弗吉尼亚州	1 525
17	Army and Navy Academy 海陆军校	All-boys	加利福尼亚州	1 520
18	St' Thomas More School 圣托马斯中学	All-boys	康涅狄格州	1 520
19	Missouri Military Academy 密苏里军校	All-boys	密苏里州	1 511
20	The Phelps School 菲尔普斯中学	All-boys	宾夕法尼亚州	1 508

纽约市排名第一的史蒂文森高中

对于大部分向往优质公立高中的纽约家庭来说，学生八年级的时候，也就是相当于中国大陆初中二年级的时候，还有一次机会可以通过考试，进入纽约市教育机构专门设立的位于曼哈顿的史蒂文森高中、布朗克斯技术高中和布鲁克林技术高中，每年招生总人数可达5 000名左右，专门为常春藤大学联盟培养理科候选人。

女儿读八年级时，亨特高中已经拥有了两年前千里挑一选来的学生不再继续录取新生。大部分家长和学生还沉浸在两年前成功的喜悦中，换一个角度说，也是背负了继续挑战自我的一个包袱。我们夫妇深知孩子的潜力，更希望她有不断竞争的动力，这个时候的女儿，基本还是听从家长的想法，全家一起开始了考取史蒂文森高中的竞赛，结果当然是如愿以偿。

史蒂文森高中毕业生在全美一流大学中的信誉如虹，每年考取哈佛大学、普林斯顿大学、耶鲁大学和麻省理工学院的就有30～50名，其他常春藤大学的就更多了，全美排名30位左右的纽约大学是史蒂文森高中毕业生的基本去向，可见它不愧是一所百年名校。

说实在的，美国高中的教学要求不是很高，下面所列的数学题目，可以请我们的高一读者同学尝试解答一下，这就是美国大学入学考试的基本水准，大家应该对考取美国的大学充满自信，唯一的要求是你得保持一定的解题速度。上述从幼儿园到高中的移民教育内容，对于已经移民美国的家庭具有一定的借鉴；而对于直接将孩子送往美国留学的家庭，请仔细阅读接下来的几节内容。

小贴士：美国高中试题举例

第一题

A special lottery is to be held to select the student who will live in the only deluxe room in a dormitory. There are 100 seniors, 150 juniors, and 200 sophomores who applied. Each senior's name is placed in the lottery 3 times; each junior's name, 2 times; and each sophomore's name, 1 time. What is the probability that a senior's name will be chosen?

◉(A) $\dfrac{1}{8}$

◉(B) $\dfrac{2}{9}$

◉(C) $\dfrac{2}{7}$

◉(D) $\dfrac{3}{8}$

◉(E) $\dfrac{1}{2}$

Correct Answer: D

第二题

NOONTIME TEMPERATURES IN HILO，HAWAII

Mon	Tue	Wed	Thu	Fri	Sat	Sun
66	78	75	69	78	77	70

The table above shows the temperatures, in degrees Fahrenheit, in a city in Hawaii over a one-week period. If m represents the median temperature, f represents the temperature that occurs most often, and a represents the average (arithmetic mean) of the seven temperatures, which of the following is the correct order of m, f, and a?

◉(A) $a < m < f$

◉(B) $a < f < m$

◉(C) $m < a < f$

◉(D) $m < f < a$

◉(E) $a = m < f$

Correct Answer：A

第三题

The projected sales volume of a video game cartridge is given by the function, in dollars; an da is a constant. If according to the projections, 100 000 cartridges are sold at ＄10 per cartridge, how many cartridges will be sold at ＄20 per cartridge?

◉(A) 20,000

◉(B) 50,000

◉(C) 60,000

◉(D) 150,000

◉(E) 200,000

Correct Answer：C

第四题

In the xy-coordinate plane above, line ℓ contains the points $(0,0)$ and $(1,2)$. If line m (not shown) contains the point $(0,0)$ and is perpendicular to ℓ, what is an equation of m?

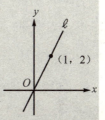

◉(A) $y=-\dfrac{1}{2}x$

◉(B) $y=-\dfrac{1}{2}x+1$

◉(C) $y=-x$

◉(D) $y=-x+2$

◉(E) $y=-2x$

Correct Answer：A

第五题

Note：Figure not drawn to scale.

If two sides of the triangle above have lengths 5 and 6, the perimeter of the triangle could be which of the following?

Ⅰ. 11

Ⅱ. 15

Ⅲ. 24

◉(A) Ⅰ only

◉(B) Ⅲ only

◉(C) Ⅲ only

◉(D) Ⅱ and Ⅲ only

◉(E) Ⅰ, Ⅱ, and Ⅲ

Correct Answer：B

第六题

If $x>1$ and $\dfrac{\sqrt{x}}{x^3}=x^m$, what is the value of m?

◉(A) $-\dfrac{7}{2}$

◉(B) -3

◉(C) $-\dfrac{5}{2}$

◉(D) -2

◉(E) $-\dfrac{3}{2}$

Correct Answer：C

第七题

If k is divisible by 2，3，and 15，which of the following is also divisible by these numbers?

◉(A) $k + 5$

◉(B) $k + 15$

◉(C) $k + 20$

◉(D) $k + 30$

◉(E) $k + 45$

Correct Answer：D

做一套完善的大学申请材料：
准备迈入大学

本节的标题是"准备迈入大学"，毫不掩饰意图，期待读者在全面阅读有关内容之前，直接清晰地获得一个信号，美国的大学人人可上，只要学生家长充满自信。

我们应该回避涉及"考大学"话语时，经常使用的"人生拼搏"或者"背水一战"等诸如此类的表达句式，不要过分吓着孩子。在孩子进入大学之前，家庭的每位成员其实都很辛苦，而且敏感。十几年养育下来，好不容易等到了可以独立起飞的关键时刻，谁不想自己的孩子往高处飞？

但是，人人可以上大学，与能够顺利进入自己心仪已久的理想大学，这样两种结局还是有区别的。大学申请需要专业指导或技巧引导。

美国大学的申请材料，基本上可以归纳成"3－3－3－1"方案，即一份完美的申请材料取决于 4 个部分，平时成绩占 30%，统考成绩占 30%，才艺推荐占 30%，还有 10% 就是来自前辈的指导与自己的执着了。

对于在中国文化背景下成长起来的学生及其家长，准备去美国上大学，首先需要摆脱中国式的思维方式。中国考生的常规印象中，高三时那场恐怖的高考，至今仍然是"一考定终身"的魔咒，难以摆脱。各地媒体上登载了太多令人心酸的报道。这种人才选拔方式，脱胎于中国古代的科举制度，时过境迁，已经日显迂腐，不仅缺乏科学性，而且也太不讲人性了。

另一方面，大家也千万不要把曾经流传的风言风语，如"在美国读书很轻松"这样的讹传当成真相，这是一种相当不负责任的片面误导。

美国的大学入学准备其实是一项系统工程，渗透在人才培养的全部过程中。一个希望进入理想大学的学生，其家庭必须提前好几年就要开始筹划，否则临时抱佛脚解决不了任何问题。这样一种优质的家庭教育计划，不仅仅包括常规理解的学生教育标准，即从小到大，好好读书，夯实基础这样的基本要求；更主要强调家庭培养子女的过程中，应经在孩子的人格、才艺和知识等多方面，进行了大量的投资与努力。在这里，我想引用一段美国高中学生对中国高考的思考，换一种视角看问题，但它确实有助中国学生与家长的换位思考。引用这篇美国十二年级高中毕业生的普通短文，也有助从一个侧面了解美国文化下长大的十七八岁华裔孩子，他们写作的基本文字能力正是每位大学候选人必须相互了解比较的平面。

这篇文章不再翻译成汉语，那样读懂了也毫无意义。建议每位阅读本书的美国大学申请人，最好把它读下来，这是一篇常规大学申请材料中很普通的作文，有助于你了解申请的难易程度。

In the race to get into a good college, those who were brave enough this year to fill in Jiao Tong University or Fu Dan University this year must be spending these past few days happily exclaiming to everyone they meet. That's because this year, too few highly qualified people applied for the top two universities in Shanghai. What resulted was a humanities score cut off lower than that of Tong Ji & Chai Jing University, both considered less prestigious schools.

A reason for the small applicant pool this year is the way that the college exams are set up. Each student gets to put down their top three choices. But it isn't advisable to fill in Jiao Tong as first and Tong Ji as second. If the student doesn't get into Jiao Tong, his score won't even be considered for Tong Ji since many students fill in Tong Ji as their first choice.

Since college acceptance is dependent only upon this one test score, many students were understandably nervous about applying for a top tier school and finally only getting into a school on the bottom of the heap. For students who've been through it before, the memories for those days still lay fresh in their minds. Yu Junjia, now finishing his third year at University of Shanghai for science and technology says, "The day before the results came out, I sat at home and stared at the wall to avoid throwing up whenever I thought of the test."

The Chinese exam for college entrance, ironically called "Gao Kao", which means high school exam, is the only criteria for college entrance. Every student's past, present, and future is determined by that one test. My steriously drawn lines split aspiring students into different colleges.

On the other hand, I applied for college in America and it felt much less stressful. Even getting the results to my college entrance exam, the SAT, only made me anxious, slightly sweaty, maybe even a bit cross-eyed. But I didn't feel too terrible knowing that I could always take it over if I did badly. Besides, I had another year worth of writing essays and perfecting my character to make myself more appealing to the admissions officers.

In the American system, the college selection process stretches on for basically all of high school, where even freshmen in high school worry about how their grades might affect their future. It's true that the process becomes much more subjective, much more difficult for everyone involved. Instead of my personality being represented by a number, I am now a compilation of countless essays, interview profiles, activities and other bits and pieces of information.

I become much more difficult to understand. Yet, it gives me room to maneuver. I don't have to depend on one test taken over three days to determine the rest of my life. I can use everything I've done my entire life to build my future. In doing so, I found myself admitted into Harvard.

One of my friends, James Gerien-Chen, didn't do all that well on his SAT's scoring a 2 190 out of 2 400, with roughly 15% of other high school kids doing better than him. Yet he's an amazing cellist, having played for people such as the mayor of New York City. He's also a half Irish half Taiwanese boy who's extremely talented at Japanese, having won the American national Japanese championships all four years of high school. Recently, he went to Japan as a winner of the contest and met members of the royal family. Because he was given the chance to be more than a number, he got into top schools such as Georgetown and Princeton and Duke. He would never have gotten that opportunity if his test scores were the only ones that mattered.

To judge a student as a number is almost irresponsible. Universities are missing out on so many students who could provide them with a fresh sense of direction or even better, something more to offer than adeptness at understanding derivatives and adages under time pressure. Adopting a system that gives them the chance to see students outside the purely academic can loosen the pressure on students during the Gao Kao. That will also prevent good students from being too scared to apply to their favorite schools. Besides, everyone should recognize that there's more to life and to a student than simply scoring well on tests.

一、大学申请表格

如何着手备齐未来的大学申请材料？让我们先从一份典型的大学

申请基本表格开始,逐一解释。选用哈佛大学 2010 年的版本可能是个不错的选择,哈佛大学的要求都搞明白了,其他大学也就差不离了,这样的自我期许必须树立。

哈佛大学本科入学申请表格的基本信息部分,清晰明了,一般具有高中英文水平的学生,基本上都可以独立填写。这里仅将可能涉及的专门概念的条款稍作解释。

第一部分第三行的社会安全号码(US Social Security Number),相当于中国的身份证号码,此号有时也缩写为"SSN♯"。一般中国学生不用填写,也不用将中国的身份证号码填上,毫无意义。如果你已经在美国生活过一段时间,有社会安全号码,填上也无妨,这里主要是为申请政府助学金的学生安排的。

第二部分的最终入学决定(Decision Plane)部分,有些专用名词的含义必须区别清楚,但只有哈佛大学等竞争特别激烈的一流大学才有这样的选项,主要是为了学校和学生双方早日约定,以免各大学重复招生,浪费效率。

2006 年 9 月 12 日,哈佛大学宣布从 2008 年秋季开始,取消实行了长达 30 年之久的提前录取招生政策,随后跟进的有普林斯顿大学和弗吉尼亚大学。但不到 5 年的时间内,哈佛大学与普林斯顿大学两校又相继宣布恢复提前录取,说是从 2012 年 9 月入学的新生开始,这也就意味着实际上是从 2011 年年底开始,因为提前录取是要提前进行的。而弗吉尼亚大学则更早一些,在 2010 年就恢复了这一先前被废止的制度。

2009-10 FIRST-YEAR APPLICATION
For Spring 2010 or Fall 2010 Enrollment

APPLICANT

gal name _____
Last/Family/Sur (Enter name **exactly** as it appears on official documents.)   First/Given   Middle (complete)   Jr., etc.

eferred name, if not first name (choose only one) _____   Former last name(s), if any _____

th date _____ ○ Female ○ Male   US Social Security Number, if any _____
mm/dd/yyyy   Optional, unless applying for US Federal financial aid with the FAFSA form

mail address _____   IM address _____

rmanent home address _____
Number & Street   Apartment #

City/Town   State/Province   Country   ZIP/Postal Code
rmanent home phone (_____) _____   Cell phone (_____) _____
Area Code   Area Code

different from above, please give your current mailing address for all admission correspondence.

rrent mailing address _____
Number & Street   Apartment #

City/Town   State/Province   Country   ZIP/Postal Code
your current mailing address is a boarding school, include name of school here: _____

one at current mailing address (_____) _____   (from _____ to _____)
Area Code   (mm/dd/yyyy)   (mm/dd/yyyy)

FUTURE PLANS

ur answers to these questions will vary for different colleges. If the online system did not ask you to answer some of the questions you see in this section, this college ose not to ask that question of its applicants.

llege: _____   Deadline: _____
mm/dd/yyyy

try Term: ○ Fall (Jul-Dec)   ○ Spring (Jan-Jun)

cision Plan: ○ Regular Decision   ○ Rolling Admission
              ○ Early Decision   ○ Early Decision II
              ○ Early Action   ○ Early Action II
              ○ Restrictive Early Action ○ Early Admission
                                          juniors only

reer Interest: _____

Do you intend to apply for need-based financial aid?   ○ Yes ○ No
Do you intend to apply for merit-based scholarships?   ○ Yes ○ No
Do you intend to be a full-time student?   ○ Yes ○ No
Do you intend to enroll in a degree program your first year? ○ Yes ○ No
Do you intend to live in college housing? _____
Academic Interests: _____
_____
_____

DEMOGRAPHICS

US citizen
Dual US citizen
US permanent resident visa (Alien registration # _____)
Other citizenship (Visa type _____)
t any non-US countries of citizenship _____
_____
w many years have you lived in the United States? _____
ace of birth _____
City/Town   State/Province   Country
st language _____
mary language spoken at home _____

tional The items with a gray background are optional. No information you ovide will be used in a discriminatory manner.

rital status: _____
Armed Services veteran? ○ Yes ○ No

1. Are you Hispanic/Latino?
○ Yes, Hispanic or Latino (including Spain) ○ No
   Please describe your background _____
2. Regardless of your answer to the prior question, please select one or more of the following ethnicities that best describe you:
○ American Indian or Alaska Native (including all Original Peoples of the Americas)
   Are you Enrolled? ○ Yes ○ No If yes, please enter Tribal Enrollment Number _____
   Please describe your background _____
○ Asian (including Indian subcontinent and Philippines)
   Please describe your background _____
○ Black or African American (including Africa and Caribbean)
   Please describe your background _____
○ Native Hawaiian or Other Pacific Islander (Original Peoples)
   Please describe your background _____
○ White (including Middle Eastern)
   Please describe your background _____

图 5-1 哈佛大学本科入学申请表格 I（第一页）

　　提前录取,顾名思义,就是大学提前录取学生,使这些高中生早于通常录取考生的时间就知道自己被大学录取了。提前录取至少有两大好处:第一,高校可以在第一时间吸引优秀的学生,一般来说,越是优秀的学生,被提前录取的几率越高,同时也提前保证了高校新生的入学率;第二,站在学生的立场上,早早获知自己被心仪的大学提前录取,自然是一件令自己和家庭都会感到很美好的事情,而且在后来的学习中,也不必有太大的压力了。

　　所谓提前录取(Early Admission),总体上是对政策或制度的统称。在美国,高中生是可以同时申请多所大学的,通常需要在每年的 11 月将申请表提交给大学。一般来说,学生会在第二年的 3 月底前获知是否被录取。但在现实生活中,很多学生在当年的 12 月就知道自己是否被录取了。这就是大学实施的提前录取政策在起作用。

　　提前录取政策在实施的时候,实际上分为两种办法:一种是提前决定(Early Decision);另一种是提前行动(Early Action)。虽然两者都是学生获准被高校录取,但却有所不同。简单来说,前者有附加条件,而后者没有附加条件。具体来说,"提前决定"至少有两个附加条件:第一,在高中生按常规申请的几所大学中,只能申请一所大学的"提前决定";第二,一旦高中生被该大学录取,就必须撤回对其他大学的申请,而且要到该大学就读,否则所受到的惩罚是非常严厉的——所有的大学都不会再录取他/她。而"提前行动"与"提前决定"的申请过程大体一样,其最大的不同就是:即使你被申请的大学提前录取了,你也可以不去该大学就读。

　　值得一提的是,此次哈佛大学与普林斯顿大学宣布恢复的,全部都是"提前行动",这意味着,考生虽然提前报考了哈佛大学或者普林斯顿大学，但并不意味着录取后一定要入学，不去也不用承担什么后果。举例来说，被普林斯顿大学提前录取了，但后来自己在正常录取中又被哈佛大学录取了，那么，如果考生心仪的大学是哈佛大学，那么他/她仍然可以放弃普林斯顿大学而转投哈佛大学的门下。就此而言，学生可以在自己被录取的大学之间进行选择，比较哪所大学给予更多的奖/助学金，哪所大学更适合自己、更有利于自己的成长，从而在此基础之上作出自己的最终选择。

美国的家庭结构形式多样，所以此表出现的分类很多。但中国学生可以根据自身情况，如实填写家庭细节，美国的个人信息保密工作还是值得信任的。需要强调的是，在美国，一个好的家庭背景有助于录取人员进一步考虑你的被录取机会，这并不涉及公正问题，对于大部分优秀的大学而言，私立办学的性质给予了学校人才为上的理念和可操作性。比如说，作为一名哈佛大学的本科入学申请人，若你的祖父母、父母或哥哥、姐姐为哈佛校友，则申请人被哈佛录取的机会会大得多；如果你的伯、叔、舅、姑、姨和表兄弟、表姐妹等亲属也是美国一流大学的校友，设法将这样的信息提供给校方，不会给你带来负面的影响。这种家族成员选择同一所大学的情况，是大学欢迎的传统（Legacy）模式，录取机会大增。

填写一份完美的受教育背景资料非常重要。因为美国的大学依托强大的私立教育体制，他们主观上更愿意录用来自某些特定高中的学生，这样的招生制度并不能简单被归类于"戴了有色眼镜招生"，更不能简单搬用中国的招生理念来对号入座。大学历年积累的该高中学生在大学和毕业后的统计数据，让大学对某些高中更有好感，依据是科学的，符合人才培养的基本规律。反过来，由于一流大学在每所高中的招生名额有限，有时候反而增加了高中学生间对特定大学的竞争程度，这倒是让家长与学生们要未雨绸缪、量力而行了。但是,总体而言,在美国排名较前的高中里,毕业生升入一流大学的机会,在同等条件下,比其他高中要有优势。最起码,大学主动上门介绍自己,互相间了解交流的机会就多得多。

对于中国高中生而言,设法主动提供自己的高中信誉是明智的,特别是历史悠久的高中,提供学校几十年前或者百年老校名,肯定比用枯燥乏味的现校名有用,说不准有一位你并不了解的知名校友,至今还留在美国大学的纪念册上,那样的话,你一不小心就沾光了。比如说,现在的上海市第三女子中学的名字,肯定比不上该校的两个前身圣玛利亚女中和中西女中这两个校名如雷贯耳,那里曾经名人辈出,名扬海外。

有关统考成绩,即 ACT/SAT/AP(大学预修课程)的内容,我们在上文有关高中的章节中谈得很详细了,除了考试中心已经直接将成绩单寄往几所你首选的大学以外,如果还有较多学校申请的话,如实填写就是。值得强调的是,大学会照顾到你最好的统考成绩,但是一次获得高分,与考了几次才获得高分,在录取人员心目中的意义是不同的,所以,如何发挥最佳考试水平,一次通过,是最重要的。如果你之前没有在美国上过高中,英语能力测试托福和雅思的成绩就很关键了,不过申请美国大学,托福成绩更被看重些。

哈佛大学本科入学申请表格第四页的内容主要涉及课外能力,我们会在下文中重点介绍。值得提醒的是,由于政治体制的差别,有关同学的政治面貌、三好学生、积极分子等奖励内容,最好不要出现在表上。好在一些国际通行的学生组织活动,如模拟联合国等国际活动、国际间文化活动的获奖等其他课余活动值得罗列。总之,这部分内容的重要性不亚于考试成绩,要严肃对待。

FAMILY

...ase list both parents below, even if one or more is deceased or no longer has legal responsibilities toward you. Many colleges collect this information for demo-
...phic purposes even if you are an adult or an emancipated minor. If you are a minor with a legal guardian (an individual or government entity), then please list that
...ormation below as well. If you wish, you may list step-parents and/or other adults with whom you reside, or who otherwise care for you, in the Additional Information
...tion **online**, or on an attached sheet **if applying via mail**.

...usehold

...ents' Marital Status (relative to each other): ○ Never married ○ Married ○ Widowed ○ Separated ○ Divorced (date _____)
mm/yyyy

...h whom do you make your permanent home? ○ Parent 1 ○ Parent 2 ○ Both ○ Legal Guardian ○ Ward of the Court/State ○ Other

...rent 1: ○ Mother ○ Father ○ Unknown	**Parent 2:** ○ Mother ○ Father ○ Unknown
...Parent 1 living? ○ Yes ○ No (Date deceased _____ mm/yyyy)	Is Parent 2 living? ○ Yes ○ No (Date deceased _____ mm/yyyy)

...t/Family/Sur _____ First/Given _____ Middle _____ Title (Mr./Ms./Dr., etc.)	Last/Family/Sur _____ First/Given _____ Middle _____ Title (Mr./Ms./Dr., etc.)
...untry of birth _____	Country of birth _____
...me address **if different** from yours	Home address **if different** from yours
_____	_____
_____	_____
...me phone (_____) _____ Area Code	Home phone (_____) _____ Area Code
...mail _____	E-mail _____
...cupation _____	Occupation _____
...me of employer _____	Name of employer _____
...lege (if any) _____	College (if any) _____
...gree _____ Year _____	Degree _____ Year _____
...duate school (if any) _____	Graduate school (if any) _____
...gree _____ Year _____	Degree _____ Year _____

...gal Guardian (if other than a parent)

...ationship to you _____

...t/Family/Sur _____ First/Given _____ Middle _____ Title (Mr./Ms./Dr., etc.)

...me address **if different** from yours

_____

_____

...me phone (_____) _____ Area Code

...nail _____

...upation _____

...me of employer _____

...ege (if any) _____

...ree _____ Year _____

...duate school (if any) _____

...ree _____ Year _____

Siblings

Please give names and ages of your brothers or sisters. If they have attended or are currently attending college, give the names of the undergraduate institution, degree earned, and approximate dates of attendance. If more than three siblings, please list them in the Additional Information section **online**, or on an attached sheet **if applying via mail**.

Name	Age	Relationship
College Attended _____		
Degree Earned _____ or Expected	Dates _____ yyyy-yyyy	

Name	Age	Relationship
College Attended _____		
Degree Earned _____ or Expected	Dates _____ yyyy-yyyy	

Name	Age	Relationship
College Attended _____		
Degree Earned _____ or Expected	Dates _____ yyyy-yyyy	

图 5-2 哈佛大学本科入学申请表格 II (第二页)

ACADEMICS

Secondary Schools

Current or most recent secondary school attended _____

Entry Date _____ Graduation Date _____ School Type ○ public ○ charter ○ independent ○ religious ○ home scho|
        mm/yyyy   *mm/dd/yyyy*

Address _____ CEEB/ACT Code _____
        Number & Street

_____
        City/Town   *State/Province*   *Country*   *ZIP/Postal Code*

Counselor's name (Mr./Ms./Dr., etc.) _____ Counselor's Title _____

E-mail _____ Phone (_____) _____ Fax (_____) _____
        Area Code *Number* *Ext.*   *Area Code*   *Number*

List all other secondary schools, including summer schools as well as summer and other programs, you have attended, beginning with 9th grade.

School Name & CEEB/ACT Code	Location (City, State/Province, ZIP/Postal Code, Country)	Dates Attended (mm/yyyy
_____	_____	_____
_____	_____	_____
_____	_____	_____

If you received college counseling or assistance with your application process from a community-based organization (such as Upward Bound, Questbridge, HEOP, etc.),

please specify. _____

If your secondary school education was or will be interrupted, check all that apply and provide details in the Additional Information section or on an attached sheet.

○ did/will graduate late   ○ did/will change secondary schools   ○ did not/will not graduate

○ did/will graduate early   ○ did/will take time off   ○ did/will receive GED Date: _____ (Official scores must be sent from the testing agency.)
                                                    mm/yyyy

Colleges & Universities List all colleges/universities at which you have taken courses for credit; list names of courses taken, grades earned, and credits earned i| the Additional Information section **online**, or on an attached sheet **if applying via mail**. Please have an official transcript sent from each institution as soon as possible|

College/University Name & CEEB/ACT Code	Location (City, State/Province, ZIP/Postal Code, Country)	Degree Candidate? Yes No	Dates Attended (mm/yyyy)	Degree(s) Earned
_____	_____	○ ○	_____	_____
_____	_____	○ ○	_____	_____
_____	_____	○ ○	_____	_____

TESTS

Be sure to note the tests required for each institution to which you are applying. The official SAT, ACT, TOEFL, MELAB and/or IELTS scores from the appropriate testin| agencies should be sent as soon as possible.

ACT Tests	Date taken/ to be taken	English	Math	Reading	Science	Composite	Writing	Date taken/ to be taken	English	Math	Reading	Science	Composite	Writing

SAT Reasoning Tests	Date taken/ to be taken	Critical Reading	Math	Writing	Date taken/ to be taken	Critical Reading	Math	Writing	Date taken/ to be taken	Critical Reading	Math	Writing

SAT Subject Tests	Date taken/ to be taken	Subject	Score	Date taken/ to be taken	Subject	Score	Date taken/ to be taken	Subject	Score
	Date taken/ to be taken	Subject	Score	Date taken/ to be taken	Subject	Score	Date taken/ to be taken	Subject	Score

AP/IB Tests	Date taken/ to be taken	Subject	Score	Date taken/ to be taken	Subject	Score	Date taken/ to be taken	Subject	Score
	Date taken/ to be taken	Subject	Score	Date taken/ to be taken	Subject	Score	Date taken/ to be taken	Subject	Score
	Date taken/ to be taken	Subject	Score	Date taken/ to be taken	Subject	Score	Date taken/ to be taken	Subject	Score

TOEFL/IELTS/MELAB	Date taken/ to be taken	Test	Score	Date taken/ to be taken	Test	Score	Date taken/ to be taken	Test	Score

AP-3/2009-

图 5-3　哈佛大学本科入学申请表格Ⅲ（第三页）

onors Briefly list any academic distinctions or honors you have received since the 9th grade or international equivalent (e.g. National Merit, Cum Laude Society).

Grade level or post-graduate (PG)					Honor	Level of Recognition			
9	10	11	12	PG		School	State/ Regional	National	Inter- national
○	○	○	○	○	_____	○	○	○	○
○	○	○	○	○	_____	○	○	○	○
○	○	○	○	○	_____	○	○	○	○
○	○	○	○	○	_____	○	○	○	○
○	○	○	○	○	_____	○	○	○	○

ACTIVITIES

xtracurricular Please list your **principal** extracurricular, community, volunteer and family activities and hobbies **in the order of their interest to you**. Include pecific events and/or major accomplishments such as musical instrument played, varsity letters earned, etc. **To allow us to focus on the highlights of your ctivities, please complete this section even if you plan to attach a résumé.**

Grade level or post-graduate (PG)					Approximate time spent		When did you participate in the activity?		Positions held, honors won, or letters earned	If applicable, do you plan to participate in college?
9	10	11	12	PG	Hours per week	Weeks per year	School year	Summer		
○	○	○	○	○	____	____	○	○		○

ctivity

○	○	○	○	○	____	____	○	○	_____	○

ctivity _____

○	○	○	○	○	____	____	○	○		○

ctivity

○	○	○	○	○	____	____	○	○	_____	○

ctivity _____

○	○	○	○	○	____	____	○	○		○

ctivity

○	○	○	○	○	____	____	○	○	_____	○

ctivity _____

○	○	○	○	○	____	____	○	○		○

ctivity

Work Experience Please list **paid** jobs you have held during the past three years (including summer employment).

Specific nature of work	Employer	School year	Summer	Approximate dates (mm/yyyy - mm/yyyy)	Hours per week
_____	_____	○	○	_____	____
_____	_____	○	○	_____	____
_____	_____	○	○	_____	____
_____	_____	○	○	_____	____

图 5-4 哈佛大学本科入学申请表格 Ⅳ (第四页)

WRITING

Short Answer Please briefly elaborate on one of your extracurricular activities or work experiences in the space below or on an attached sheet (150 words or fewer).

_____

_____

_____

_____

Personal Essay Please write an essay (250 words minimum) on a topic of your choice or on one of the options listed below, and attach it to your application before submission. **Please indicate your topic by checking the appropriate box.** This personal essay helps us become acquainted with you as a person and student, apart from courses, grades, test scores, and other objective data. It will also demonstrate your ability to organize your thoughts and express yourself.

○   ❶ Evaluate a significant experience, achievement, risk you have taken, or ethical dilemma you have faced and its impact on you.

○   ❷ Discuss some issue of personal, local, national, or international concern and its importance to you.

○   ❸ Indicate a person who has had a significant influence on you, and describe that influence.

○   ❹ Describe a character in fiction, a historical figure, or a creative work (as in art, music, science, etc.) that has had an influence on you, and explain that influence.

○   ❺ A range of academic interests, personal perspectives, and life experiences adds much to the educational mix. Given your personal background, describe an experience that illustrates what you would bring to the diversity in a college community, or an encounter that demonstrated the importance of diversity to you.

○   ❻ Topic of your choice.

Disciplinary History

① Have you ever been found responsible for a disciplinary violation at any educational institution you have attended from 9th grade (or the international equivalent) forward, whether related to academic misconduct or behavioral misconduct, that resulted in your probation, suspension, removal, dismissal, or expulsion from the institution? ○ Yes ○ No

② Have you ever been convicted of a misdemeanor, felony, or other crime? ○ Yes ○ No

If you answered yes to either or both questions, please attach a separate sheet of paper that gives the approximate date of each incident, explains the circumstances, and reflects on what you learned from the experience.

Additional Information If there is any additional information you'd like to provide regarding special circumstances, additional qualifications, etc., please do so in the space below or on an attached sheet.

_____

_____

_____

_____

SIGNATURE

Application Fee Payment If this college requires an application fee, how will you be paying it?

○ Online Payment   ○ Will Mail Payment   ○ Online Fee Waiver Request   ○ Will Mail Fee Waiver Request

Required Signature

○ _I certify that all information submitted in the admission process—including the application, the personal essay, any supplements, and any other supporting materials—is my own work, factually true, and honestly presented. I authorize all schools attended to release all requested records covered under the FERPA act, and authorize review of my application for the admission program indicated on this form. I understand that I may be subject to a range of possible disciplinary actions, including admission revocation or expulsion, should the information I've certified be false._

○ _I acknowledge that I have reviewed the application instructions for each college receiving this application. I understand that all offers of admission are conditional, pending receipt of final transcripts showing work comparable in quality to that upon which the offer was based, as well as honorable dismissal from the school. I also affirm that I will send an enrollment deposit (or the equivalent) to only one institution; sending multiple deposits (or the equivalent) may result in the withdrawal of my admission offers from all institutions. [Note: students may send an enrollment deposit (or equivalent) to a second institution where they have been admitted from the waitlist, provided that they inform the first institution that they will no longer be enrolling.]_

Signature ✎ _____ Date _____

                                                mm/dd/yyyy

> _The Common Application, Inc., and its member institutions are committed to fulfilling their mission without discrimination on the basis of race, color, national origin, religion, age, sex, gender, sexual orientation, disability, or veteran status._

AP-5/2009-1

图 5-5 哈佛大学本科入学申请表格 V（第五页）

THE COMMON APPLICATION
For Undergraduate College Admission

2009-10 INTERNATIONAL SUPPLEMENT IS
For Spring 2010 or Fall 2010 Enrollment

You may leave all school contact information (bottom of page 2) blank *if* you are stapling this International Supplement to the Secondary School Report before mailing. Please type or print in black ink. Check specific college information in our Requirements Grid or online to ensure a member institution uses this form. This form should only be completed by secondary schools using non-US educational systems. **International schools using an AP curriculum exclusively need not complete this form.**

TO THE APPLICANT

○ Female
○ Male

Legal name _____
Last/Family/Sur *(Enter name **exactly** as it appears on official documents.)*   First/Given   Middle (complete)   Jr., etc.

Birth date _____ Social Security # _____ - ___ - _____
mm/dd/yyyy   *(Optional)*

Address _____
Number & Street   Apartment #   City/Town   State/Province   Country   ZIP/Postal Code

School you now attend _____ CEEB/ACT code _____

TO THE SECONDARY SCHOOL COUNSELOR

What is the primary language of instruction in your secondary school? _____

Is promotion within your educational system based upon standard examinations (for example: Abitur, GCSE/A-Level, ICSE/ISC, etc.) given at the end of lower and/or senior secondary school by a state or national examinations board? ○ Yes ○ No

If yes: Please attach an official copy of this student's lower secondary examination results. If the student has already taken senior secondary leaving exams, please include an official copy of the results. If this applicant's senior secondary leaving exam results are not yet available, please indicate predicted results on the reverse. If you have already forwarded these results with the Secondary School Report, you do NOT need to attach another copy to this form.

If no: Please attach an official transcript of this student's academic record for the final three years of secondary school, including courses taken and marks/grades in those courses. If you have already forwarded a full transcript with the Secondary School Report, you do NOT need to attach another copy to this form.

Senior secondary leaving examinations

Date of exam (month/year)	Examining board	Academic subject	Predicted result	Actual result
		Overall result		

Please indicate the marking or grading scale used in your school and its approximate equivalence to the A-F scale commonly used in the United States:

A (Excellent) _____ B (Very Good) _____ C (Average) _____ D (Poor) _____ F (Failing) _____

Counselor's name (Mr./Ms./Dr., etc.) _____
Please print or type

Signature ✎ _____ Date _____
                                                                                        mm/dd/yyyy

Title _____ School _____

School address _____
City/Town   State/Province   Country   ZIP/Postal Code

Counselor's phone (_____) _____ Counselor's fax (_____) _____
Area Code   Number   Ext.   Area Code   Number

Secondary school CEEB/ACT code _____ Counselor's e-mail _____

© 2009 The Common Application, Inc.   IS-1/**2009-10**

图 5 - 6 国际学生补充表格

申请表第五页的入学写作，是空间极大也及其重要的部分，写作内容、角度和写法，非常值得研究，我们同样会在后面的章节重点介绍。

除了上述 5 页基本表格，每位申请者还要依据自身情况，填写不同的补充材料。下面针对中国籍申请者，还是以哈佛大学为例，逐一罗列相关材料。

首先，对于中国高中生，或者高中阶段是在中国度过的学生，需要填写如下一份国际学生补充表。此表主要涉及学籍和成绩，要由校长或教务长等主要学校人员填写和签名。美国学校已经逐步了解中国式管理方法，所以盖上学校大印，也是不错的一道手续。另外，最好附上英文版的学习课程和成绩，以便录取人员自行评估整体学习内容。

其次，老师的评价是一项至关重要的内容，此表共两页，可以请了解熟悉你的班主任、校长或其他老师填写。关键是，老师要另外专门为你撰写一份个性化、有特色的推荐信，信中既能让录取人员感受到老师与学生相识的程度，也能看出老师对你的真实评价。当然，此信的英文水准也在一定程度上表现了你的学校信誉与老师评语的价值。所以，到底请哪位老师写推荐信，应该好好有所准备。在美国学生中，一般先自己将所有值得书写的履历和成绩，整理成有序的材料，找个时间详细与老师深入探讨一次，以便老师加深对你的了解，推荐信会更加有血有肉。最后必须强调的是推荐信的私密性，所以这份表格与推荐信最好直接由老师寄往学校。

下面附上推荐信一封供读者了解。①

---

① 推荐信来源：http://businessmajors. about. com/od/samplerecommendations/a/RecSample3. htm。

To Whom It May Concern：

Cheri Jackson is an extraordinary young woman. As her AP English Professor, I have seen many examples of her talent and have long been impressed by her diligence and work ethic. I understand that Cheri is applying to the undergraduate business program at your school. I would like to recommend her for admission.

Cheri has outstanding organizational skills. She is able to successfully complete multiple tasks with favorable results despite deadline pressure. As part of a semester project, she developed an innovative collaborative novel with her classmates. This book is now being considered for publication. Cheri not only headed the project, she ensured its success by demonstrating leadership abilities that her classmates both admired and respected.

I must also make note of Cheri's exceptional academic performance. Out of a class of 150 students, Cheri graduated with honors in the top 10. Her above-average performance is a direct result of her hard work and strong focus.

If your undergraduate business program is seeking superior candidates with a record of achievement, Cheri is an excellent choice. She has consistently demonstrated an ability to rise to any challenge that she must face.

To conclude, I would like to restate my strong recommendation for Cheri Jackson. If you have any further questions regarding Cheri's ability or this recommendation, please do not hesitate to contact me using the information on this letterhead.

Sincerely,

Professor William Dot

2009-10 TEACHER EVALUATION

For Spring 2010 or Fall 2010 Enrollment

TE

TO THE APPLICANT

After completing all the relevant questions below, give this form to a teacher who has taught you an **academic** subject (for example, English, foreign language, math science, or social studies). **If applying via mail**, please also give that teacher stamped envelopes addressed to each institution that requires a Teacher Evaluation.

○ Femal
○ Male

Legal name _____
Last/Family/Sur *(Enter name **exactly** as it appears on official documents.)*   First/Given   Middle (complete)   Jr., etc.

Birth date _____ Social Security # _____
mm/dd/yyyy   (Optional)

Address _____
Number & Street   Apartment #   City/Town   State/Province   Country   ZIP/Postal Code

School you now attend _____ CEEB/ACT code _____

IMPORTANT PRIVACY NOTICE: Under the terms of the Family Educational Rights and Privacy Act (FERPA), after you matriculate you *will* have access to this form and all other recommendations and supporting documents submitted by you and on your behalf after matriculating, unless at least one of the following is true:

1. The institution does not save recommendations post-matriculation *(see list at www.commonapp.org/FERPA)*.
2. You waive your right to access below, regardless of the institution to which it is sent:

○ Yes, I do waive my right to access, and I understand I will never see this form or any other recommendations submitted by me or on my behalf.
○ No, I do *not waive* my right to access, and I may someday choose to see this form or any other recommendations or supporting documents submitted by me or on my behalf to the institution at which I'm enrolling, if that institution saves them after I matriculate.

Signature ✎ _____ Date _____

TO THE TEACHER

The Common Application membership finds candid evaluations helpful in choosing from among highly qualified candidates. You are encouraged to keep this form in your private files for use should the student need additional recommendations. Please submit your references promptly, **and remember to sign below**.

Teacher's name (Mr./Ms./Dr., etc.) _____ Subject taught _____
Please print or type

Signature ✎ _____ Date _____
mm/dd/yyyy

Secondary school _____

School address _____
Number & Street   City/Town   State/Province   Country   ZIP/Postal Code

Teacher's phone (_____) _____ Teacher's e-mail _____
Area Code   Number   Ext.

Background Information

How long have you known this student and in what context? _____

What are the first words that come to your mind to describe this student? _____

List the courses you have taught this student, noting for each the student's year in school (10th, 11th, 12th; first-year, sophomore; etc.) and the level of course difficulty (AP, IB, accelerated, honors, elective; 100-level, 200-level, etc.).

_____

图 5-7　老师评价的表格 I

No basis		Below average	Average	Good (above average)	Very good (well above average)	Excellent (top 10%)	Outstanding (top 5%)	One of the top few I've encountered (top 1%)
	Academic achievement							
	Intellectual promise							
	Quality of writing							
	Creative, original thought							
	Productive class discussion							
	Respect accorded by faculty							
	Disciplined work habits							
	Maturity							
	Motivation							
	Leadership							
	Integrity							
	Reaction to setbacks							
	Concern for others							
	Self-confidence							
	Initiative, independence							
	OVERALL							

aluation Please write whatever you think is important about this student, including a description of academic and personal characteristics, as demonstrated in classroom. We welcome information that will help us to differentiate this student from others. (Feel free to attach an additional sheet or another reference you may e prepared on behalf of this student.)

图 5-8 老师评价的表格 II

2009-10 MIDYEAR REPORT

For Spring 2010 or Fall 2010 Enrollment

MR

TO THE APPLICANT

After completing all the relevant questions below, give this form to your secondary school counselor or another school official who knows you better. **If applying via mail**, please also give that school official stamped envelopes addressed to each institution that requires a Midyear Report.

○ Female
○ Male

Legal name _____
Last/Family/Sur *(Enter name **exactly** as it appears on official documents.)* First/Given   Middle (complete)   Jr., etc.

Birth date _____ Social Security # _____
mm/dd/yyyy   *(Optional)*

Address _____
Number & Street   Apartment #   City/Town   State/Province   Country   ZIP/Postal Code

School you now attend _____ CEEB/ACT code _____

Current year courses—please indicate title, level (AP, IB, advanced honors, etc.) and credit value of all courses you are taking this year. Indicate quarter classes taken in the same semester on the appropriate semester line.

First Semester/Trimester	Second Semester/Trimester	Third Trimester
		or additional first/second term courses if more space is needed
_____	_____	_____
_____	_____	_____
_____	_____	_____
_____	_____	_____
_____	_____	_____
_____	_____	_____
_____	_____	_____

IMPORTANT PRIVACY NOTICE: Under the terms of the Family Educational Rights and Privacy Act (FERPA), after you matriculate you *will* have access to this form and all other recommendations and supporting documents submitted by you and on your behalf after matriculating, unless at least one of the following is true:

1. The institution does not save recommendations post-matriculation *(see list at www.commonapp.org/FERPA).*
2. You waive your right to access below, regardless of the institution to which it is sent:

○ Yes, I do waive my right to access, and I understand I will never see this form or any other recommendations submitted by me or on my behalf.
○ No, I do *not* waive my right to access, and I may someday choose to see this form or any other recommendations or supporting documents submitted by me or on my behalf to the institution at which I'm enrolling, if that institution saves them after I matriculate.

Signature ✎ _____ Date _____

TO THE SECONDARY SCHOOL COUNSELOR

Please submit this form when midyear grades are available (end of first semester or second trimester). Attach applicant's official transcript, including courses in progress, a school profile, and transcript legend. (Please check transcript copies for readability.) Use both pages to complete your evaluation for this student. **Be sure to sign below.**

Counselor's name (Mr./Ms./Dr., etc.) _____
Please print or type

Signature ✎ _____ Date _____
mm/dd/yyyy

Title _____ School _____

School address _____
City/Town   State/Province   Country   ZIP/Postal Code

Counselor's phone (_____) _____ Counselor's fax (_____) _____
Area Code   Number   Ext.   Area Code   Number

Secondary school CEEB/ACT code _____ Counselor's e-mail _____

MR-1/2009-10

图 5－9　大学预修课程(AP 课程，Advanced Placement)登记表 I

ackground Information If any of the information on this page has changed for this student since the Secondary School Report was submitted, please enter the ew information in the appropriate section below. If your recommendation for this student has changed, please comment in the space below or on a separate sheet. nothing has changed, you may leave this page blank. *However, your signature is still required.*

ass rank: _____ Class size: _____ Covering a period from _____ to _____ .
(mm/yyyy) *(mm/yyyy)*

he rank is ○ weighted ○ unweighted. How many students share this rank? _____

○ We do not rank. Instead, please indicate quartile _____ quintile _____ decile _____

umulative GPA: _____ on a _____ scale, covering a period from _____ to _____
(mm/yyyy) *(mm/yyyy)*

his GPA is ○ weighted ○ unweighted. The school's passing mark is _____ .

ghest GPA in class _____ Graduation date _____
(mm/dd/yyyy)

ercentage of graduating class immediately attending: _____ four-year _____ two-year institutions

Are classes taken on a block schedule? ○ Yes ○ No
Is the applicant an IB Diploma candidate? ○ Yes ○ No
If you offer AP courses, do you limit the number a student can take? ○ Yes ○ No
How many AP courses does your school offer (in total)? _____
In comparison with other college preparatory students at your school, the applicant's course selection is:
○ most demanding
○ very demanding
○ demanding
○ average
○ below average

ow long have you known this student and in what context? _

hat are the first words that come to your mind to describe this student?

atings Compared to other students in his or her class year, how do you rate this student in terms of:

No basis		Below average	Average	Good (above average)	Very good (well above average)	Excellent (top 10%)	Outstanding (top 5%)	One of the top few I've encountered (top 1%)
	Academic achievement							
	Extracurricular accomplishments							
	Personal qualities and character							
	OVERALL							

valuation Please write whatever you think is important about this student, including a description of academic, extracurricular, and personal characteristics. We elcome a broad-based assessment that will help us to differentiate this student from others. (Feel free to attach an additional sheet or another reference you may have epared on behalf of this student.)

○ Has the applicant ever been found responsible for a disciplinary violation at your school from 9th grade (or the international equivalent) forward, whether related to academic misconduct or behavioral misconduct, that resulted in the applicant's probation, suspension, removal, dismissal, or expulsion from your institution? ○ Yes ○ No

○ To your knowledge, has the applicant ever been convicted of a misdemeanor, felony, or other crime? ○ Yes ○ No

you answered yes to either or both questions, please attach a separate sheet of paper or use your written recommendation to give the approximate date of each cident and explain the circumstances.

○ **Check here if you would prefer to discuss this applicant over the phone with each admission office.**

I recommend this student: ○ No basis ○ With reservation ○ Fairly strongly ○ Strongly ○ Enthusiastically

图 5 – 10 大学预修课程(AP 课程,Advanced Placement)登记表Ⅱ

2009-10 ARTS SUPPLEMENT
For Spring 2010 or Fall 2010 Enrollment

AR

Check specific college information in our Requirements Grid or online to ensure a member institution uses this form.

TO THE APPLICANT

○ Female
○ Male

Legal name _____
Last/Family/Sur (Enter name **exactly** as it appears on official documents.)   First/Given   Middle (complete)   Jr., etc.

Birth date _____   Social Security # _____ - ____ - _____
mm/dd/yyyy   (Optional)

Address _____
Number & Street   Apartment #   City/Town   State/Province   Country   ZIP/Postal Code

E-mail address _____   Phone (_____) _____
Area Code

School you now attend _____   CEEB/ACT code _____

ARTS MEDIUM

Please indicate your area of interest and provide supplementary materials, as required.

○ **Music**   Instrument _____   Voice (part) _____   Composition _____

World Music Tradition _____   Song Writing _____   Other _____

○ **Theater**

○ **Dance**

○ **Visual Arts and Film**

INSTRUCTIONS

If you've made a substantial commitment of time and energy to one or more of the arts and you wish to have that considered as part of your application, please:

❶ Complete this form.

❷ Have an instructor who is familiar with your work send us a letter of recommendation.

❸ Enclose a 10-minute CD or DVD with this form that demonstrates contrasting examples of expression and technique. Please do not submit videotapes.
List the contents of the CD or DVD here:

Music

❹ Attach a résumé to this form that summarizes your experience with instrument(s), voice, and/or composition, giving years studied, name(s) of teacher(s) or group(s), repertoire, and awards/honors received.

Theater and Dance

❹ Attach a résumé to this form that summarizes your experience, giving years studied, name(s) of teacher(s) or group(s), repertoire, special programs, and awards/honors received.

Visual Arts and Film

❹ Attach a résumé to this form that summarizes your experience, giving dates, institutions or programs, and awards/honors received. Include a brief description of each course or workshop attended, and describe any related experiences.

No materials will be reviewed until all components of your portfolio arrive. Please send copies only; many schools do not return supplementary materials.

Signature ✎ _____   Date _____
mm/dd/yyyy

AR-1/**2009-10**

图 5-11 才艺补充登记表

　　由于美国的大学从学生十一年级，就是相当于中国的高二和高三上半学期，就已经开始接受申请，甚至发出录取信，所以，下面这份大学预修课程成绩表格非常重要，是你高中最后阶段的学习成绩和学校评语。特别是那些已经被学校提前录取的同学，千万不能放松高中最后阶段的自我要求，一旦大学发现你的以往申请材料与此不符，随时可以取消你的录取资格。

　　而对于尚在等待大学录取信的同学，这份表格又是你的最后机会。由于录取信迟迟未到，拒绝信也从来没有收到过，表明你的申请材料还在候选人名单中，如果你在高中最后阶段，大学预修课程选修很多，而且成绩优秀，表明了你是一位既有追求，又有能力的学生，这份最后的表格，将是你脱颖而出、绝地反攻的唯一机会了。

　　准备好了上述材料，现在，就轮到展示你课外才艺的时候了。美国的大学非常看中这个部分，由于才艺是无法临时抱佛脚获得的，所以，可以看出一个人的耐心和坚持的特点；才艺的培养需要家庭的长期投入和配合，可以反映出一个人的成长背景和家教的传统；最后，才艺人才的集中也有利整个大学的社交品味和学生管理。值得提出的是，千万不要把一位学生的才艺展示，理解为必须达到报考艺术类别或专业类别的程度，才可以呈报录取办公室。学校不会要求一位数学系的申请人，提供一流的小说或者诗歌作品，但是如果该申请者连年参加学校或者学区的作文竞赛，而且可以提名入围，即使最后没有获得金、银、铜牌，这样的成绩就已经表明你是一位不"偏食"的数学尖子，而且富于生活情趣。

　　近年来，中国家庭的富裕程度和重视教育的历史传统，让他们喊出了"不要让孩子输在起跑线上"这样的"雷人"口号。而另一方面，家长为孩子十来年的各项才艺投资,又没有渠道好好总结发表,最后到了需要整体包装申请人的阶段,要不发现原始材料无法复原,悔不当初;要不弄虚作假,最后自食苦果。所以,未雨绸缪一向是家庭教育的重要一环,是做负责任父母的主要内容。孩子从小学到中学的作品、奖状、履历和报道评语,都应该悉心收集保存。对于中国家庭来说,唯一遗憾的是,因为你希望申请的是英语为主要语种的大学,缺乏原始的英文材料才艺证据。但这也是家长尽量需要争取的空间,这里附上有关的华裔孩子才艺展示平台——《中美青少年学术前沿学报》,这是一本由美国国会图书馆登记收藏的杂志,专门刊登全球青少年在科技、艺术、文学等各领域的才艺,并愿意向大学出示有关作者的推荐证明。

以上介绍的还不是申请哈佛大学的全部表格与材料,当然,更不是涉及全美各种大学的五花八门的表格材料。对这些表格熟悉及有所了解,是为了当你收到全套大学申请表或者在线填写表格的时候有所借鉴。一切顺利的话,接下来你会在收到录取信的同时,要求填写两份专门针对外籍学生的表格,也就是在赴美留学高中或者大学、研究生都要填写的大名鼎鼎的 I-20 表格以及与学生签证有关的表格。这些将来提交给大学国际事务办公室和签证官员的材料,无非表明学生就学的学费已经落实,或者来自奖学金、助学金,大部分的情况下,留学费用来自自费筹款。过去 30 年,全球政治经济格局发生了很大变化,特别是中国的国民收入整体向上增加、人民币汇率不断上升等一系列变化,使得近年来美国政府对于中国学生的留学签证 F1 政策大大地放宽了,有关内容可以查阅本书的其他章节。

二、委托专业机构咨询大学申请细节

俗话说,好钢使在刀刃上。申请表格自己能够完美准备固然很好。

但是由于美国的大学种类繁多，专业繁多，学生情况各异，一次大学申请阶段起码要做 5～10 套有针对性的优质材料，这并非是每个学生与家庭都可以轻松应付的工程。因此，即使是美国家庭，正式申请大学之前，也要大量投入，参加不同的专业讲解会，参观大学设施，与前辈家长、学生、校友联谊交流，甚至聘用专门人员或机构，定制个性化的申请材料。通过上一节内容的介绍，我们可以发现，常规信息、平时成绩和统考成绩，这些部分的标准化程度相对比较大，除了历年积累、复习准备、及时考试以外，学生本人以外的家长和专业人士，很难对其进一步帮助。但这些材料的权重，仅占全部内容的 1/3，所以，千万不要忽视了入学写作、个人介绍和面试准备等环节，这些内容既反映了学生整体的能力，也可以结合家人、朋友和专业人员的意见建议。

三、写作短文

自我简介在申请表中的重要性很突出，常以写作几十到几百字短文的形式，要求申请人完成。我被要求替国内高中生审读过不少此类的短文，他们基本的不足之处是一致的，就是与普世价值观念的隔阂和对个性的忽视。也难怪这些孩子们，他们从小被要求写作的内容就是歌颂，通过描述自己遥远的目标来阐述宏大理想，空话谎话成了文章中的基本元素。所以，即使你立志赴美留学，在出国咨询机构的关心辅导下，要求全面真实地反映一个真实的自我时，遣词造句之间，还是难以摆脱十几年来教化的痕迹。不过此时急不得，只有靠在日常生活中回归一个独立真实的自我，才能逐渐得以解决，也就是成为世界名校真正期待的标准学生。否则，你无非就是口耳相传的学生申请材料不实的又一桩证明。此处附上美国一流大学申请材料中的写得相对成功的一

Dad left. My Mom and I were alone in an empty echoing house. My world was unraveling. I missed him.

We used to write together. I would read my essays in a high, piping voice as he made suggestions, smiling in encouragement. But once he left, I was on my own. He never got to see me win my first Scholastic Art and Writing Award in 2002. He could only congratulate me through the static of the Pacific Ocean.

I slowly grew used to a Dad who was rarely home. His departure drove me to help my Mom as much as I could, changing me from a carefree child into a responsible teenager.

In 2003, I began mentoring at Star Learning Center. I taught Brian Aponte, a half Peruvian, half Puerto-Rican eighth grader who despised McDonald's but loved everything else about America. He fought against getting shipped off to a private school in Peru; the consequence if he were unable to test out of his graffiti encrusted high school in New York City.

We had only four white walls and a flashing computer screen to keep us company as we slogged through $ hours of work. Week after week, we tried to conquer algebra, defeat reading passages and pass the citywide English test.

My main focus was his writing. He was charismatic in real life, but could never harness that quality when he set pen to paper. I watched as he struggled to turn ideas into written language, wrinkling his forehead and frowning his green—tinted hazel eyes. I worked with him as my Dad had worked with me.

In the last three weeks of the school year, Brian was rushing to finish a paper on bears in the Bronx Zoo. As he haltingly read his essay aloud, I realized what a change had occurred. He had surpassed my expectations by imbuing a dry topic with flair. We had succeeded.

The last day, Brian came peeling upstairs to tell me he had been accepted into a challenging high school. He carried a box of Entenmann's cookies under one arm and a Hallmark card in another. In painstaking print, he had written, "Thank you Joan for being a big helper... These things explain how great of a tutor you are and a friend."

The card sits on my dresser table, its edges curled from age, the words never faded. I like to imagine that Brian remembers my help in the same way as I remember my Dad's patient understanding. Mentoring began after I had conquered the pain of my Dad's frequent absence, as a way to help others triumph over their obstacles. Seeing Brian overcome his frustration with writing inspired me to continue tutoring. In more wistful moments, I wish my Dad never had to leave. But without that, I would never have helped Brian.

四、面试

对于大部分中国高中生而言，面试是生活中很少遇见的事件，但在现在，它出现了。代表大学面试申请人的，一般不会是专程从大学赶来的录取人员，而是分布在各地的大学校友组成的义务面试官，这是一项与中国大学截然不同的管理和社交机制，大学通过加强与以往校友的密切联系，上至百岁老人，下到刚走出校园的毕业生，这张巨大的社会网络，不仅为母校形成了巨大的向心力，也为学校贡献了无数的人力和财力。

面试可能就在申请人居住城市的某个咖啡馆、公园、办公室或教室里，但是对于申请人而言，事先的严肃准备，包括从服装到语调、妆容，首先都是体现了你对他人的尊重。对于海外学生，电话面试往往是唯一的选择，因此，训练你的听说能力，肯定是证明自己语言能力的最好机会。面试的时间从十几分钟到几十分钟不等，话题海阔天空，唯一可以把握的原则，就是展示一个真实、机灵和礼貌的形象，讨论的意义大于答题的形式，答案无关结局，一切尽在面试双方的互动中展露无遗。

从实际出发，选择一个有回报的专业

大学专业的选择是个综合性的问题，有个人成绩的因素，有个人兴趣的因素，有理想主义的因素，但是我们还是坚持要从现实出发。特别是一个中国普通家庭，以举家之力，将后代送到异国他乡，青年学子首先要有实现父母愿望的心理准备。从这个角度出发，可以有两种选择标准：第一，未来择业的地理标准；第二，未来择业的工资标准。其他人生理想，有待立稳脚跟，富裕起来再议不迟。

所谓择业的地理标准，比较简单，即将美国分成东、南、西、北、中五大块，五块各有其气候与经济特征，与中国的距离远近也有所不同，所以学生家庭可以依据学生是否适合寒、热、干、远等地理特点来选择学校和专业，这是一种以地理特征为主要考量的择学择业方法。

择业的工资标准完全是一种机会主义的经济学原则，即按未来3～5年热门行业为目标，选择最不会将教育投资血本无归的行业方向来选择专业。但是这种择业原则的风险在于，技术的进步可能在10年间将一门最热门的行业堕落为最无生机的行业。人在社会中，也只能边走边学边看，积极地表述为与时俱进而已。目前看来，在国内完成普通大学教育，作为一种经济上的投资完全是失败的，仅以北京与上海两大城市为例。

从北京市人力资源和社会保障局公布的 2010 年北京市劳动力市

189

场工资指导价位可以了解到,工资按"低位数、中位数、高位数"分区。应届大学生起薪低位数多在最低工资标准至 1 500 元之间徘徊,中位数多在 2 000 元上下浮动,高位数能突破 3 000 元大关的在半数以下。平均中位数为 1 937 元,而高位数可达 5 763 元。以月平均工资 1 937 元计算,应届毕业生的平均年薪为 23 244 元。上海市的工资水平和北京市的差不多。上海市人力资源和社会保障局公布的《2009 年毕业生工资指导价位》显示,2009 年毕业生最集中的三个工资段分别为 2 001～2 500 元(占 23.3%)、1 501～2 000 元(占 17.5%)和 2 501～3 000 元(占 14.8%),三者合计占总数的 55.6%。初步估计一位高中生为了考上大学的补习费用和大学期间的学费、生活费,基本无法在毕业后的短期内收回成本,达到收支平衡,更妄谈生活品质。

在美国,2010 年本科刚毕业进入职场的毕业生,平均年薪所得为 47 673 美元,比 2009 年毕业者当时的平均年收入 48 515 美元同比低了 1.7%。毕业生的起薪直接和专业挂钩,以下是一些行业的中等平均起薪年收入概况。

Engineering(工程):53 400 美元

Construction, Trades and Labor(建筑、专业工匠):51 100 美元

Energy, Oil and Gas(能源、石油、天然气):50 900 美元

Information Technology and Telecommunications(信息技术和电子通信):46 000 美元

Biotechnology and Pharmaceuticals(生物技术和药剂学):43 900 美元

Manufacturing(制造业)：42 700 美元

Insurance(保险业)：40 800 美元

Government，Military and Civil Service(政府、军职、公务员)：
40 300 美元

Business and Finance(商业和金融业)：40 200 美元

Warehouse and Logistics(仓储和物流)：39 600 美元

下文的数据主要依据美国劳工部的统计资料，①其中，2011 年 6 月在北美发行的《明报》教育专刊，较完整地总结了近年来的大学专业与收入概况，可以提供大家参考。

未来 10 年最吃香的学位

有分析师预计，未来 10 年最吃香的学位，直接与工资回报挂钩，大学生获得的学位决定第一份工作的起薪点，这也成为要读一个合适的学位的主要原因。

从 2011 到 2020 年的 10 年中，就业市场最需要的是什么样的学位呢？从美国联邦劳工部劳工数据署的 2010—2011 年度《就业前景展望》手册中的大量资料中可找到如下答案。

———————————

① 美国平均工资统计资料可从劳工部的公开信息中获得。http://www.bls.gov/bls/blswage.htm。

表 5-4　美国未来 10 年中最吃香的学位

热门学位	相关行业	平均年收入	简要分析
健保学位	医疗助理	28 300 美元	爱也好,恨也罢,一个无可争议的事实是,美国健保改革将带来更多新的就业机会,健保业已然成为美国经济成长最迅速的行业。 　　在医院控制成本的前提下,必将减少医生人数,因此大多数的白大褂将由助理医生穿上。而受到人口老龄化的影响,促使健保需求愈发强烈,健保学位从未如此吃香过。 　　根据美国白宫和联邦劳工部预测,健保业成长速度将是其他行业的几乎两倍,在美国成长最快的五个工作中,有三个将来自健保业。
	医疗记录及保健资料管理员	30 610 美元	
	注册护士	62 450 美元	
商科学位	会计师	59 430 美元	技术创新与科技进步正在不断改变人们的生活方式以及企业的经营方式。在商业世界中,唯一不变的就是改变。今天的商学院学生将是决定未来商业模式的关键。 　　瞻望商业前景,其中最吃香的学科包括管理、科学及技术顾问服务等。根据联邦劳工部预测,在商业领域,就业机会的增长幅度将达到惊人的 83%。
	管理分析师	73 570 美元	
	财务经理	99 330 美元	
教育学位	公立学校教师	47 100~51 180 美元	联邦劳工部称,教育服务是美国的第二大产业。事实上,这个行业在 2008 年共有 1 350 万名雇员,且社会对该行业的需求还将不断增强。 　　由于人口的快速增加和基础教育的普及,未来将会有更多孩子进入学校学习,这对于教育工作者而言意味着更多的就业机会。乔治城大学教育和就业中心 2010 年发表的一份报告预测,及至 2018 年,在最缺乏拥有学位和资格雇员的行业排行榜中,教育位居第二,仅排在健保业之后。
	教务主任	88 280 美元	
	高中校长	97 486 美元	

续　表

热门学位	相关行业	平均年收入	简要分析
技术学位	网络管理员	66 310 美元	拥有诸如网络管理等技术相关学位的人，将会因为他们能够掌握尖端技术而受惠，在整个经济的各个领域畅通无阻。从高科技重镇如硅谷和西雅图，到转型中心地区如得克萨斯州和北卡罗来纳州，以至全国，各个公司都在寻找优秀的科技人才来开发新的技术产品和管理电脑与网络。
	电脑科研人员	97 970 美元	
	资讯系统经理	112 210 美元	乔治城大学的报告称，在未来 8 年，光是电脑方面的专家就会有 70 万个工作职闲。据联邦劳工部预测，到 2018 年，电脑系统设计和相关服务的从业员人数比现在增长 45%。

　　注：以上所有平均收入的数额均为美国联邦劳工部发表的 2008 年中间工资。

工作最有保障的 6 个学位

　　根据美国联邦劳工部、Pay Scale 网站以及研究生管理委员会 2010 年调查的 MBA 毕业生起薪资料等数据，可以发现某些学位确实有较大的优势。

　　以下是长远来说最具工作保障和增长潜力的 6 个职业。

表 5-5　美国最具工作保障和增长潜力的 6 个学位及其相关职业

排行榜	学位	相关行业	平均年收入	简要分析
第 1 位	商科（起薪：41 100美元，职业中期薪酬：70 600 美元）	公关专家	51 280 美元	商科始终被认为是一个稳妥的学位，它能为你的就业道路打下坚实的基础，无论经济好坏都能有所保障。
		市场研究分析员	61 070 美元	尽管仍需一段时日经济才会全面复苏，但根据美国联邦存款保险公司（FDIC）的资料显示，从 2010 年 7 月至 9 月的商业贷款已有所增加，企业对资金的更多需求显示将会有更多职位空缺。根据人力资源顾问公司 APD 发表的全
		管理分析师	73 570 美元	

续 表

排行榜	学位	相关行业	平均年收入	简要分析
		管理分析师	73 570 美元	国就业报告称,在 2010 年员工少于 500 人的企业增加了 39 万个就业机会。
第 2 位	法务助理(起薪:38 400 美元,职业中期薪酬:55 000 美元)	法务助理	46 120 美元	法律行业是美国历史最悠久、最有保障的专业之一。而获得法务助理学位是投身法律行业的最佳方法。 根据美国劳工部资料显示,直到 2018 年,法律行业的就业机会增长达到 28%。因此,法务助理学位亦需求殷切。只在短短 18 个月之内,你就能取得法务助理副学士学位,投身于这个行业。当然,如果你已经有一个学士学位,你更可以在短短的半年内完成法务助理证书课程。
		保险业法务助理	52 200 美元	
		联邦行政部门法务助理	58 540 美元	
第 3 位	医疗保健管理(起薪:35 600 美元,职业中期薪酬:58 000 美元)	医院秘书	14.21 美元(时薪)	如果你想投身于既稳定又有就业保障的行业,那么可以考虑医疗保健专业。 根据劳工部资料显示,在 20 个增长最快的职业中,医疗保健业占去了其中的 10 个席位。《美国新闻与世界报道》的 2011 年最佳职业名单中,医疗保健工作仍然独领风骚。由于人口老龄化趋势的加剧,医疗保健的长远前景依然强劲,职业也更具就业保障。
		保险承报人	56 790 美元	
		医疗服务经理	80 240 美元	
第 4 位	刑事司法(起薪:35 600 美元,职业中期薪酬:58 000 美元)	警察	51 410 美元	无论经济气候好坏,美国的刑事司法系统良好的就业前景仍然是毋庸置疑的事实。 修读刑事司法应该是个万无一失的选择。根据劳工部资料显示,直至 2018 年,警务人员的就业机会将增加 10%,而那些“由于削减预算而失去工作的人,通常不难在其他领域找到工作”。此外,根据劳工部资料显示,直至 2018 年
		联邦惩教人员	53 459 美元	
		探员主管	75 490 美元	

续　表

排行榜	学位	相关行业	平均年收入	简要分析
		探员主管	75 490	感化官及惩教治疗专家的就业机会将有 19％的增长。
第 5 位	工商管理硕士（起薪：78 820美元，职业中期薪酬：97 091美元）	总经理	91 570 美元	在日益复杂的商业世界里，修读 MBA 学位是获得成功的合理策略之一。 接受更多的教育便等于拥有更多的就业机会。获得 MBA 学位可以帮助你升入管理层和获取更丰厚的薪水。2010 年 12 月《商业周刊》中一篇关于 MBA 价值的文章毫不讳言称之为"几乎令你立即富有的保证"。
		财务经理	99 330 美元	
		软件经理	126 840 美元	
第 6 位	信息系统（起薪：49 300美元，职业中期薪酬：87 100美元）	电脑系统管理员	66 310 美元	私人企业越来越依赖于利用信息系统来收集数据，展开内部和外部沟通。据 2010 年 11 月《温哥华太阳报》报道："除医疗科学之外，最大的就业机会将会是电脑和信息系统的专业人才的天下。"劳工部也有同样的乐观预测，相信至 2018 年信息系统管理人员的就业机会将有 17％的大幅上升。
		网络系统分析师	71 100 美元	
		信息系统经理	112 210 美元	

回报最高的学位

各项研究使用不同标准，包括薪资、工作满意度、福利、长远发展的机会等，确定 35 个最有回报的学位及其相关职业。

表 5-6　美国最有回报的 5 个学位及其相关职业

排行榜	学位	相关行业	平均年收入	简要分析
第 1 位	医疗保健管理硕士学位（平均年薪：60 800美元）	医疗卫生服务经理	80 240 美元	医疗保健管理硕士学位能成为最高回报学位，原因包括该行业所带来的工作满足感、高工资和优厚的福利待遇。但是，该行业远超其他行业的就业保障才是使其脱颖而出的最主要因素。

续　表

排行榜	学位	相关行业	平均年收入	简要分析
第1位	医疗保健管理硕士学位（平均年薪：60 800美元）	医疗卫生服务经理	80 240美元	2010年由企业雇问公司Challenger，Gray & Christmas对人力资源专业人士所作的一项调查显示，医疗保健管理硕士学位在最有可能让你获得录用的名单上也高居榜首。而许多拥有高技术的医疗保健行政人员，在该行业迅速发展之际成为吃香一族，帮助管理层确保业务运作畅顺。
第2位	国际商业学士学位（平均年薪：73 700美元）	营运分析师	69 000美元	在现今的全球经济环境下，没有一个学位比国际商业更切合需求。据2010年Pay Scale的一项报告，国际商业击败了一直以来最受欢迎的商科和医疗保健学位，成为最令人有满足感的大学专业。就业保障是该专业另一个吸引之处，随着跨国企业的业务关系日渐复杂，国际商业毕业生比其他人有更大的发展机会。根据爱荷华大学教育政策与领导学系的一项研究，当大学毕业生被问及他们对自己的薪水的满意程序时，商业学位持有者傲视群雄，该研究历经25年完成，对30个公营和私营机构的大学专业和工作满意度间的关连进行分析。
		管理分析师	73 570美元	
		工业生产经理	83 290美元	
第3位	会计学（平均年薪：77 500美元）	核数师	59 430美元	在大学学习会计能助你投身于会计或财务事业，这两个专业增长迅速，有良好晋升机会和优厚的薪酬。有多项研究得出的结论显示，如果你的大学学位和未来工作相关，对你在毕业后的工作满意度有很大的影响。一般来说，人们都喜欢做他们擅长的工作。如果你有数学头脑，攻读会计学位可以让你获得个人和专业的满足感。
		金融分析师	73 150美元	
		财务经理	99 330美元	

排行榜	学位	相关行业	平均年收入	简要分析
		财务经理	99 330 美元	在 Pay Scale 的 2010 年大学专业满意度调查中，会计学位仅次于化学工程和管理资讯系统学位。
第 4 位	信息系统学位（平均年薪：87 100 美元）	电脑系统管理员	66 310 美元	通称 IT 的信息科技业很庞大，但简称为 IS 的信息系统则更庞大。信息系统可以帮助企业消除业务和电脑世界之间的隔阂，一些当今最成功的公司便是建立在这个基础上。 如果你热爱互联网和电脑，信息系统可能是最合你心意的一个专业。美国劳工部预测，直至 2018 年，信息系统员工和管理人员的就业前景令人鼓舞，因为新科技推动下该行业急需新雇员。
		网络系统分析师	71 100 美元	
		资讯系统经理	112 210 美元	
第 5 位	教育学位（平均年薪：54 900 美元）	初中职业教育	47 870 美元	和其他高回报学位不同，教育学位并非因为高薪而上榜，而是工作满足感和工作带来的快乐。 根据大都会人寿保险 2009 年的一项研究，现在的教师比过去 25 年任何时候更满意自己的职业，衡量指标包括薪资、获得社会的承认和尊重等。芝加哥大学 2007 年一项研究发现，最有成就感的工作皆与服务他人有关，教育行政人员和教师在有关排行榜上均名列前茅。
		中学特殊教育教师	51 340 美元	
		小学校长	85 907 美元	

较易获聘任的几个学位

根据全国大学与雇主协会（NACE）资料，大学选修的专业是决定毕业后就业情况的最大因素。总结来自联邦劳工部的薪酬数据和其他相关调查，以下 5 种学位有可能让你在毕业后被聘用的胜算更高。

表 5-7 美国较易获聘任的 5 个学位及其相关职业

排行榜	学位	相关行业	平均年收入	简要分析
第 1 位	会计学士学位	会计师	59 430 美元	由国会通过的新的会计法规使这个稳当的学位变得更有价值。根据 NACE 在 2010 年的调查,47%攻读会计专业者在毕业前便获得聘用机会。 根据 Universum 集团 2010 年一项调查,商学院学生心目中的理想雇主名单中,四大会计师事务所毕马威(KPMG)、安永(Ernst & Young)、普华永道(Pricewaterhouse Coopers)以及德勤(Deloitte)仅次于网络巨擘谷歌,但却领先于如苹果电脑、微软、高盛公司之上。
		个人理财顾问	69 050 美元	
		金融分析师	73 150 美元	
第 2 位	商业学士学位	保险承保人	56 790 美元	在经济困难时期企业必须找到出路,他们将需要新的员工去担当这项职责。NACE 指出,超过45%的修读商业专业的学生,在毕业前便找到工作。 据联邦教育部统计,在 2008 年颁授的所有本科学位中,商业学位占了高达 21%。
		行政服务经理	73 520 美元	
		财务经理	99 330 美元	
第 3 位	电脑/信息系统学位	电脑支援专家	43 450 美元	根据 NACE,在 2010 年获得电脑及资讯系统专业者,其中超过44%的学生毕业以前便找到至少一个工作机会。 大公司如 Facebook 和苹果电脑已经扩大了在硅谷的招聘工作,这是在这个信息科技 IT 产业的原产地,自 2010 年 9 月近两年来第一次看到就业机会增加。
		网络系统分析师	71 100 美元	
		电脑科学家	97 970 美元	
第 4 位	工程学士学位	土木工程师	74 600 美元	工程科学生不仅在毕业前便轻而易举地找到工作,他们的报酬亦十分丰厚,由 NACE 进行的一个独立调查显示,10 大收入最高的专业中工程占去了 8 席。
		化学工程师	84 680 美元	
		石油工程师	108 020 美元	

续　表

排行榜	学位	相关行业	平均年收入	简要分析
第 5 位	医科学士学位	医疗助理	28 300 美元	医疗保健业前景一片光明。根据 NACE 统计，近 39% 的医疗科学专业学生在 2010 年毕业前便获得了工作机会。美国劳工部估计，至 2018 年之前，医疗保健将创造超过 300 万个新的就业机会。 　　许多医疗保健职业，例如保健医疗技术员和医疗助理，只需有一个副学士学位便有资格申请。
		医疗资讯技术员	30 610 美元	
		注册护士	62 450 美元	

副学士大专学位工作也有好前途

　　听起来难以置信？这是千真万确的事，以下就是 6 个只需两年制副学士学位即可胜任的优差。

表 5-8　美国 6 个只需两年制副学士学位即可胜任的职业

职业	所需学位	简要说明	平均薪酬
人力资源助理	工商管理两年制副学士学位	几乎每一个组织，从私人企业到教育机构以至政府部门，皆需要人力资源工作人员处理人事问题。如果你认为这项工作适合你，攻读工商管理学两年制副学士学位将对你加入这个行业有帮助。从担任人力资源助理开始，你的职责为协助雇主保持员工记录，包括员工福利记录。	根据劳工部资料为 36 810 美元。持有两年制学位，加上你的技能和一些工作经验，可能获升迁人力资源专家的职位，平均年薪为 86 500。
医务助理	医务助理两年制副学士学位	美国劳工部预计，至 2018 年前，医务助理的就业增长将会大大高于平均水平。想投身这个发展蓬勃的职业，你需要具有医务助理两年制学士学位。作为医务助理，你将要负责办公室管理和临床工作，包括更新医疗记录和记录病人生理数据。	根据劳工部资料为 28 300 美元，收入最高者每年平均薪酬超过 39 570 美元。医务助理薪金会基于经验、技术水平和地点而有所不同。

续 表

职业	所需学位	简要说明	平均薪酬
公司法务助理	法务助理两年制副学士学位	想要踏进法律界,但所花时间比起攻读法学博士短得多;修读两年制法务助理副学士学位可以帮你做到这点。美国劳工部预计从 2008 年至 2018 年间,法务助理职位将增长 28%,尤其是在私人企业方面,预计将雇用更多的法务助理帮助处理法律事务。	根据 PayScale.com 网站资料,工资范围是 46 086～70 260 美元。
网页设计师	网页设计师	如果你热爱网页设计,修读平面设计副学士学位,可能是助你发挥创意的第一步。作为一个网页设计师,你将会设计网站来迎合你的目标顾客,为客户有效传达信息。由于现时几乎每个人都使用网络,未来 10 年的就业机会应该相当乐观。	根据 PayScale.com 网站资料,工资范围是 30 878～50 918 美元。
簿记文员	会计两年制副学士学位	劳工部预计从现时至 2018 年将会有超过 21 万份新增会计职业。修读为期两年的会计副学士学位将会是投身会计行业的第一步。有了这个学位,你有望成为簿记文员,工作责任包括维持会计记录,处理应付账款,以及维持整个公司的账目。	根据劳工部资料为 32 510 美元,收入最高者平均超过 49 260 美元。请记住,大多数企业通过内部升迁来填补监督和管理职位,所以一旦你已经累积经验,便可能有资格晋升为一名会计师或核数师,届时平均年薪为 59 430 美元。
急诊室或创伤科护士	护理两年制副学士学位	急诊和创伤科护士是注册护士(RN)专职照顾有生命危险或紧急情况的病人。修读护理副学士学位,让你得到这一行业所需要的技术和临床技能训练。该学位课程也助于准备执照考试成为注册护士。	根据 PayScale.com 资料,急诊室护士的薪金范围是 50 241～73 271 美元。

未来 10 年增长最快的职业

　　根据联邦劳工部最新公布的从 2008 年到 2018 年的就业增长预测，以及晋升机会、工资数据和工作满意度等其他因素，以下介绍 20 多个不同行业的职位，除了预计将在未来 10 年中以高于平均水平的速度增长外，从业者的收入还能达到高于中位数的水平。同时介绍一下这些职位相关的学位和资历要求。

表 5 - 9　美国未来 10 年增长最快的职业

行业门类	相关职业	简　要　分　析
商务行业	会计师	劳工统计局预测 2008 年至 2018 年的会计师和审计师就业增长率为 22％，为现时的 129 万份就业机会再增加多 27.94 万位职位。尽管当前经济衰退，劳工统计局预计，会计师人数增长速度将高于全国平均就业增长水平。由于政府推出更多复杂的金融法规，因此对会计师的需求将会增加。 　　2009 年会计师和审计师中位数年薪为 60 340 美元，其中最高薪金的 10％的会计师收入超过 104 450 美元，而最底层的 10％收入则少于 37 690 美元。 　　要成为会计师，会计师学士学位是首要的条件。想成为公共会计师，你可能需要先成为注册会计师，亦即是要参加美国注册会计师协会的统一考试。大多数州份都要求至少 150 小时的相关课程，才有资格参加考试。
	精算师	精算师的就业机会在未来 10 年会迅速攀升。2008 年精算师的数目为 1.97 万人，在接下来 10 年数目增长达 4 200 人，涨幅超过 20％。保险业对精算师的需求将保持稳定，医疗保健和咨询公司将越来越依赖于精算师所具备的技能。 　　2009 年精算师的薪酬中位数为 87 210 美元。收入最低的 10％的收入则少于 51 950 美元，而收入最高的 10％的收入则逾 158 240 美元。精算学学士学位新毕业生预期起薪约为 56 000 美元。 　　要成为精算师，你需要具有学士学位和主修财务或数学专业。有志者应考虑主修数学、统计学、经济学，甚至精算科学学位，当前约有 100 个学校提供该学位。

续　表

行业门类	相关职业	简要分析
商务行业	精算师	有些雇主或会支付由意外险精算学会和精算师协会提供的证书课程,如果你通过考试,带来加薪的机会将相当高。有一些数据表明,越来越多的雇主在聘请员工时希望雇用已经通过初步的考试应征者。
	财务顾问	未来 10 年这将是一个增长较快的行业,2008 年至 2018 年预料增长速度超过 30%。2008 年财务顾问约有 20.84 万人,其中约三分之一是自雇人士。即将退休的婴儿潮时期出生的 7 800 万人,预计将会为该咨询行业创造强劲的就业机会。不过,许多投资者质疑财务顾问和他们的律师的价值。同时许多互联网站有日益强大的咨询工具,已足以应付消费者的需求。 　　2009 年中位数年薪为 68 200 美元,收入最低的 10% 少于 33 790 美元,收入最高的 10% 的年薪超过 166 400 美元。很多财务顾问同时获得大量奖金,这并不包括在工资数据内。 　　财务顾问必须持续进修及保持走在时代尖端的技能,拥有专业知识是赢取客户的胜算所在,有意投身该行业者必须拥有学士学位,拥有更高级学位更佳。
	金融分析师	2008 年至 2018 年之间金融分析师的就业机会预计将增长 20%,远高于所有职业的平均数。在 2008 年现存职位为 25.06 万,10 年内将增加 4.96 万个新职位。但是对新的分析师而言,这些职位的竞争仍然激烈。 　　该行业薪金优厚,2009 年 5 月中位数年薪包括一大笔奖金在内的总收入为 73 670 美元。收入最高者年收入为 139 350 美元。 　　必须拥有学士学位,而主修金融、工商管理、会计学、统计学或经济学专业者更佳。许多金融分析师攻读金融或商业管理的硕士学位。可能需具执照,但大多数是由雇主支付。
	物流员	物流是一个相对狭窄的领域,但因供应和分配系统日益复杂,该领域的就业增长很可能高于平均水平,按劳工部估计 2008 年至 2018 年就业增长率为 20%。 　　大学毕业生一般的入门级薪酬大约是 40 500 美元,2009 年所有物流员的中位数薪金均达到约 68 000 美元。这行业最高薪的 10% 收入超过 104 500 美元。 　　想入行者必须拥有学士学位,主修如商业、供应一连锁性管理、处理工程或工业工程。当物流员晋升到管理层

续　表

行业门类	相关职业	简要分析
商务行业	物流员	后,许多会攻读 MBA 或各类专业的证书。工作经验十分重要,物流员亦要跟上不断变化的技术,如 RFID 追踪系统或新的库存控制软件。许多物流员具有军方背景,因为在不利条件下搬运材料为军队的强项,这项训练有助他们迎接商业挑战。
	会议策划员	2008 年在全国范围内,会议和会议策划者的就业人数为 5.66 万人,预计在未来 10 年就业增长速度将会超过所有行业平均速度,就业人数将会跳升 16%,这要感谢越来越多的全球性公司日益重要的会议所赐。 在 2009 年,会议及会议策划者中位数工资为 44 780 美元,基本上收入介于 25 000~75 000 美元之间。 投身该行业,拥有学士学位较佳。虽然某些学校提供会议管理学位,但实践经验可能是助你找到工作的最重要因素。拥有学士学位,再加上一些会议策划经验将会是最好的求职配搭。
	公共关系专家	2008 年至 2018 年公共关系专家职位预计将增加超过 6.6 万个,比例为 24%。公关专家去年平均年薪约为 51 960 美元,而最低的 10% 的收入少于 30 520 美元,最高的 10% 的收入为 96000 以上。 大多数公关专家具有通信、新闻、公共关系或相关领域学士学位。很多新闻从业人员由于不满其职业的待遇,转而投向公关行业中寻找出路,更因此而获得较佳的就业前景。很多公司在聘请员工时会考虑雇用在其专业领域已有一些实践经验的求职者。
	销售经理	根据劳工部统计资料预计,2008 年至 2018 年整体销售经理的职位预计将增加 5.18 万个,即增加 5 个百分点。企业视聘请一线销售经理为一项投资,因为公司依赖他们来增加销售额。这些受到青睐的职位往往竞争激烈。 该职位待遇优厚,2009 年 5 月销售经理中位数年薪为 96 790 美元,奖金数额随时相等于工资的 10% 或以上。工资差距可以很大,取决于销售经理的责任和服务时间,以及公司规模和地点,销售额版图,以及属于哪一行业。2009 年 5 月,最低的 10% 的销售经理赚取 47 660 美元,而最高的 10% 的收入为每年 166 400 美元以上。通常在大都市地区金融投资公司任职销售经理者赚取的工资位最高之列。

续　表

行业门类	相关职业	简　要　分　析
商务行业	销售经理	想要成为销售经理,必须具有大学学位,获得工商管理硕士学位更佳,但是也请留意,该行业比较重视工作经验多于所接受的教育,入职者通常由低做起,从销售行列开始,逐渐晋升为经理级别。
	培训专家	该行业前景乐观,就业机会方面预计会猛增 5.05 万个职位,即超过 23%,至 2018 年时将会达到 26.7 万个职位。 　　在 2009 年培训和发展专家的中位数年薪是 52 120 美元。最高的 10% 的收入年薪超过 85 860 美元,而最低的 10%,年薪收入约 30 120 美元。 　　投身这一行业的学历要求十分参差,可以需要具有人力资源或相关事业学士学位,并有修读培训和发展课程。获得实习机会将有助于找到第一份工作。
创作和服务行业	商业机师	到 2018 年这一行业的就业机会预计将增长 19%。据估计,此行业将会增加 7 300 个新的就业机会。由于同业中的合并和削减,使很多下岗机师目前正在竞争就业机会。但是当经济好转,空中交通量回升,以及许多年老飞行员退休后,此情况将得到纾缓。 　　2009 年商业机师平均年收入为 65 840 美元。刚入行机师必须清楚了解,在区域航空公司任职通常工资低和需长时间工作。你还要为自己支付训练的费用,这方面的开支可能很昂贵。 　　许多机师在军队中取得他们的驾驶飞机训练,亦有一些人在民用飞行学校取得有关训练。目前,大部分进入该行业者拥有大学学位,这亦是有利于求职者获得聘任的优越条件。负责驾驶运载旅客或运输货物飞机的机师,必须具有商业机师执照,以及由美国联邦航空局 FAA 颁发的仪表飞行等级执照。
	博物馆员	在未来的几年里,博物馆员的数量将上升 23%,高于所有职业平均增长率。到 2018 年,新职位增加应会达到 2 700 个。 　　在过去的几年里,一些博物馆一直在挣扎求存,在裁减员工后获留任者往往须肩负额外工作负担。因此,在经济全面复苏前,馆员职位的竞争可能较激烈。 　　该职位的薪酬取决于雇用机构或博物馆的规模和信誉。在 2009 年馆员年收入中位数约为 48 000 美元,50% 中间收入者年薪为 35 000~65 000 美元。最高的 10% 的

行业门类	相关职业	简 要 分 析
创作和服务行业	博物馆员	管理员收入年薪超过 83 000 美元。不过,这行业往往需要热爱该工作的人担任,有时甚至工资低微任职者也甘之如饴。 大多数博物馆都需要应征者具有相关专业学历,如艺术史或考古,或在博物馆研究方面的硕士学位。享负盛名的博物馆可能要求应征者具有博士学位。如欲在保护专业领域担任馆员,应选修化学课程,这将有助于做好入行准备。这项工作还需要专业领域的工作经验。博物馆员还必须具备优秀的写作能力,撰写目录和博物馆宣传品。具有领导能力和业务经验更佳,因为撰写拨款建议书,是博物馆馆长的重要工作之一。
	电影和视频编辑	预计该行业就业竞争激烈。在2008年该行业的在职人员为2.55万人。虽然美国国内的电影编辑职位到2018年预计将增加3 000个,但希望从事电影和电视行业的人数却远远超过职位空缺。只有最熟练、高能力、并善于利用技术者会觅得高薪厚职,或自雇者须具备以上条件才会得到全职工作。 2009年,电影和视频编辑中位数年收入为50 790美元,最高的10%的薪酬达到6位数字。从事电影和视频业者薪酬最高者,年收入中位数约69 000美元。自雇者每年的收入波动很大。如同许多创作行业,入行时通常收入较低,直到你建立地位或证明自己的实力比同行优胜情况才会得到改善,这可能需要数年时间。 大多数电影和视频编辑工作均要求大学本科学历,包括录像和电脑技术课程。雇主通常要求申请者具有良好的电影艺术眼光、想象力和创造力,以及对编辑软件和摄影技术有深入的了解。
	赌场经理	2008年至2018年赌场主管和赌场经理职位预计会猛增12%,略高于所有职业的平均水平。赌场经理通常有较大责任和赚钱较多。2008年全国只有大约62 00名赌场经理,赌场主管职位则高出许多,约40 900个,由于经济不景气,使拉斯维加斯赌业不振,但越来越多的州份却希望以博彩业来增进财源。 2009年赌场主管收入中位数年薪近48 000美元,另一方面,专责人力资源、雇用和培训的赌场经理,收入中位数是67 380美元,薪酬最高可达到115 000美元以上,而收入最低者约为30 000美元。

续　表

行业门类	相关职业	简要分析
创作和服务行业	赌场经理	此行业没有严格的学历要求,但很多主管和赌场经理均有荷官经验,他们在职业或赌博业学校接受赌博规则、程序和法例的训练。如果你想升至管理层,大专以上学历是必要的。想当荷官的话需获得负责临管赌场的州府委员会发出的执照。
	暖气、空调和制冷技工	2008 年至 2018 年,暖气、空调和制冷技术员预计将增加 8.66 万个职位,升幅为 28%,近年来供过于求的住宅建筑是该行业的一个福音,而住宅空调制冷系统一般经过 10～15 年便需要更换。环保和节能的暖气和空调系统需求增加,将需要更多的技术员安装和提供有关服务。许多现职的技术人员已届退休年龄,承包商都在寻求技术工人,以应付需求,估计商用空调和制冷行业每年需要额外 5.07 万名技术工人。 　　时薪中位数为年薪 19.76 美元,即每年约 41 100 美元。最低的 10% 的收入为时薪 12.38 美元以下,而最高的 10% 收入为时薪 31.53 美元以上。该行业最高薪的工种是汽车制造业、发电装置、输电和配电等。 　　技术人员通常受过职业学校或社区学院提供的技术训练。课程为期六个月至两年不等。当学徒亦是进入该行业另一途径。一些州和地方政府要求技术工必须领取牌照,而负责购买或使用制冷计者,必须具有妥善处理该物品的证书。由于空调制冷系统技术不断发展,工人必须持续接受培训。
	口译/翻译人员	劳工部预计到了 2018 年,口译和笔译人员就业增长达 22%。经济日趋全球化,以及在美国日益庞大的非英语人口,使该行业的需求不断增加。2008 年口译和笔译方面有超过 5 万份工作,实际人数可能更高,因为这行业有很多人是断续工作的。西班牙语的翻译就业机会稳固,预计随着美国拉美裔人口的增加,对医疗保健和法律口译及笔译人才的需求将相当迫切。其他语言的需求同样会提高,包括中文、韩文、日文、阿拉伯语、波斯语、法语、意大利语、德语,甚至非洲国家语言。 　　薪酬与所需语言和所关事项有很大关系。需求高或任职工数不足领域的语言,以及需翻译比较复杂的议题,往往收入较高。2009 年中位数年薪为 40 860 美元,中位时薪 19.65 美元。薪水介于 22 810～74 150 美元。需要能很流利说至少两种语言(包括母语)。双语环境中长大

续　表

行业门类	相关职业	简要分析
创作和服务行业	口译/翻译人员	的求职者自有优势，但并非必要条件。某些翻译人员需学士学位才能获得工作，而另一些只需要完成与工作有关的具体培训课程。联邦、州和市法院对某些语言的口译人员规定必须具有专业证书。如具备深厚的研究和分析能力，以及良好记忆力则更为理想。
医疗保健行业	按摩治疗师	由于按摩疗法越来越受欢迎，此行业就业增长速度预计将高于平均水平，根据劳工部预测，2008 年到 2018 年，增长率约为 19％。水疗和按摩诊所如雨后春笋般涌现，以满足按摩服务日益增加的需求，也为按摩治疗师创造了众多就业机会。2008 年约有 12.24 万份按摩治疗师工作，有一半以上是自雇人士。 　　按摩治疗师需具执照，但不需要具有学位。2009 年平均年薪 35 230 美元，中位数时薪 16.94 美元。通常有既定客户的自雇按摩治疗师收入最高。 　　大多数州都要求按摩治疗师完成正规教育课程，并通过考试获得执照，但各处标准和要求差别很大。各学院或大学提供的课程，规定约需 500 小时学习时间以完成课程。
	体育运动教练	体育教练需求日益增加，特别是高中，但另一方面专业及大学体育队伍教练的就业竞争也相当激烈。2008 年共有 16 300 个体育教练职位，到 2018 年预计将攀升至 22.4 万个，增长率达 37％，远远高于所有职业平均增幅。由于流动率低，求职者可能要到新成立的健身中心、医院和学校中找寻工作机会。 　　大部分体育教练为全职工作，并享有福利。2009 年中位年薪超过 41 000 美元，根据经验、职责和工作环境，工资会有差别。收入最低者低于 25 500 美元，收入最高者则超过 65 000 美元。 　　最低入职要求是拥有学士学位，但许多体育教练持有硕士或博士学位。大多数州份都要求体育教练持有执照。雇主会支付一些持续教育培训以确保体育教练取得所需的有效执照。高中体育教练如需教学，可能也需要教师证书。
	实验室技术员	劳工部预计临床实验室技术员的数量，从 2008—2018 年将增长约 16％，增加约 2.5 万份工作，将高于平均水平。该行业退休数目和流失率高。预计私人实验室以及医务所的就业机会将会迅速增长。

续　表

行业门类	相关职业	简要分析
医疗保健行业	实验室技术员	工资以时薪计算,2009 年中位数年薪是 36 030 美元。薪酬最高者,收入可超过 55 210 美元。 该职业的教育成本较低。对于入门级的工作,可能只需副学士学位或完成证书课程,并在工作中学习一些技能。
	牙科卫生员	这是迅速增长并具有大量就业机会的行业。根据美国劳工部的资料,2008 年共有 17.4 万份卫生员工作,到 2018 年预计将攀升至 23.7 万份,增幅达 36%,远高于所有行业的平均预期。牙齿护理需求预计增加,此外新一代人们比年长一辈更多聘用卫生员,因而造成大量工作机会。由于就业市场紧张,一些卫生员(尤其是刚入行者)抱怨很难找到工作。除传统工作以外,牙科卫生员或可在教学领域找到工作机会。 牙科卫生员每小时工资约 32 美元。刚入行者,最低工资每小时约 21 美元。最好工资的牙科卫生员时薪达 44 美元。2009 年中等年薪约 67000 美元。 全国约 300 个口腔卫生课程中大部分颁授副学士学位。毕业后需通过笔试和临床考试,才得到认可资格。有志从事研究或教学职务者,必须完成学士或硕士学位课程。医务所提供大部分工作机会,通常不需要更高学历。
社会服务行业	神职人员	美国目前似乎不缺乏神职人员。2008 年约有 67 万个神职人员职位,劳工部预计未来 10 年该职位数量将上升 13%。小型教区的就业机会较佳,但薪酬会略低。 2009 年中位数收入为 42 950 美元,但工资范围非常大,从不到 22 940 美元到超过 75 320 美元不等。 不同教派之间对入职者的教育要求有很大的差别。许多业内人士具有硕士以上学位。一些宗教团体不需要神职人员获得正规培训。
	法庭速记员	该行业的就业前景非常乐观。据劳工数据署统计,2008—2018 年这行业将增长 18%,高于所有职业的平均水平。由于为听力障碍人士提供电视直播字幕和翻译服务的需求不断增长,该行业的需求亦相应增加。 薪酬会基于不同的专业/经验和认证而有区别,2009 年法庭速记员的中位数年薪为 47 810 美元。根据劳工部统计,法庭速记员收入介乎 25 410 美元以下至 89 240 美元以上。除薪金外,法庭速记员亦赚取每页转录费。 有超过 150 个培训课程让有志成为法庭速记员者选

续　表

行业门类	相关职业	简　要　分　析
社会服务行业	法庭速记员	择,他们可以通过社区学院、大学、网上和家庭学习课程等取得资格。大多数学院课程为期至少两年。毕业后可以再进修一个专业领域的证书。每个州对执照规定各不相同,但大多数州都规定法庭速记员须具专业注册速记员证明书。
	教育行政管理人员	虽然就业机会前景乐观,但因国内不同地区而有差异,大部分工作机会在西部和南部地区。根据劳工部统计,2008 年教育行政人员有 44.54 万个职位,其中约一半在小学或中学。2008—2018 年就业增长幅度预计为 8％。由于此行业有大量预期的退休人士,部分职位较少人员申请,加上就学年龄人口增长,求职者会有良好就业机会。 　2009 年幼儿园行政管理人员中位数年薪达 41 060 美元。小学和中学校行政管理人员包括校长在内,薪金约 85 220 美元。学院和大学行政管理人员薪酬约 82 800 美元,2009 年收入最高者工资超过 162 170 美元。福利通常包括优厚的医疗和退休金计划。以及每年 4～5 个星期的休假。行政管理人员的其他福利包括自己和家人取得免学费优惠。 　大多数行政管理人员,尤其是公立学校,须具硕士或博士学位,以及经教室验。公立学校的校长通常必须领取州府认证资格。私人托儿所管理人须具备学前教育证书或州执照,但不一定需要有学位。由于工作需要与他人合作,因此具有良好沟通技能的行政管理人员较为优胜。
科技行业	生物医学工程师	根据劳工部预测,2008—2018 年生物医学工程师就业预计增长将高达 72％,增加近 1.2 万个就业机会。由于婴儿潮一代步入老年,医疗手术需求相应增加,加上医疗技术方面的日新月异,该行业有较大的需求空间。 　劳工部报告指出,2009 年生物医学工程师中位数年薪为 78 860 美元。收入最高的年薪超过 123 000 美元,而收入最低的不到 50 000 美元。 　一些生物医学工程师拥有机械或电子工程学位,而新一批学生则选修生物医学学位。有志于研究和开发工作者,通常需要具备研究生学位。

续　表

行业门类	相关职业	简　要　分　析
科技行业	土木工程师	劳工部预测,土木工程师在未来 10 年就业增长约为 24%,大大高于平均水平。即大约 6.8 万个新职位。美国的基础设施完善,但亦有很多设施急需修理,因此对土木工程师有迫切的需求。整体人口增长亦将使现有社区持续扩张,新的社区亦会不断成立。 　　2009 年土木工程师中位数年收入为 76 590 美元。薪酬最高的 10% 土木工程师年收入超过 118 000 美元,而收入最低 10% 的年收入低于 50000 美元。 　　入职者须具土木工程学士学位。许多雇主要求入职者通过标准专业考试并获得认可执照。有志于技术项目和晋升管理层者,需要获得硕士学位,从事教学工作者须具博士学位。
	电脑软件工程师	根据劳工部的预期,2008 年至 2018 年电脑软件工程师职位将有大幅增长,新增职位达到 29.52 万个,或超过 32% 的增幅,远高于所有职业的平均水平,这是由于公司不断整合新技术和自行设计软件所致。由于企业增加如网络安全和移动技术的开支,因此某些具体的应用程式工程师比较吃香。 　　鉴于各电脑软件工程师的经验、教育和技术技能不同,薪金差异有可能很大。2009 年该类中位数年收入介于 87 480～93 470 美元。该职位的大部分工作需要至少具备电脑科学或相关领域的学士学位,更复杂的工作通常需要硕士学位。 　　这行业的金科玉律是对业内编程语言如 C++、Java 和 C# 有深入的认识,同时要掌握按不同行业所需的其他高度专业化程式。这一行业不但需要员工具有专业技术,还要理解复杂的软件系统功能,并善于与公司内技术和业务团队之间进行沟通。

现在，试想你们全家已经成功移民美国，或者你的孩子已经在美国留学，作为家庭主要成员的家长又该如何启动移民初期的生活呢？百姓的日子无非由衣食住行和柴米油盐构成，我们就从生活细节一一道来。

社会福利与居民责任的身份证：社会安全号码的办理

宽泛地讲，社会安全号码就是美国的身份证号码，有时还会特别指明，某些持卡人不得用此号码来申请正式工作，比如外国留学生。此证的办理需要一定的条件，有时候，绿卡也只是办理此证的前提条件之一。为了帮助部分读者的特殊需要，特将有关官方要求附上。

图 6-1 社会安全卡

SOCIAL SECURITY ADMINISTRATION
Application for a Social Security Card

Applying for a Social Security Card is free!

USE THIS APPLICATION TO:

- Apply for an original Social Security card
- Apply for a replacement Social Security card
- Change or correct information on your Social Security number record

IMPORTANT: You MUST provide a properly completed application and the required evidence before we can process your application. We can only accept original documents or documents certified by the custodian of the original record. Notarized copies or photocopies which have not been certified by the custodian of the record are not acceptable. We will return any documents submitted with your application. For assistance call us at 1-800-772-1213 or visit our website at www.socialsecurity.gov.

Original Social Security Card

To apply for an original card, you must provide at least two documents to prove age, identity, and U.S. citizenship or current lawful, work-authorized immigration status. If you are not a U.S. citizen and do not have DHS work authorization, you must prove that you have a valid non-work reason for requesting a card. See page 2 for an explanation of acceptable documents.

NOTE: If you are age 12 or older and have never received a Social Security number, you must apply in person.

Replacement Social Security Card

To apply for a replacement card, you must provide one document to prove your identity. If you were born outside the U.S., you must also provide documents to prove your U.S. citizenship or current, lawful, work-authorized status. See page 2 for an explanation of acceptable documents.

Changing Information on Your Social Security Record

To change the information on your Social Security number record (i.e., a name or citizenship change, or corrected date of birth) you must provide documents to prove your identity, support the requested change and establish the reason for the change. For example, you may provide a birth certificate to show your correct date of birth. A document supporting a name change must be recent and identify you by both your old and new names. If the name change event occurred over two years ago or if the name change document does not have enough information to prove your identity, you must also provide documents to prove your identity in your prior name and/or in some cases your new legal name. If you were born outside the U.S. you must provide a document to prove your U.S. citizenship or current lawful, work-authorized status. See page 2 for an explanation of acceptable documents.

LIMITS ON REPLACEMENT SOCIAL SECURITY CARDS

Public Law 108-458 limits the number of replacement Social Security cards you may receive to 3 per calendar year and 10 in a lifetime. Cards issued to reflect changes to your legal name or changes to a work authorization legend do not count toward these limits. We may also grant exceptions to these limits if you provide evidence from an official source to establish that a Social Security card is required.

IF YOU HAVE ANY QUESTIONS

If you have any questions about this form or about the evidence documents you must provide, please visit our website at www.socialsecurity.gov for additional information as well as locations of our offices and Social Security Card Centers. You may also call Social Security at 1-800-772-1213. You can also find your nearest office or Card Center in your local phone book.

图 6－2 社会安全号码申请说明 I（免费、可申请、可更换）

EVIDENCE DOCUMENTS

he following lists are examples of the types of documents you must provide with your application and are not all
clusive. Call us at 1-800-772-1213 if you cannot provide these documents.

IPORTANT : If you are completing this application on behalf of someone else, you must provide evidence that
hows your authority to sign the application as well as documents to prove your identity and the identity of the
erson for whom you are filing the application. We can only accept original documents or documents certified by
e custodian of the original record. Notarized copies or photocopies which have not been certified by the
ustodian of the record are not acceptable.

vidence of Age

general, you must provide your birth certificate. In some situations, we may accept another document that
hows your age. Some of the other documents we may accept are:

- U.S. Hospital record of your birth (created at the time of birth)
- Religious record established before age five showing your age or date of birth
- Passport
- Final Adoption Decree (the adoption decree must show that the birth information was taken from the original birth certificate)

vidence of Identity

ou must provide current, unexpired evidence of identity in your legal name. Your legal name will be shown on
e Social Security card. Generally, we prefer to see documents issued in the U.S. Documents you submit to
stablish identity must show your legal name AND provide biographical information (your date of birth, age, or
arents' names) **and/or** physical information (photograph, or physical description - height, eye and hair color,
c.). If you send a photo identity document but do not appear in person, the document must show your
ographical information (e.g., your date of birth, age, or parents' names). Generally, documents without an
xpiration date should have been issued within the past two years for adults and within the past four years for
hildren.

s proof of your identity, you must provide a:

- U.S. driver's license; or
- U.S. State-issued non-driver identity card; or
- U.S. passport

you do not have one of the documents above or cannot get a replacement within 10 work days, we may accept
her documents that show your legal name and biographical information, such as a U.S. military identity card,
ertificate of Naturalization, employee identity card, certified copy of medical record (clinic, doctor or hospital),
ealth insurance card, Medicaid card, or school identity card/record. For young children, we may accept medical
cords (clinic, doctor, or hospital) maintained by the medical provider. We may also accept a final adoption
ecree, or a school identity card, or other school record maintained by the school.

you are not a U.S. citizen, we must see your current U.S. immigration document(s) and your foreign passport
ith biographical information or photograph.

/E CANNOT ACCEPT A BIRTH CERTIFICATE, HOSPITAL SOUVENIR BIRTH CERTIFICATE, SOCIAL
ECURITY CARD STUB OR A SOCIAL SECURITY RECORD as evidence of identity.

vidence of U.S. Citizenship

general, you must provide your U.S. birth certificate or U.S. Passport. Other documents you may provide are a
onsular Report of Birth, Certificate of Citizenship, or Certificate of Naturalization.

vidence of Immigration Status

ou must provide a current unexpired document issued to you by the Department of Homeland Security (DHS)
howing your immigration status, such as Form I-551, I-94, I-688B, or I-766. If you are an international student or
xchange visitor, you may need to provide additional documents, such as Form I-20, DS-2019, or a letter
uthorizing employment from your school and employer (F-1) or sponsor (J-1). We CANNOT accept a receipt
howing you applied for the document. If you are not authorized to work in the U.S., we can issue you a Social
ecurity card only if you need the number for a valid non-work reason. Your card will be marked to show you
annot work and if you do work, we will notify DHS. See page 3, item 5 for more information.

图 6 - 3 社会安全号码申请说明 II (提供年龄和合法身份证明材料)

HOW TO COMPLETE THIS APPLICATION

Complete and sign this application LEGIBLY using ONLY black or blue ink on the attached or downloaded form using only 8 ½" x 11" (or A4 8.25" x 11.7") paper.

GENERAL: Items on the form are self-explanatory or are discussed below. The numbers match the numbered items on the form. If you are completing this form for someone else, please complete the items as they apply to that person.

4.   Show the month, day, and full (4 digit) year of birth; for example, "1998" for year of birth.

5.   If you check "Legal Alien Not Allowed to Work" or "Other," you must provide a document from a U.S. Federal, State, or local government agency that explains why you need a Social Security number and that you meet all the requirements for the government benefit. NOTE: Most agencies do not require that you have a Social Security number. Contact us to see if your reason qualifies for a Social Security number.

6., 7. Providing race and ethnicity information is voluntary and is requested for informational and statistical purposes only. Your choice whether to answer or not does not affect decisions we make on your application. If you do provide this information, we will treat it very carefully.

9.B., 10.B. If you are applying for an original Social Security Card for a child under age 18, you MUST show the mother's and father's Social Security numbers unless the mother and/or father was never assigned a Social Security number. If the number is not known and you cannot obtain it, check the "unknown" box.

13. If the date of birth you show in item 4 is different from the date of birth currently shown on your Social Security record, show the date of birth currently shown on your record in item 13 and provide evidence to support the date of birth shown in item 4.

16. Show an address where you can receive your card 7 to 14 days from now.

17. WHO CAN SIGN THE APPLICATION? If you are age 18 or older and are physically and mentally capable of reading and completing the application, you must sign in item 17. If you are under age 18, you may either sign yourself, or a parent or legal guardian may sign for you. If you are over age 18 and cannot sign on your own behalf, a legal guardian, parent, or close relative may generally sign for you. If you cannot sign your name, you should sign with an "X" mark and have two people sign as witnesses in the space beside the mark. Please do not alter your signature by including additional information on the signature line as this may invalidate your application. Call us if you have questions about who may sign your application.

HOW TO SUBMIT THIS APPLICATION

In most cases, you can take or mail this signed application with your documents to any Social Security office. Any documents you mail to us will be returned to you. Go to https://secure.ssa.gov/apps6z/FOLO/fo001.jsp to find the Social Security office or Social Security Card Center that serves your area.

图 6-4　社会安全号码申请说明Ⅲ(填表须知,包括年龄、种族、性别等个人资料)

PROTECT YOUR SOCIAL SECURITY NUMBER AND CARD

rotect your SSN card and number from loss and identity theft. DO NOT carry your SSN card with you. eep it in a secure location and only take it with you when you must show the card; e.g., to obtain a new b, open a new bank account, or to obtain benefits from certain U.S. agencies. Use caution in giving ut your Social Security number to others, particularly during phone, mail, email and Internet requests u did not initiate.

PRIVACY ACT STATEMENT
Collection and Use of Personal Information

ections 205(c) and 702 of the Social Security Act, as amended, authorize us to collect this formation. The information you provide will be used to assign you a Social Security number and sue a Social Security card.

he information you furnish on this form is voluntary. However, failure to provide the requested formation may prevent us from issuing you a Social Security number and card.

/e rarely use the information you supply for any purpose other than for issuing a Social Security umber and card. However, we may use it for the administration and integrity of Social Security rograms. We may also disclose information to another person or to another agency in accordance ith approved routine uses, which include but are not limited to the following:

1. To enable a third party or an agency to assist Social Security in establishing rights to Social Security benefits and/or coverage;

2. To comply with Federal laws requiring the release of information from Social Security records (e.g., to the Government Accountability Office and Department of Veterans' Affairs);

3. To make determinations for eligibility in similar health and income maintenance programs at the Federal, State, and local level; and

4. To facilitate statistical research, audit or investigative activities necessary to assure the integrity of Social Security programs.

/e may also use the information you provide in computer matching programs. Matching programs ompare our records with records kept by other Federal, State, or local government agencies. formation from these matching programs can be used to establish or verify a person's eligibility or Federally-funded or administered benefit programs and for repayment of payments or elinquent debts under these programs.

omplete lists of routine uses for this information are available in System of Records Notice 0-0058 (Master Files of Social Security Number (SSN) Holders and SSN Applications). The otice, additional information regarding this form, and information regarding our systems and rograms, are available on-line at www.socialsecurity.gov or at any local Social Security office.

his information collection meets the requirements of 44 U.S.C. §3507, as amended by Section 2 of the aperwork Reduction Act of 1995 . You do not need to answer these questions unless we display a alid Office of Management and Budget control number. We estimate that it will take about 8.5 to 9.5 inutes to read the instructions, gather the facts, and answer the questions. You may send comments n our time estimate to: SSA, 6401 Security Blvd., Baltimore, MD 21235-6401. **Send only comments elating to our time estimate to this address, not the completed form.**

图 6 - 5　社会安全号码申请说明Ⅳ（个人隐私条款与社会安全卡号的保护）

SOCIAL SECURITY ADMINISTRATION
Application for a Social Security Card

Form Approved
OMB No. 0960-0066

		First	Full Middle Name	Last
1	**NAME** TO BE SHOWN ON CARD			
	FULL NAME AT BIRTH IF OTHER THAN ABOVE	First	Full Middle Name	Last
	OTHER NAMES USED ON YOUR SOCIAL SECURITY CARD			

2 Social Security number previously assigned to the person listed in item 1 ➔ ☐☐☐ — ☐☐ — ☐☐☐☐

3 **PLACE OF BIRTH** (Do Not Abbreviate) City _____ State or Foreign Country _____ | Office Use Only FCI | **4** **DATE OF BIRTH** _____ MM/DD/YYYY

5 **CITIZENSHIP** ➔ (Check One)
☐ U.S. Citizen
☐ Legal Alien Allowed To Work
☐ Legal Alien **Not** Allowed To Work(See Instructions On Page 3)
☐ Other (See Instructions On Page 3)

6 **ETHNICITY** Are You Hispanic or Latino? (Your Response is Voluntary) ☐ Yes ☐ No

7 **RACE** Select One or More (Your Response is Voluntary)
☐ Native Hawaiian ☐ American Indian ☐ Other Pacific Islander
☐ Alaska Native ☐ Black/African American ☐ White
☐ Asian

8 **SEX** ➔ ☐ Male ☐ Female

9
A. MOTHER'S NAME AT HER BIRTH ➔	First	Full Middle Name	Last Name At Her Birth

B. MOTHER'S SOCIAL SECURITY NUMBER (See instructions for 9 B on Page 3) ➔ ☐☐☐ — ☐☐ — ☐☐☐☐ ☐ Unknown

10
A. FATHER'S NAME ➔	First	Full Middle Name	Last

B. FATHER'S SOCIAL SECURITY NUMBER (See instructions for 10B on Page 3) ➔ ☐☐☐ — ☐☐ — ☐☐☐☐ ☐ Unknown

11 Has the person listed in item 1 or anyone acting on his/her behalf ever filed for or received a Social Security number card before?
☐ Yes (If "yes" answer questions 12-13) ☐ No ☐ Don't Know (If "don't know," skip to question 14.)

12 Name shown on the most recent Social Security card issued for the person listed in item 1 ➔ | First | Full Middle Name | Last Name |

13 Enter any different date of birth if used on an earlier application for a card ➔ _____ MM/DD/YYYY

14 **TODAY'S DATE** _____ MM/DD/YYYY

15 **DAYTIME PHONE NUMBER** _____ Area Code _____ Number

16 **MAILING ADDRESS** (Do Not Abbreviate) | Street Address, Apt. No., PO Box, Rural Route No. City | State/Foreign Country | ZIP Code |

I declare under penalty of perjury that I have examined all the information on this form, and on any accompanying statements or forms, and it is true and correct to the best to my knowledge.

17 **YOUR SIGNATURE** ▶

18 **YOUR RELATIONSHIP TO THE PERSON IN ITEM 1 IS:**
☐ Self ☐ Natural Or Adoptive Parent ☐ Legal Guardian ☐ Other Specify _____

DO NOT WRITE BELOW THIS LINE (FOR SSA USE ONLY)

NPN			DOC	NTI	CAN		ITV
PBC	EVI	EVA	EVC	PRA	NWR	DNR	UNIT

EVIDENCE SUBMITTED	SIGNATURE AND TITLE OF EMPLOYEE(S) REVIEWING EVIDENCE AND/OR CONDUCTING INTERVIEW
	DATE
	DCL DATE

图 6-6 社会安全号码申请说明 V (表格简明却事关一生)

做明明白白的纳税人
是新移民的第一课

2011 年年初,一篇关于《月入万元税负多少?》的文章,在网上引发高度关注。大致意思是,国内中产白领月收入 1 万元,要交 14％个税、12％公积金、8％养老保险、4％医疗失业险,之后可支配收入为 6 200 元,这些钱全部用于消费的话,还要继续为所购商品缴纳 17％增值税、28％各种杂税。总之,1 万元账面收入,最终缴税达到 6 600 元之多。关键是,很多人根本不知道在为商品流动纳税,没有为未来的失业和收入下降要求纳税返回的希望,不存在因为家人收入低下要求减税和免税的法律依据。

上述数字的关键一点在于揭示了一个客观事实,低收入者被认为工资低于起征点,相当一部分人的生活是"免税"的,没有纳税,就是社会的"食利者",这是完全错误的。只要人们在社会中生活,只要消费,收入再低的社会一员,也在不断地纳税,从自来水到牙膏,从馒头到公交车票,无一不是标上了含税的价格销售给消费者的,只是我们的体制对此含混模糊,往往单向夸大了社会对贫困者的救济。理论上说,穷人富人都是纳税人,他们缴税能力有所差别,但在社会属性上都是平等的纳税人,同样支撑了国家经济生活。

新移民来到美国以后,第一件事情,就是理直气壮地行使和享受纳税人的义务与权利。

　　比如说,你来到超市,购买了一车的主食和副食品,这些作为民生的必需品,收银条上显示的就是食品的价格总和,没有格外的支出。此时,假如你是一位暂时失业者,或者你的父母亲年老已经不再工作,没有收入,就有机会在社会福利部门办理社会保障卡。购买食品时,这些消费金额就会直接从社会保障卡的账上扣除,根据社会福利部门的核定,每人每月食品券的金额在数百美元之间,足够一个正常消费者过上粗茶淡饭的日子;假如你无法抵御琳琅满目的食物诱惑,顺手拿了巧克力、冰淇淋、糖果等,对不起,结账的时候,你在纽约市要在所有商品基本价格的基础上,支付 8.25% 的消费税,至于你购买了食物以外的其他商品,如无特别注明,所有商品均得支付 8.25% 的消费税,有时还有饮料罐等环保回收费用。

　　上述这几笔费用,不是商家的收入,而是商家代政府征收的税收,到时候会一分不少进入国库,如有差错,商家要自掏腰包吃"赔账",还要支付巨额罚款。美国的制度设计使得商家既要为政府打工,还要为政府尽职,政府倒是省了不少征税的成本。

　　作为新移民,一位从中国初来乍到的消费者,开始的时候,也许你并不习惯处处缴税的生活,日子一长,也就习以为常了。但你千万不要自作聪明,与卖主商量漏税的事宜,这些不良记录,终有一天会露出马脚,让你后悔不迭。关键是,当你坐上纽约的公交车,可以感受到它的舒适整洁,当你乘坐纽约的地铁,可以感觉到它的快捷通顺。你也许会责怪纽约的百年地铁老旧,不如新鲜出炉的上海轨道交通时尚,但你一旦知道纽约的公交地铁可以免费换乘,多付几美元就可以 24 小时无限制出入,也没有头班车末班车的困扰,你开始明白,8.25% 的消费税是很实惠的。开车上路的时候,总有不需交纳过桥费、隧道费和高速费的

Register #3 Transaction #975356
Cashier #60830173 3/16/12 2:28PM

```
              WELLNESS+ SAVINGS
          Dscnt Card#: 95XXXXX3803
    1 BR LIP APPL LP CA6546           0.74 T
      SALE 1/0.74, Reg 1/2.99
      Discount 2.25-
    1 BR ES QUARTET DP TPPTY880       1.24 T
      SALE 1/1.24, Reg 1/4.99
      Discount 3.75-
    1 BR ES QUARTET FRT SD 8802       1.24 T
      SALE 1/1.24, Reg 1/4.99
      Discount 3.75-
    1 BR ES QUAD 8807A                1.24 T
      SALE 1/1.24, Reg 1/4.99
      Discount 3.75-
    1 BR ES QUAD 8804C                1.24 T
      SALE 1/1.24, Reg 1/4.99
      Discount 3.75-
    1 BR ES QUARTET PT TONE 880       1.24 T
      SALE 1/1.24, Reg 1/4.99
      Discount 3.75-
    1 PR LASH MATRIX BLK              1.62 T
      SALE 1/1.62, Reg 1/6.49
      Discount 4.87-
    1 PR LASH MATRIX BRN              1.62 T
      SALE 1/1.62, Reg 1/6.49
      Discount 4.87-
    1 MERCHANDISE                     1.00-
      MANUF COUPON
    1 MERCHANDISE TAXABLE             1.00-
      MANUF COUPON
    1 MAY STIL LINR BLK BLK           7.49 T
    1 MAY GL LOTS VERY BLACK 41       2.79 T
      SALE 1/2.79, Reg 1/5.59
      Discount 2.80-

  12 Items          Subtotal       18.46
                         Tax        1.59
                       Total       20.05
      * CASH PAYMENT *             20.05
                    Tendered       20.05
                 Cash Change          .00

  Your wellness+ Savings:          33.54
```

图6-7 收据清楚地列出了收费总额、政府税收额以及本次购物优惠额　221

路段,即使有,也是 25 美分、50 美分和 1 美元的小额,便宜得让你吃惊。终于有一天,你的车技已经保证你可以上任何一条州际高速公路的时候,你会安静地感受到,虽然一年需要支付的地产税、联邦税、州税和市税总计达到成百上千美元,但你或是你的家人、朋友生活在一个有序、整洁和安宁的环境中,我的感觉就是等于买了一张全年的公园门票。

重视 4 月 15 日,美国报税截止日

接下来,我们就要仔细讨论每年 4 月 15 日的报税大限之日。按照美国的风俗,这一天,一位打扮成卡通纳税官的人物会在邮局门口,任由来往报税人赶在报税截至日前邮寄税表时发泄不满,正如美国宪法先驱托马斯·杰斐逊所言,发泄归发泄,纳税归纳税,日子归日子,来年照旧。

一般来讲,大部分的美国工作有收入人士,包括永久绿卡居民和美国公民,每年都要依法报税,合理要回当年多余缴税,当然,也有交了好运另有横财的人,要补交个人所得税。原因在于,美国的合法员工都会在求职时填写一张 W-2 申请表格,雇主按照 W-2 表格上的要求,早已将你的收入一部分缴到联邦和本州的税务部门,就等你每年的 4 月 15 号去结账!即使这样严格的缴税程序和时间要求,还是有相当比例的纳税人没有及时报税,延误了大量的退税额度,其中肯定也有不少代缴税额。

当你正式在美国打工,哪怕是在美国校园打工,在雇主处一定要完成 W-2 表格的填写,每年 1 月份,雇主会主动将个人收入汇总在 W-2 表格上,供你向联邦和州政府报税所用。不光在经济上,W-2 表格同时也是一份法律保障，表明了你的神圣纳税人资格，即使你一生没有加入美国国籍，没有选举美国总统的资格，但纳税人的资格足以保障你行使选民的权利，选举当地社区的各类公职人员，为保障你的家庭与孩子权利发出声音。

每年 4 月 15 日之前，你必须亲笔在你的联邦个人所得税 1040 表格上和本州的个人所得税表上签名并寄出，很多人搞不清或者懒得逐一搞清税务法规，这时可以聘请会计师帮你理财，这也是合法的。所以，这个季节是会计师的繁忙季节，一般会收取几十到几百美元的服务费，帮你填妥 1040 主要表格和其他相关的附表，有时会多达几十页，如果你是投资移民的候选人，恐怕没有会计师的协助，你是无法通过日后移民局的复核的。现在，电脑技术已经部分取代了会计师的工作，收入单纯的纳税人基本不用将自己的隐私向会计师一一详述了。

22222	Void ☐	a Employee's social security number	For Official Use Only ▶ OMB No. 1545-0008		
b Employer identification number (EIN)			1 Wages, tips, other compensation	2 Federal income tax withheld	
c Employer's name, address, and ZIP code			3 Social security wages	4 Social security tax withheld	
			5 Medicare wages and tips	6 Medicare tax withheld	
			7 Social security tips	8 Allocated tips	
d Control number			9	10 Dependent care benefits	
e Employee's first name and initial	Last name	Suff.	11 Nonqualified plans	12a See instructions for box 12
			13 Statutory employee ☐ Retirement plan ☐ Third-party sick pay ☐	12b
			14 Other	12c
				12d
f Employee's address and ZIP code					

15 State	Employer's state ID number	16 State wages, tips, etc.	17 State income tax	18 Local wages, tips, etc.	19 Local income tax	20 Locality name

Form **W-2** Wage and Tax Statement **2011**

Copy A For Social Security Administration — Send this entire page with
Form W-3 to the Social Security Administration; photocopies are **not** acceptable.

Department of the Treasury—Internal Revenue Service
**For Privacy Act and Paperwork Reduction
Act Notice, see back of Copy D.**

Cat. No. 10134D

Do Not Cut, Fold, or Staple Forms on This Page — Do Not Cut, Fold, or Staple Forms on This Page

图 6-8 W-2 表格

Form 1040

Department of the Treasury—Internal Revenue Service

U.S. Individual Income Tax Return 2010 (99) IRS Use Only—Do not write or staple in this space.

For the year Jan. 1–Dec. 31, 2010, or other tax year beginning , 2010, ending , 20 | OMB No. 1545-0074

Name, Address, and SSN

PRINT CLEARLY

Your first name and initial | Last name | Your social security number

If a joint return, spouse's first name and initial | Last name | Spouse's social security number

See separate instructions.

Home address (number and street). If you have a P.O. box, see instructions. | Apt. no.

▲ Make sure the SSN(s) above and on line 6c are correct.

City, town or post office, state, and ZIP code. If you have a foreign address, see instructions.

Checking a box below will not change your tax or refund.

Presidential Election Campaign ▶ Check here if you, or your spouse if filing jointly, want $3 to go to this fund . . . . . ▶ ☐ You ☐ Spouse

Filing Status

Check only one box.

1 ☐ Single
2 ☐ Married filing jointly (even if only one had income)
3 ☐ Married filing separately. Enter spouse's SSN above and full name here. ▶
4 ☐ Head of household (with qualifying person). (See instructions.) If the qualifying person is a child but not your dependent, enter this child's name here. ▶
5 ☐ Qualifying widow(er) with dependent child

Exemptions

6a ☐ Yourself. If someone can claim you as a dependent, **do not** check box 6a . . . . . .
b ☐ Spouse
c Dependents:

(1) First name Last name	(2) Dependent's social security number	(3) Dependent's relationship to you	(4) ✓ if child under age 17 qualifying for child tax credit (see page 15)
			☐
			☐
			☐
			☐

If more than four dependents, see instructions and check here ▶ ☐

d Total number of exemptions claimed . . . .

Boxes checked on 6a and 6b
No. of children on 6c who:
• lived with you
• did not live with you due to divorce or separation (see instructions)
Dependents on 6c not entered above
Add numbers on lines above ▶

Income

Attach Form(s) W-2 here. Also attach Forms W-2G and 1099-R if tax was withheld.

If you did not get a W-2, see page 20.

Enclose, but do not attach, any payment. Also, please use Form 1040-V.

7 Wages, salaries, tips, etc. Attach Form(s) W-2 . . . . . . | 7
8a Taxable interest. Attach Schedule B if required . . . . . . | 8a
b Tax-exempt interest. **Do not** include on line 8a . . | 8b
9a Ordinary dividends. Attach Schedule B if required . . . . . . | 9a
b Qualified dividends . . . . . | 9b
10 Taxable refunds, credits, or offsets of state and local income taxes . | 10
11 Alimony received . . . . | 11
12 Business income or (loss). Attach Schedule C or C-EZ . . . . | 12
13 Capital gain or (loss). Attach Schedule D if required. If not required, check here ▶ ☐ | 13
14 Other gains or (losses). Attach Form 4797 . . . . | 14
15a IRA distributions . | 15a | b Taxable amount . . . | 15b
16a Pensions and annuities | 16a | b Taxable amount . . . | 16b
17 Rental real estate, royalties, partnerships, S corporations, trusts, etc. Attach Schedule E | 17
18 Farm income or (loss). Attach Schedule F . . . . | 18
19 Unemployment compensation . . . . | 19
20a Social security benefits | 20a | b Taxable amount . . . | 20b
21 Other income. List type and amount _____ | 21
22 Combine the amounts in the far right column for lines 7 through 21. This is your **total income** ▶ | 22

Adjusted Gross Income

23 Educator expenses | 23
24 Certain business expenses of reservists, performing artists, and fee-basis government officials. Attach Form 2106 or 2106-EZ | 24
25 Health savings account deduction. Attach Form 8889 . | 25
26 Moving expenses. Attach Form 3903 . . . . . . | 26
27 One-half of self-employment tax. Attach Schedule SE . | 27
28 Self-employed SEP, SIMPLE, and qualified plans . . | 28
29 Self-employed health insurance deduction . . | 29
30 Penalty on early withdrawal of savings . . . . | 30
31a Alimony paid b Recipient's SSN ▶ | 31a
32 IRA deduction . . . . | 32
33 Student loan interest deduction . . . . . | 33
34 Tuition and fees. Attach Form 8917 . . . . . | 34
35 Domestic production activities deduction. Attach Form 8903 | 35
36 Add lines 23 through 31a and 32 through 35 . . . . ▶ | 36
37 Subtract line 36 from line 22. This is your **adjusted gross income** . . . . . ▶ | 37

For Disclosure, Privacy Act, and Paperwork Reduction Act Notice, see separate instructions. Cat. No. 11320B Form **1040** (2010)

图 6－9 联邦个人所得税 1040 表格 Ⅰ

Tax and Credits	38	Amount from line 37 (adjusted gross income)	38	
	39a	Check if: ☐ **You** were born before January 2, 1946, ☐ Blind. ☐ **Spouse** was born before January 2, 1946, ☐ Blind. } **Total boxes checked ►** 39a		
	b	If your spouse itemizes on a separate return or you were a dual-status alien, check here ► 39b☐		
	40	**Itemized deductions** (from Schedule A) **or** your **standard deduction** (see instructions) . .	40	
	41	Subtract line 40 from line 38	41	
	42	**Exemptions.** Multiply $3,650 by the number on line 6d	42	
	43	**Taxable income.** Subtract line 42 from line 41. If line 42 is more than line 41, enter -0- . .	43	
	44	**Tax** (see instructions). Check if any tax is from: **a** ☐ Form(s) 8814 **b** ☐ Form 4972 .	44	
	45	**Alternative minimum tax** (see instructions). Attach Form 6251	45	
	46	Add lines 44 and 45 . . . . ►	46	
	47	Foreign tax credit. Attach Form 1116 if required . . .	47		
	48	Credit for child and dependent care expenses. Attach Form 2441	48		
	49	Education credits from Form 8863, line 23	49		
	50	Retirement savings contributions credit. Attach Form 8880	50		
	51	Child tax credit (see instructions)	51		
	52	Residential energy credits. Attach Form 5695 . . .	52		
	53	Other credits from Form: **a** ☐ 3800 **b** ☐ 8801 **c** ☐	53		
	54	Add lines 47 through 53. These are your **total credits**	54	
	55	Subtract line 54 from line 46. If line 54 is more than line 46, enter -0- . . . . ►	55	
Other Taxes	56	Self-employment tax. Attach Schedule SE	56	
	57	Unreported social security and Medicare tax from Form: **a** ☐ 4137 **b** ☐ 8919 . .	57	
	58	Additional tax on IRAs, other qualified retirement plans, etc. Attach Form 5329 if required . .	58	
	59	**a** ☐ Form(s) W-2, box 9 **b** ☐ Schedule H **c** ☐ Form 5405, line 16 . .	59	
	60	Add lines 55 through 59. This is your **total tax** . . . . ►	60	
Payments	61	Federal income tax withheld from Forms W-2 and 1099	61		
	62	2010 estimated tax payments and amount applied from 2009 return	62		
	63	Making work pay credit. Attach Schedule M	63		
If you have a qualifying child, attach Schedule EIC.	64a	**Earned income credit (EIC)**	64a		
	b	Nontaxable combat pay election	64b			
	65	Additional child tax credit. Attach Form 8812 . . .	65		
	66	American opportunity credit from Form 8863, line 14 . .	66		
	67	First-time homebuyer credit from Form 5405, line 10 . .	67		
	68	Amount paid with request for extension to file ˙. . .	68		
	69	Excess social security and tier 1 RRTA tax withheld . . .	69		
	70	Credit for federal tax on fuels. Attach Form 4136 . . .	70		
	71	Credits from Form: **a** ☐ 2439 **b** ☐ 8839 **c** ☐ 8801 **d** ☐ 8885	71		
	72	Add lines 61, 62, 63, 64a, and 65 through 71. These are your **total payments** . . . . ►	72	
Refund	73	If line 72 is more than line 60, subtract line 60 from line 72. This is the amount you **overpaid**	73	
	74a	Amount of line 73 you want **refunded to you.** If Form 8888 is attached, check here . ►☐	74a	
Direct deposit? ► *See instructions.*	b	Routing number |_|_|_|_|_|_|_|_|_| ► **c** Type: ☐ Checking ☐ Savings		
	► d	Account number |_|_|_|_|_|_|_|_|_|_|_|_|_|_|_|_|_|		
	75	Amount of line 73 you want **applied to your 2011 estimated tax ►**	75		
Amount You Owe	76	**Amount you owe.** Subtract line 72 from line 60. For details on how to pay, see instructions ►	76	
	77	Estimated tax penalty (see instructions)	77		

Third Party Designee	Do you want to allow another person to discuss this return with the IRS (see instructions)? ☐ **Yes.** Complete below. ☐ **No**
	Designee's name ►＿＿＿＿＿ Phone no. ►＿＿＿＿＿ Personal identification number (PIN) ► |_|_|_|_|_|

Sign Here	Under penalties of perjury, I declare that I have examined this return and accompanying schedules and statements, and to the best of my knowledge and belief, they are true, correct, and complete. Declaration of preparer (other than taxpayer) is based on all information of which preparer has any knowledge.			
Joint return? *See page 12.*	Your signature	Date	Your occupation	Daytime phone number
Keep a copy for your records.	Spouse's signature. If a joint return, **both** must sign.	Date	Spouse's occupation	

Paid Preparer Use Only	Print/Type preparer's name	Preparer's signature	Date	Check ☐ if self-employed	PTIN
	Firm's name ►			Firm's EIN ►	
	Firm's address ►			Phone no.	

图 6 - 10　联邦个人所得税 1040 表格 Ⅱ

购房和租房：日常生活中最大宗的买卖

住房和土地，是中国文化中安身立命之所在，它们在美国同样也很重要，但是花了钱就可以办到，而且花多花少都可以办到。

首先，美国法律不会对外国人购房租房设立任何障碍，甚至在某种程度上欢迎世界各地的房地产客商和用户，共同促进当地的房地产市场，为美国国民提供源源不断的房地产税收来源。

从程序上来说，购房租房还需要一个房产经纪人从中斡旋，既有利于转递信息，也方便讨价还价，因为这样的大宗交易，不开价还价，是不可思议的行为。历来房屋经纪与广告信息来自当地的报纸和门店，网络发达起来后，即使你还身处北京、上海等待移民，有关信息也可以一目了然。一般来说，美国的经纪人还是规范运作的，他们的从业培训和执照都是在法律的监督下有序执行的。比如说，该保密的信息和该公开的资料，绝对不得含糊，中介不能在买卖过程中暗自交易，上下家通吃，但是他的工作基本也是有利润保障的，就拿纽约州来讲，一般房产交易的中介费是成交价的 6％，向双方或者卖方收取。租房中介费为一个月的房租额，向承租方收取。

无论购房还是租房，你都可以聘请律师，中介也有统一的法律文件供双方签约。目前，纽约市的房产律师最低收费在 300～500 美元就可以帮助新移民解决购房过程中的法律问题。租房总额较小，是否聘请律师自己可以决定，除非你是向华人房东寻租，否则大型公寓的规则、种类和服务条款也够新移民摸索一阵的，最好从租用华人房东的公寓开始你的移民新生活。

具体来讲，美国的公寓分股份公寓（Apartment）、产权公寓（Condo）、独栋别墅（House）三种。从法律上讲股份公寓是不得出租的，业主委员会委托管理公司对所有危及股东利益的行为予以制止，但有时对股东的亲朋好友临时暂居，也会人情化地网开一面，关键是大家事先要有心理准备。产权公寓可以大到上千户的大楼，也可小到个人投资的两三套公寓，都可以合法出租。至于别墅房东愿意将多余的空间出租给他人，法律上没有障碍，但在管理和安全设施方面必须符合房屋管理当局的规定，如人口密度、水电负荷、地下空间的利用管理等，承租人必须事先考虑妥当，以免日后发生纠纷。

至于房租，基本与上述产权形式无关，主要取决于地段、面积和实施。比较笼统而言，曼哈顿市中心 700 平方尺（约 70 平方米使用面积）的一室一厅，月租 2 500～3 000 美元，到了公交地铁一小时车程以外的生活区，相同的条件，1 000 美元左右就可以租下了。上述大小的房产，曼哈顿的产权公寓可以在 50 万～70 万美元成交，比较上海、北京的房产市场，投资回报率相当诱人，到了一小时车程以外的地区，10 万～20 万美元也可以觅得，如果你确实被当地的房产吸引，50 万～70 万美元的曼哈顿中心公寓价格，就可以在一小时车程以外的地区换取一栋独立洋房，既享受了生活，也开始了房产出租生意。

医疗保险与
就医保健

　　新移民和留学生初到美国，人地两生，不像在国内，有了问题随时可以找到社会关系，就算临时抱佛脚，往往也可以渡过危机。

　　在美国这片陌生的土地上，你当然可能也会有个把可以随时叫得应的亲友，无线通讯发达的手机时代，也为通过电话与亲友随时保持沟通提供了技术便利。但是，在美国这个市场经济发达的社会里，人人都在为自己的生存或者更好的生活奔波，真正拿出大把的时间与你分担生活细节与烦恼的，实在也是不多。"时间就是金钱"的口号在这里不是理论，而是看得见摸得着的纸币。临时找人一两次救急没问题，次数多了，恐怕你自己也不好意思再打扰别人了，这或许就是我们形成美国社会人情淡漠的印象的原因之一。

　　但市场决定一切的经济制度，同时也是解决上述问题最好的途径。只要一开始建立好了法定关系，你再也不用整天琢磨人情社会中的一些潜规则，满世界找人、托人、用人再回报人。因为你是合法定居在美国的，不管长期还是短期，在你办妥了社会安全卡，或者办妥了入学手续，有了稳定的居所之后，接下去首先需要关注的问题，应该就是就医与保险了。

　　如果你有足够的钱，当然很好，报纸上到处都是销售保险的经纪人广告，从医疗保险、人寿保险、汽车保险、信用卡保险，到承诺投资回报红利的各种保险方案，不一而足，日日翻新，这是这个行当的市场模式与合理规则。但是如果你钱不多，又希望有个保险计划解决当下的健康保障，也还有许多其他方案。

比如，一旦有了稳定的工作，有了一份稳定的收入，但你又嫌商业保险太贵，自己年轻力壮，还不需要花太多的钱在医疗保险上，那就可以先尝试加入当地的工会组织，这个机构不光维护会员的职业保障和职业福利，同时也有一定的就医保险，就是说，一笔保险费承担了生活中的好几种意外问题。比如司机工会、车衣工会等社会最基本的工种，都有相应的员工组织。中国赴美的新移民较多在大学或者医院从事实验室工作，作为技术人员可以在纽约市加入1199工会，每月缴纳少量的费用，就可以将职位、就医和退休等困扰你多时的问题，找到一个对口的法定机构，随时要求他们提供服务。

留学生的医疗保险基本在入学注册时已经办妥，但是你必须及时将你的免疫接种记录转换成美国版本。中国学生几乎每人都接种过卡介苗等各种常见传染病的疫苗，必要的时候，要及时递交给有关机构作为自己健康的凭证。在中国的时候，大家对自己结核菌感染皮试阳性一个＋、两个＋，或者甲肝、乙肝血清呈阳性反应见怪不怪，但美国医生对这两种传染性疾病会表现得如临大敌。这也难怪他们，美国社会人群中，这些传染病感染率很低，所以对这类病的免疫力普遍较低，因而医生们不得不对血清试验阳性的就诊者采取全面的体检，以确定他是患者还是健康携带者。所以，在这个时候，找到一位会讲汉语的华裔医生作为你的家庭医生是首选的方案，起码双方在语言和文化上相互共鸣。其次，医学英语即使对于一个托福考了满分的人来讲，也是头大的事，更不要说你临时遇上了过堂般的询问与质疑，常常答非所问，会讲汉语的华裔医生基本可以消除你的这类烦恼。

找一位合适自己的医生，其实与找一家合适自己的医疗保险基本上是同步的。在一些经济发达、实力雄厚的州市，初来乍到者还是有许多不错的选择，比如纽约州的非营利性亲情保健计划（Affinity Health Plan，网址是 http://affinityhealth.org/page/home.html）就是针对低收入人群、儿童和青少年、新移民、少数民族等特殊人群，提供免费或者收费低廉的医疗保险计划。

在纽约市，亲情保健计划还特别提供了中文服务，他们承诺的特色服务包括以下方向。

1. 日常的健康警示。对于青壮年人士而言，平时有了专业的健康提示，就可以自我保健。很多人在国内也很少去医院，没病没灾的，也确实很少需要求医，有人提供健康关爱就足够了。

2. 疫苗接种。季节性的疫苗接种倒是非常有用的疾病预防措施，特别是对于在大流量的人群中提供服务型工种的人士，有了这项贴心服务，可以解除后顾之忧。

3. 一次性电话预约就诊。对于新来乍到的人士，与中文电话接线员通话，基本可以将你的要求表述清楚，应急的时候是较好的求助来源。

4. 就近服务。刚到美国，往往人生地不熟，加上没有驾照，或不会开车，这时若有接线员告诉你，医生就在附近，步行或者坐公交车就可以去就诊，是再好不过的帮助了。

5. 过敏哮喘治疗。来到一个新的环境，空气质量和你原来居住的地方有所不同，尤其是绿化环境极好的地方，花粉等外源性蛋白质经常会引起流鼻涕、打喷嚏等症状，过敏治疗就相当贴心了。

6. 怀孕跟踪关怀。意外怀孕了，年轻男孩和女孩都没有经验，父母又不在身边，这时妇产科医生的忠告就是唯一的来源，他们的检查和判断，可以及时帮助需要的人。

7. 敦促乳房筛检。美国的生活方式与营养状况似乎与乳腺肿瘤有相当大的关联性，同时他们的诊断与治疗水平也是世界最高的。对于有家族病史的 25 岁以上女性，或者所有 35 岁以上的女性，半年做一次筛检绝对不是坏事。

8. 急诊、牙科和眼科服务。在商业保险中，这几项诊治服务都需要另外购买，而且费用可能与基本医疗保险一样昂贵。亲情保健计划将他们合并在一起，非常划算。

值得提醒的是，华人社区中，有一些自以为聪明的家庭，将老人单独划为一户，老人名下没有房产、收入和存款，于是向联邦政府申请老人福利，希望获得额外的食品券、住房津贴、零用钱和医疗保险等。如果不是经得起核实的低收入人士，一旦被有关部门发现，上述补助肯定泡汤，说不定还会导致吊销全家的移民资格。所以，一定要入乡随俗、遵纪守法。尤其是在美国经济走下坡路的时候，美国政府肯定会在消除浪费、提高福利效率、追究非法所得等方面加大力度。

美国是个宗教信仰极其宽松和广泛的国度。热闹的商业区街道上，不时会有教会人士或者教会学校的学生在传道，特别是通过给新移民提供生活方便，希望新移民加入他们的教会家庭。可以客观地下这样一个结论，他们的热情都是发自内心的，就看你是否承受得了。改革开放以后来到美国的中国留学生和各类移民，基本上都是无神论者，面对传教人士的过分热情与宗教情结，一般很难在第一时间接受。但是，生活的窘迫，比如，签证出现问题，找不到经济担保人，住房无法落实，生病缺钱，哪怕就是周末没有交通工具，无法去超市采购日常生活用品这样的琐事，热心的教会，特别是在大城市以外的边远地区，无处不在的教会人员确实成为初到美国者的最大救助者。他们慢慢与新移民成为朋友，新移民然后从不自觉到自觉地走向教会，成为教友也就顺理成章。教会这种社会的基本架构，确立了美国社会福利的草根资源。

比如，赖先生是一位马来西亚移民，初看上去与平常人无异，实际上患有严重的心理障碍，是个忧郁症患者，教会几次帮他解决工作机会，最后他连超市仓库理货、清理垃圾这样的工作都无法完成，一日三餐与住房均出现问题。最后，他所在教会的人员直接为他在教堂里安排了临时生活，并没有简单地把他送往政府救济机构，以免再给他的移民身份雪上加霜。约翰是一位欧洲移民，与我做了十年的邻居。他四十出头还是独身，父亲是德国人，母亲是英国人，双亲早已过世，世上几乎没有亲人。他平时开一辆厢式货车从事物流业务，热情幽默，其实患有严重的先天性心脏病，但他从来不会麻烦邻里也没有诉说过自己的危机，就依靠着类似亲情保健计划这样的基本医疗保险维持着生命健康。

老爸老妈的
新移民生活

　　鉴于本书的目标读者群是有实力赴美投资移民的家庭和送子女出国留学的家庭，有关新移民来美国后的生活方式，就有了比较广泛的选择。比如，在语言和环境都需要适应的开始几个月，你可以吃老本，也可以像大多数来自底层投亲靠友的移民一样，靠体力挣钱，男性技术工种如泥瓦、水电、木工，手艺好的，每天 150～200 美元，打个下手也有100 美元，这样的建筑工地伙计，只要你有足够的体力，唐人街上你起个大早基本上都会有工头把你领走，中午包饭，8 小时后原地送回，几天下来，可能就建立起固定的雇佣关系了。没有手艺的，去菜市、餐馆打个下手，每月可挣上 2 000 美元。如果会点管理和厨艺，你就比对着手艺工匠的收入，与老板慢慢讨论工资吧。女性最多的是去成衣厂打工，技术工种不同，工资可以从每月 5 000～6 000 美元到 1 万～2 万美元不等，小到唐人街的成衣厂，大到名牌作坊里为名媛淑女赶制晚礼服。如果不愿出门，自己在家为年轻夫妇看个孩子，每月也有千儿八百美元的收入，而且自家的杂务也没有耽误。

　　老爸老妈毕竟曾是读书做事，有头有脑的主儿，几个月下来，开始琢磨起生意上的事。对他们来讲，做房东是第一项有自信的活儿，投资收益上面已经谈及，许多富二代"游"学美国期间，一不小心，将房地产买卖做成主业，也算留学一回，游学成功。不过，在美国做房东与国内不一样,你千万不可把自己当大款,要万事自己动手,省下人工就是收入。有手艺的老爸可以先从装修自家开始,大型超市里的五金工具到五金材料,既便宜又规范,将自个的房子出租以后,可以在《世界日报》上每月花 200 美元登个专业维护房屋的小广告,揽上一单活便有 100～200 美元的收入,那是最基本的生意了,一个月若有个 10～20 趟上门生意,便可开始计划扩大经营。

老妈也别闲着,当年的英文老底翻出来重新操练,先做个房屋中介的助理,也从自家的生意开始,练英文和"煲电话"全当一锅煮了,好在美国的电话费极便宜,固话全包手机晚上全包,用打电话的方式练口语,效果肯定比上英文补习班还好,拿出当年死记硬背的本领,人生难得又搏一回,考上地产执照,运气好的话,第一年卖出一栋房就有 3 万美元进账,小日子就过得挺舒坦了。

表 6-1 美国小本生意规模及收益

经营项目	成本	员工人数	月营业额
中餐馆	4 万～40 万美元	4～20 人	10 万～100 万美元
指甲店	4 万～10 万美元	2～6 人	2 万～30 万美元
开出租车	2 万～4 万美元	自任司机	1 万～3 万美元
百货小摊拉	5 000 美元	自己经营	1 万美元
美发店	2 万～10 万美元	2～4 人	2 万～20 万美元
蔬果杂货小摊位	3 000 美元	自己经营	2 万美元
旅游订票业务	5 000 美元	1～2 人	10 万～30 万美元
搬运业务	2 000 美元	2～3 人	2 万～3 万美元
园艺清理业务	5 000 美元	1～2 人	1 万～2 万美元
艺术绘画销售摊位	2 000 美元	自己经营	1 万美元
课后补习游乐班	2 000 美元	自己经营	3 000～1 万美元
跳蚤市场周末摊位	2 000 美元	自己经营	2 000～1 万美元

三餐不用愁，
就怕吃多了

　　前文集中篇幅介绍了在美国生活的主要支出，住房的消费和由此产生的商机，讨论了几项可以迅速获得收入的方式，这样再谈一日三餐，那就是基本到了享受生活的层面了。

　　一日三餐可以自己买来原料加工，在时间就是金钱，每小时最低收入可以达到7～10美元的美国，在唐人街上3.99美元可以获得三菜一汤的中式快餐或者5美元一份的美式快餐，自己做饭，烧还是不烧，真的成了一个值得快速计算的成本效益心算题。将下厨当成一种享受的事，绝不是矫情。

　　无论唐人街上的中式副食品超市，还是西式的食品大卖场，整车整车地将食品和其他日用品采购回家，曾经成为娱记在"报屁股"上感叹明星海外生活奢侈的依据，其实这只是普通美国老百姓日常生活的场景。一方面是货物充足，价格便宜；另一方面，也是时间宝贵，没有人愿意天天逛菜市场，浪费时间、精力、汽油和宝贵的悠闲享受机会。比较阅读下面这份中国家庭的日常采购清单，你就会深有体会。

　　　上海青菜：0.59～0.79美元/磅

　　　大白菜：0.39～0.49美元/磅

　　　韭菜：0.79～1.19美元/磅

黄瓜:0.59～0.79美元/磅

带皮猪腿肉:1.29～1.59美元/磅

五花肉:1.99～2.19美元/磅

里脊肉:2.49/2.99美元/磅

排骨:1.59～1.99美元/磅

冰冻带鱼:2.49～2.99美元/磅

活杀鲤鱼:2.19～2.49美元/磅

游水石斑鱼:3.99～4.99美元/磅

游水大龙虾:3.99～5.99美元/磅

走地鸡:2.49～2.79美元/磅

冰冻鸡腿:0.49～0.69美元/磅

鸡蛋:0.99～1.49美元/12只

新鲜牛奶:2.59～3.29美元/加仑

香蕉:0.49～0.69美元/磅

橙子:1.00美元/四个

苹果:1.00美元/2个

西瓜:5.99美元/个

……

　　除了自己下厨,外出饮茶吃饭也是海外移民们热衷的生活方式,其内涵不仅在于填饱肚子,我曾经专门研究过这个现象。

　　在上海经营早茶生意,餐饮业主往往血本无归。原因之一,可能是上海人饮茶归饮茶,与美食无关,特讲究品茶味。我曾在师母处品过一回天目湖白茶,由于是临时尝新,毫无心理和生理准备。结果,我被那位惊心动魄的茶仙弄得丢魂失态的逸事，一直成为朋友间的谈资。清茗入口的感觉分为三个层次：两颊溢香，舌尖鲜美；舌根醇厚；最终失声叫绝，以致在相当长一段时间里，拒绝进食任何茶点。其结局是，我被授予知遇懂行的角色，奖赏白茶二两，回家独自享用。事后得知，此茶属特供产品，来自天目湖畔唯一的两株茶树，采摘前后，必派专人守护，以防不测。

到了上海的"后花园"，饮茶与美食的关系就暧昧起来，不过也仅止于嘴上过瘾的程度。陆文夫的《美食家》记载了一段消逝的姑苏韵味："那爿大茶楼上有几个和一般茶客隔开的房间，摆着红木桌、大藤椅，自成一个小天地。那里的水是天落水，茶叶是直接从洞庭东山买来的，煮水用瓦罐，燃料用松枝，茶要泡在宜兴出产的紫砂壶里。吃喝吃喝，吃与喝是一个不可分割的整体，称得上美食家的人，无一不是陆羽和杜康的徒弟的……美食家们除掉早点之外，决不能单独行动，最少不能少于四个，最多不得超过八人，因为苏州菜有它一套完整的结构。比如说开始的时候是冷盆，接下来是热炒，热炒之后是甜食，甜食的后面是大菜，大菜的后面是点心，最后以一盆大汤作总结。这台完整的戏剧一个人不能看，只看一幕又不能领略其中的含意。所以美食家们必须集体行动。先坐在茶楼上回味昨天的美食，评论得失。第一阶段是个漫谈会。会议一结束便要转入正题，为了慎重起见，还不得不抽出一段时间来讨论今日向何方……"

但是到了广州、香港，情况又大不一样。气候闷热，日长夜短，千万不能怠慢了清晨的东升旭日。茶楼的老主顾就是街坊，各就各位，次序井然，不知底细的，还以为他们是去写字间报到。麻将得失，汇市行情，楼市风云，股市起伏肯定是茶客们话题的主要内容；马经六合彩，新开豆腐店,婚嫁月下老,娱乐八卦事,也属商情关键;至于有些头脸的,说不定心情大好,透露些许政情内幕与并购行情,碰巧了,几个时辰后股市开锣,股票抛出,今日早茶的开销肯定是值了。

到了异国的唐人街,早茶自然是有的吃的,但内容与形式正式了许多,开始延伸意义完全不同的内容。早茶唤作"Dim Sum",这倒也好记,就是粤语"点心"的谐音。这点心可不仅是小吃的意思,精美的菜单上,从油条米粉到龙虾鲍鱼,一应俱全。关键是,确定早茶的日期和出席人员,颇费周折。

在这里,喝茶吃饭是要预约的,哪怕对方是老公老婆、宝贝儿子、亲生闺女,一个个日程满满,车程遥遥,如非事先敲定时间,殊难赴约。然后就是通知父母、岳父母,把所有想得到的长辈老人一起约上。再指定男女晚辈,临时充任司机,到时候专程上门接送,不得有误。这样的家族性活动,年年讲,月月办。对老人们来说,周末的早茶活动,已经成为一场不亚于家族盛会的重大仪式,当然也是节假日的红包授收典礼。从满月的宝宝到十来岁的小字辈,届时肯定要全数出场,请安磕头,点香祭祀,一切按日月时辰有序安排。这些中国大陆城市已经绝迹的大家庭例会,长幼尊卑的血缘称谓和礼仪规范,竟在大洋彼岸的异国他乡,改头换面地延绵规范起来。礼仪之邦的文明遗产,居然假座饭肆酒廊得以传承,人头攒动的食客中,更有不少洋媳妇和洋女婿,他们除了汉语还有些不够流畅,味蕾的精细程度和筷子的灵巧程度,绝对已经超过了家族的长辈们,华夏文明得以在西方隔代融合,实属有缘。

纽约的茶楼商家,不仅比上海的幸运,生意兴隆,而且也因此浸染些许儒商风范。它绝对不会因为客家人口众多,占位太久,过程太长而大光其火。聪明的老板料到你下周还会准时光临,只不过是换了一个聚会的由头。于是,千年茶史,也被海外华人补充了一页。

所以,到了美国,出外派对成为一种文化,是生活的调剂,也是文化的延伸。特别是每年高中毕业前夕的成年派对,在美国就是一个少年成人,一个家庭盛会,一场婚礼前奏般的预演,千万不要忽视了这道风景。

图 6 - 12　成年派对

购车太容易，科技
也会绑架你

以纽约等大城市为例，每月住的费用最大，吃的花费每人 100～200
美元足够，接下来就是出行的费用。由于是大城市，公共交通系统很发
达，尽管有人出于自珍自爱，不断揭露纽约地铁系统的老旧肮脏，但是
千万不要忘了，这是一个建造于 100 年前，至今还在正常使用的公共服
务系统，硬件是老化了，需要不断更新维护，服务质量还是能保持市民
的日常需要，这样的工程和服务在全世界还找不到一个可以与之比拟
的系统。比如，它 24 小时运转，不需要担心赶不上末班车；纽约地铁有
地下 3 层，24 条线路，468 个车站，2010 年共运送了 16 亿人次；地铁和
地面公交免费换乘，几乎可以把乘客送到城市任何一个角落。目前，搭
乘地铁和巴士的一次费用是 2.25 美元，但他还有买十送一、单日无限
票、月票等多种选择方案。尽管纽约公共交通系统无法让人人满意，但
它也算百年功臣，竭尽全力了。

关键是，纽约的公共交通让市民尤其是新移民不必把买车开车作
为出门的依赖，就是来客人，来自异国的老人，也可以到处去游玩。当
然，面对满大街的新车和二手车销售推广，来自新兴国度的移民们，总
会摩拳擦掌，过一把尽情享受底价名车的瘾，这些内容，听多了也不稀
奇，倒是提醒富裕了的新移民要有另外的心理准备。

相比纽约房产地产的飙升，这里的车市好像平稳很多，总价也可以

承受。又熬过了新移民最初几年的艰难岁月,人民币与美元之间的汇率敏感障碍消失了,诸事克己奉简的祖辈教诲淡漠了,善待自己身心的宽容心态形成了,移居纽约的朋友们纷纷开始购置高档的汽车。

笔者是 2003 年购置了最新款的梅赛德斯-奔驰 E320 汽车的。无忧无虑地开上了几年新款好车后,以至有了机会,还特别喜欢拿一辆最普通、最陈旧的小车过瘾,既像是怀旧,又像是展示车技,国内的朋友们都误以为我是"超脱"了。

自从开上新购置的 E320,每隔两三个月,我就会驾车去梅赛德斯-奔驰服务中心。或是验车,或是养车,哪怕新车无恙,我也愿意与特约维护代表聊聊,获得一些驾车的专业指点,了解一下更新款的产品信息,试驾几款将来可能会被我占有的跑车。更何况,那里还可以参观专卖礼品,享用免费点心饮料。几年的免费保养期过后,我开始减少拜访梅赛德斯-奔驰服务中心的次数。但爱车在我的小心维护下,一如新嫁娘,里外可人。

但是,问题开始逐一出现了。

首先是每天发动引擎之后,方向盘上方的电子显示屏一天不拉地提示你,已经过期多少天,你尚未主动拜访梅赛德斯-奔驰服务中心。几年来,与梅赛德斯-奔驰服务中心几十次的交流,我已经知道新车保养期后的特约服务收费标准,就像上医院就诊一样,先交挂号费 240 美元,诊断结果出来后,如选择继续维修,人工是按小时计算的,每小时 200 美元;材料一律用特约产品,同类同款的零件,比市场销售价上浮 100%。你也可以选择听了诊断意见后开车走人。但是,恕不提供书面报告,法律规定,那是它们的知识产权。

就我这样的老司机,怎会接受这样的霸王服务! 想当年初为车夫,别说开车,就连修车也一起向师傅讨教了,换机油,换轮胎,换刹车片,全都自己动手,照样年检过关,安全无恙。如今年龄渐长,钱袋渐肥,又开上了新款奔驰车,车身上下钻进钻出,当然不成体统,违反本文开篇的生活原则。但是,到华人同胞开设的车行去享受价格合理的保养服务,还是可行的。就是车载显示屏上的过期提醒日日上升,预示麻烦就在眼前。

夏天将至,某日,我开始感觉闷热,车载冷气机拒绝工作了。我及时开去熟识的车行。这次,就连手熟心细的师傅也无能为力了,他的诊断结果是,制冷剂压力正常,压缩机工作正常,电路感应器功能正常,就是电脑主机板进入锁定程序,唯一的治疗出路,就是请梅赛德斯-奔驰服务中心重新启动电脑程序,告诉电脑,一切正常。电脑程序属于知识产权,购车费用中并没有将其买断。看来,开好车必须继续向服务中心进贡。

电脑时代的科技生活,仅在开车诸事上被绑架,倒也罢了,毕竟服务中心的设施与服务内容是一流的。只是,各行各业的成功人士,驾驶梅赛德斯-奔驰车的不少。由这伙精英使着性子来,到处卖弄这样的概念:科技就是现代生活,科技应该主导生活。流行开来,就是下列这样的日子。

儿子用上了电脑,老爸非常得意,下一辈终于出息了。谁知期末汇报,考试科目门门亮红灯,原来电脑用来玩网游了。

老妈每周就医,领回丸剂十数种。每晚饭后,当众设坛,数数,分类,送口,用水,吞咽。神色庄严,时辰精准,不得打扰。

世博未来实践区,有数码便具一架,实物展示,三维诠释。晨起、勿饮、小解、大便,液晶数码当场报告,旭日惊魂,晚霞担忧。

转基因水稻,说是还在科学家的试验田里;说是还在政府的有效监管下;说是承担喂饱未来空腹的重任。现实是,两湖大地的粮农已经开始播种不用施肥施药的稻谷了。确定未来有那么多健康的孩子需要喂养吗?

这样的日子,到底是祸是福,一时难以明辨。日常生活被绑架了,倒是确定无疑。

后 记
曼哈顿法则，"狼狗式"生存

将衣食住行谈完以后，最后，我还想提示读者一项最主要的新移民生存法则——不要懦弱，因为这里还是一个保留了丛林法则的生态社会。

日前，有位老友半夜来电咨询：怎么办？

原因是，他那位刚在美国大学毕业，好不容易在纽约上州（Upstate New York）找到一份工作，才安顿下来三个月的宝贝女儿，突然接到老板指令，要她立即转到曼哈顿的分支机构上班。

我说，你的宝贝正处在三岔路口，她或许又是一头乖乖喂狼的羊，或者借机突变，成为曼哈顿岛上虎口夺食的狼。

纽约曼哈顿，其性格就是一条疯狂掀浪的经济巨鳄，外表则是一座形似狼脚印的天然岛屿。曼哈顿真的有狼，这是 2006 年 3 月的一篇新闻报道。

一名晨练者在绿荫茂密的中央公园，发现了一条郊狼。警方接到报警后，动用大批警力，甚至动用了直升机，最后在公园某个角落里捕获了这条茶色郊狼。工作人员称其"哈尔"，大约 1 岁，小狼身手敏捷，"逃亡"过程中曾跳入水中，躲到桥下，还曾到冰面溜冰，翻越 2.4 米高的栅栏。警方最后不得不发射麻醉弹，将其逮住。

害怕人类却又仿效人类,喜爱"探险",正是野狼的特色。动物学家研究发现,中秋月明之夜,它们结集在旷野,仰天长叹,直到东方既白,月色稀薄,方才散去。这种宗教般的虔诚,比自诩传承中秋文化的人类,有过之而无不及。

哈尔并非第一条来到中央公园的郊狼。几年前,也曾有一只郊狼溜到中央公园来"观光"。与溜进曼哈顿的哈尔一样,郊狼进城不是轻松的旅游,一路历经坎坷。这种年幼的郊狼心理上还不成熟,喜欢尽情耍闹,对于草地感到很新奇,想探个究竟,结果却得到一个更大的教训。

近年来,美国的城市郊区出现越来越多的小郊狼。纽约郊区野狼数量剧增始于 20 世纪 70 年代。1997 年,曾一度发现 15 只郊狼。当时人们并没有在意这一现象,直至居民不断报告,家养宠物和家禽常常无端消失,有关部门介入调查发现原来都是郊狼惹的祸。有关专家对于郊狼"移居"郊区发表见解:郊狼长期接触人类,慢慢会丧失对人类的恐惧感。

这些冒险精神的特征和正视教训的精神,正是新一代留学生移民必须向郊狼学习的关键部分。比如,在老板提出新的工作要求时,你实在没有必要在第一时间无条件答应。作为一名正式雇员,无论是外国雇员还是实习员工,你还是具备一定的谈判优势和法定权利。

你不必害怕老板。老板属于人类,特别是经济市场原则下的老板,具有天生的弱点。假定老友女儿的老板,是一个正经的老板,他在这个时候突然安排你接手新的项目,表明在他那边发生了意外的变故,而你恰好是他目前员工中,最有可能协助他低成本解决危机的首选方案。此刻你只当听话的乖乖女,无条件去新址上班,正中老板下怀,而你将面临利益损失,获益的机会瞬息即逝,不符合双赢原则。

你有几项考虑:第一,老板一时难以找到工作能力和工资支出相匹配的员工立即顶替该项工作,所以找到你;第二,你目前的工作内容和报酬,只能适应目前的生活环境与安置,否则就有新的费用出现,损害了你的利益;第三,雇佣合同上面确定了你的工作地点和合法权利与义务。这样合情合理的分析以后,你就有了时间与空间,重新厘清与老板协商的条件。

这种狼性的苏醒,属于天性。但在我们这一代人身上,失而复还的过程,极具历史感。

有学者专门研究所谓的 20 世纪 60 年代生人,即专指 80 年代大学毕业,90 年代崭露头角,在文化性格、学术追求和社会生活中,构建出与父兄长辈很不相同风格的一代。他们受传统思想束缚最少,收入最多,拥有汽车、购买住房最多,正在成为市场经济中最为活跃、最具有实力和最具发展潜力的中间阶层。其实,他们业已进入开始总结、提炼自己与上下两代不同的个性,塑造和显示自己的特质的生命阶段。

"文化大革命"后恢复高考,60 年代生的人作为第一批直接从高中考入全国重点大学的应届生,与最早入学的 1977 级、1978 级大学生同处一个校园,往往自惭形秽。他们中最小的,也在工厂或者农村锻炼过,富有社会阅历。学长中最大的,则是"老三届"高中生,饱经"文化大革命"创伤。学兄学姐在大学生活中表现出来的技能特长,已具备师长辈的水准。事实上,其中有不少,就是被我的几位同窗唤作叔、舅、姨、姑的长辈。

在前辈眼中,我们是不折不扣的幸运儿:刚摆脱洗脑运动的心理折磨和一穷二白的生理磨难,就赶上在合适的年龄,开始大学生活;刚开始重建社会体制,提倡现代化发展,我们上学免交所有费用,还享受零用钱和回家路费等补助,一旦毕业,人人都安排一份体面的工作,享受国家事业单位干部待遇。

所以,我 24 岁,就幸运地开始在上海交通大学任教。像我这样一路顺利走来的教师,最大的特点,就是听话。我们年龄老大不小,思维相当天真,没有一丁点儿社会经验,整个就是保育院流水线上出品的最完美的设计杰作。

出国以前，我们对美国的了解完全是书生式的，别人如何讲，我们就如何信。那时，真正可供选择的用于了解当今真实美国的资料并不多。在我的书架上，有一套20世纪80年代流行的"五角丛书"，这套书共有几百册，每册仅售5角钱。它是西式快餐还未流行时，完全按照快餐式阅读方式直接进入我们生活的精神快餐，又便宜又丰盛。现在我们吃饱了，开始意识到，质量是快餐的最大软肋，营养失衡，我们开始戏称它为垃圾食品，但对于无知的食客，它口感极好，最易满足馋嘴的饥不择食者。这个时候，《这就是美国》出现了，我就是哪个被吃坏了肚子的"馋嘴猫"。

1987年5月，《这就是美国》首版印数35.6万册，印数代表了一部作品的影响力，但这个巨额数字也只是那个时代的特色，当时拥有这样辉煌成绩的作家有上百位，所以也不以为奇。比照现在的作家，作品首发3 000册是常规，如果可以达到《这就是美国》的零头，即6 000册，那就会被媒体捧成畅销一族了。作为这本9万字畅销书的读者，我与作者素昧平生，无意与他凭白纠结，自己在此新评旧书，只为反思20年前的那段历史。

首先我得感谢《这就是美国》的作者徐先生，他是"文化大革命"后最早赴美的大陆留学生之一。他无疑是我们敬仰的先驱性楷模。《这就是美国》总体上给我描述了一个多彩多姿的美式人间天堂，不知作者是否也被自己的热情所迷惑，或者早已开始对旧作有所遗憾，后悔草率作出结论，但是当年，该书协助我满怀憧憬地登上了飞往纽约的航班。否则，如果我们过早地接触到美国的真实生活状态，登机前很有可能再现我的童年噩梦——发生在上海火车站前，知识青年上山下乡运动高潮时期，生离死别的"杯具"一幕；或者，我就干脆临阵脱逃出虹桥机场，打道回府了。《这就是美国》这本书共有52个小节，基本上没有让我产生恐惧、警觉，或者需要自卫反击的条件反射。就算略有涉及，对一名白手起家的留学生移民，也如隔靴搔痒不值一提。

《这就是美国》一书比较有劝告性的篇章内容,如下所列:

《人人爱听的假话》　　　　　《师生恋的障碍》

《赌客招揽术》　　　　　　　《在迷幻药的阴影下》

《银行信用卡陷阱》　　　　　《洋记官僚主义》

《美国居,大不易》　　　　　《汽车甘苦经》

而让人信心饱满的篇章,如下所列:

《雅皮——美国之梦的新一代》　《大学生经济独立非难事》

《工商界里博士多》　　　　　《抽奖游戏与黄金梦》

《五花八门的彩票中奖游戏》　《结婚要二人,离婚靠一人》

《疯狂的娱乐》　　　　　　　《不欺暗室的公德心》

《邻里守望相助监督岗》　　　《残疾人也能过正常的生活》

《铁丝网里的"天堂"》　　　　《教会——社会的大家庭》

《天堂里的乞丐》　　　　　　《免费周游美国》

《谁赚的钱最多》　　　　　　《菜场优惠价》

该书的其他文字,大抵赞赏有余,批评有限。这样一本直面当今美国世俗生活的书籍,对于一个书生气十足、涉世未深的赴美预备生而言,诱惑可想而知。

现在,我被运到了纽约,成了一头真正的"迷途羔羊"。

纽约的自然生态确实良好,否则,郊狼就不会出现。在这片生物竞争的天地里,饱受片面舆论误导的留学生,如果类似上述篇章阅读太多,则中毒也深，再不能及时醒悟自赎自救的话，几乎就会成为被送来垫底喂食的迷路羔羊。这种深刻体验在留学生深入其境之前是来不及认识的，只有在时间中慢慢自学，蜕化以至敏锐。

生态学家迈克尔·波伦讲过一种科学依据：如今在美洲仅存 1 万头狼，而狗作为狼的表亲，却有 5 000 万只。从保存生物种群的生态意义上讲，狗比自己那野性未灭的同类狼要成功得多，原因之一，就是狗在与人为伍的 1 万年进化历史中，它们掌握了人类的需要和欲望、人类的情感和价值观念，狗将所有这些融入它的基因，成为它们聪明的生存繁衍策略的重要部分。现在，喂狼喂狗的羊，肯定是没人愿意充当了，但是人生原则到底选择狼，还是选择狗，这是个问题。

有一位早期的留学生，牢牢体验把握了"狼狗式"纽约生存法则，如今成了成功人士，他就是第一位参与《西贡小姐》演出的华裔主演，《西贡小姐》是 20 世纪最后 10 年风靡纽约市曼哈顿百老汇的一出音乐歌舞剧，华裔演员王洛勇则是该剧的男主角。洛勇出生于洛阳，确实神勇无比。从送报纸、送外卖、扛杂活、带孩子和刷房子，到开始进入演艺圈做形体教练、无声配角、临时救场龙套和小戏主角，历经了 9 年美国式磨砺。1995 年 7 月 4 日，美国国庆日的当晚，王洛勇正式亮相百老汇《西贡小姐》大舞台，开创了连续几年、主演上千次皮条客的演艺巨星生涯。

那时，我们的巨星在皇后区的可洛娜街坊相对稳定地定居下来。一栋红砖尖顶的独立洋居（Townhouse）成为洛勇转战百老汇的后方基地。步行几个街道，就是他每日搭乘的地铁 7 号线。他必须保证在《西贡小姐》开演之前，完成当天的所有热身——开喉、化妆、着装。如果当天有人请假，注定就会遇上临时的替补演员，导演肯定安排额外的走场配合。临时要找个好替补，确实很难，而洛勇又是个特认真的主演，所以当天的阵前操练，就有可能延续到大幕拉开之前，真是一刻也不得闲。王洛勇深刻理解面前的临时替补与大腕巨星配戏时的复杂情绪，他当初也是如此，熬过9年等待。何况，就是刚刚搭乘的地铁7号沿线，还有许许多多连百老汇替补机会还没有轮上的各类艺人，正在面对几个最多几十个的过路的乘客，极力展示才华，也是向百老汇展示潜力，最起码要挣回当天的饭钱。

地铁7号线是一条将新移民送往梦想的交通干线，一头连着曼哈顿中城，一头延伸到了华人集聚的法拉盛街坊。搭乘这条地铁的华裔居民相对多些，但是，绝大多数的乘客，还是来自南美洲的"西班牙语裔"、东欧东正教地区的移民，或南亚印度洋地区移民。途经74大街、42大道和时代广场转乘点时，上下班客流成百上千，也是各类艺人展示特技的黄金舞台。下午5点，地铁深处的表演开场了。黑人男生四重唱，击掌就是伴奏，和声就是共鸣，渴了就呷口清咖，原创歌声就像咖啡一样苦涩悠长；俄罗斯裔的手风琴与银勺杂耍，居然可以组成一台戏，打击节奏与手风琴旋律在幽默诙谐中自成一体；南美的排箫声中，秃鹰被呼来唤去，伦巴舞谢幕的时候，方才发现，"女舞伴"原来又是一尊道具。

这些百老汇的替补们，基本上是幸运的。联邦宪法第一修正条款规定，个人拥有公共表达自由。所以，只要你的"粉丝"还没有拥挤到对交通客流造成恶性影响，当值的警察上班前也没有跟老婆或女友、上司和税务官怄气，他基本上也是一边履行公务，一边偷着乐，不会踢场子。这些智慧的艺人们，将个人意志的表达与日常生计融合，演化成一种生活方式，赢得路人的尊重。于是，提供自由创作与思想表达的基础有了，就到了挑战艺术的骄傲和艺术家清高的时刻。20世纪80年代末，一位来自中国国内直辖市交响乐团的首席小提琴手，带头走下来了。他每日定点定时开始小提琴独奏，只当是借来一尺空间，完成操练房里的日常功课。但他的功底与激情，开始感染每天在此等候的"粉丝"，音乐是会传染的，琴盒中的捐款也日日丰厚，当他的琴弦下流淌出中国名曲《阳光照耀着塔什库尔干》或者

《春节序曲》时,我相信,此刻的他动情了,眼角泪光闪现。几年后,他在纽约市购置了两处房产,告别了从皇后区通向百老汇路上的预演,我也失去了下班路上的音乐享受。

现在,轮到我们的百老汇巨星疲倦了。每年 365 天,地铁往返。每天下午出发,深夜归巢。每场两小时重复几千遍标准化的台词、歌曲、舞蹈。我们或许可以赞赏他的坚韧,但无法体会艺术家生命中创造力的危机感。百老汇舞台确实风光和荣耀,但每日被地铁艺术的活力所感染,洛勇的艺术创新细胞被深深刺激了。王洛勇向往故土,他决定离开,告别《西贡小姐》的舞台,激荡另一片红尘,开始《智取威虎山》。

七八年前,我最后一次拜访王氏旧居。那天,王老太太独自在家,她像往常一样,一边为来客制作中原面食,一边与来客唠叨家常。我转交了他儿子托付的一缕黑发,这是老太太的越洋嘱托。老太太的"艺术"已经上升到宗教的层面,相信黑发具备超越自然的信仰功能,足以让儿子与母亲沟通信息。明天是个黄道吉日,老太太会独自展现她的"艺术"。

图书在版编目(CIP)数据

到美国去:投资移民与二代培育实用指南/方向著.
—杭州:浙江大学出版社,2012.5
ISBN 978-7-308-09919-6

Ⅰ.①到… Ⅱ.①方… Ⅲ.①移民－概况－美国
Ⅳ.①D771.238

中国版本图书馆 CIP 数据核字(2012)第 081404 号

到美国去:投资移民与二代培育实用指南

方　向　著

策 划 者	蓝狮子财经出版中心
责任编辑	王长刚
出版发行	浙江大学出版社
	(杭州市天目山路 148 号　邮政编码 310007)
	(网址:http://www.zjupress.com)
排　　版	杭州大漠照排印刷有限公司
印　　刷	杭州杭新印务有限公司
开　　本	710mm×1000mm　1/16
印　　张	16.5
字　　数	190 千
版 印 次	2012 年 5 月第 1 版　2012 年 5 月第 1 次印刷
书　　号	ISBN 978-7-308-09919-6
定　　价	39.00 元